Praise for *The White-Haired Girl*

"Moving . . . compelling . . . memorable . . . graphic and poetic . . . set down with unflinching honesty. The blinding confusion, the terror, the injustices, the secret doubts and fragile hopes are described in arresting detail. A gripping account that reads like fiction." *—Monterey Peninsula Herald*

"Wrenching . . . Sun has written an authentic document of growing up in Maoist culture." *—Publishers Weekly*

"One of the most touching books on China's struggle to survive the excesses of the Cultural Revolution." *—Marin Independent Journal*

"Highly readable . . . recommended . . . this book is an important contribution." · *—Library Journal*

"A colorful memoir . . . lends a tangible horror to the aftermath of national madness." *—San Jose Mercury News*

"Refreshing . . . compelling and effective. *The White-Haired Girl* succeeds in its multi-dimensionality."
—Pacific Reader, Asian Pacific North American Book Review

The
White-Haired
Girl

BITTERSWEET ADVENTURES
OF A LITTLE RED SOLDIER

JAIA SUN-CHILDERS AND
DOUGLAS CHILDERS

PICADOR USA ✹ NEW YORK

Design by Junie Lee

Library of Congress Cataloging-in-Publication Data

Sun-Childers, Jaia.
    The white-haired girl / by Jaia Sun-Childers & Douglas Childers.
      p. cm.
    ISBN 0-312-15691-X
    1. China—History—1949- —Fiction.   I. Childers, Douglas.
II. Title.
    PS3569.U49W48   1996
813'.54—dc20
                              95-44498
                              CIP

First Picador USA Paperback Edition: August 1997

10 9 8 7 6 5 4 3 2 1

Dedication

To those who lived this story, and endured our dark history,
especially Mama, Ba, and my elder brother;
To the beautiful and courageous Chinese People;
To the Infinite Source that blesses our journey;
We offer this book, with love.

As the tiny worm
spins out her life
to the last silken thread . . .

And the candle
burning in his own flame
is consumed in the dark . . .

So we will not stop
until all our tales
are told.

Contents

Acknowledgments

Our heartfelt thanks to Terry Patten, Dan Millman, and Steve Hains, whose support and critical feedback made this a better book.

Many thanks to our agent, Gina Maccoby, and our editors, Hope Dellon, Jenny Notz, and Kelley Ragland at St. Martin's Press, and George Witte at Picador.

We also thank, for their love, support, and contributions, Shivaun Mahoney, Joao Lopes, Katherine Costello, Anthony and Stephanie Nichols, Deborah Easley, Tina Weston, Jodi Freedman, Donna Hunt, Leslie Patten, Jo Childers, Grandma Lee, George and Lois Esteban, Maxine and Steve Shore, Debbie Breitbach, Phuong, Mary, Christine and Yvonne McDermott and My Le Goldberg, Priscilla Patey, Bill and Kay Atwood, Barry, Elizabeth, Jon and Sara Ferris-Childers, Richard Crosfield, Antoinette Pernetta, Richard Pierce, and Theodore Preovolos.

The White-Haired Girl

Prologue

THE MASK

The days of exile are over, we are told. But we are all in exile . . . in exile from the heart. Now the Sweetness and Bitterness are dry words on our lips, tasteless and indistinguishable. Black and white change before our eyes. Good and bad, bled of morality, shift and dance to a changing tune. We smell danger in the wind and conform at once to an arbitrary consensus which survival requires: We live in fear, like a flock of birds always hearing the arrow leave the bow. Fear tells us not only what to see but how to look, to speak, to think. To open our hearts, to reveal our hidden minds, even to share our suffering, is treason.

We live hidden, secret lives, apart from one another, desolate behind a mask of unity, wary of betrayal. The mask . . . thin, delicate, impassive . . . reveals nothing, fulfilling its purpose. What we can safely tell each other is not worth speaking. But what we must tell to live, what we must cry out like newborn children for the breath of life to enter and our hearts to beat again . . . this is dangerous, unacceptable.

Truth is our forbidden language. What lives behind the mask is taboo; it must be hidden, suppressed, denied. To survive here it seems one must die within. Truth is dangerous in a culture of lies. It is dangerous everywhere, I believe. But particularly in China, the country of my birth.

Revolutionary Cradle

Mama tells me I was the only plump baby in our compound, born in 1964, the Year of the Dragon. Ancient superstition calls me lucky on both counts. For a fat baby is our rose in the desert, and the dragon is our brightest sign. My birth marked the first harvest year after our three-year Difficult Era of famines and natural disasters that claimed nearly thirty million lives. My playmates born in those harsh years were sickly and thin.

We children moved to a live-in kindergarten when we were two because our parents worked six days a week. But we spent Sundays at home with them. My neighbors, like "Grandma" Yang and "Grandpa" Li, adored me, a little round doll, a dim-sum baby creased with fat dimples. They saw me born and watched me grow in wonder. They loved to pinch my cheeks, grab my chubby arms and legs and measure them with their fingers. They pampered me, wanting to keep me plump and growing. Sweet buns, sesame candies, and occasionally chocolate awaited me in one home or another on my Sundays home from kindergarten.

Mama, pretty and feminine, and Ba, handsome and strong, met in the prestigious Chinese Diplomatic Institute. Married on Red

Mama and Jaia, the Dragon Year baby, at forty-five days old.

October Day, 1957, the fortieth anniversary of Russia's Liberation, they were assigned to work in the Ministry of Culture on their graduation. In our living compound they were called the Beautiful Couple. And they took me, their plump dragon baby, everywhere in Beijing. I saw the city riding on Ba's shoulders. And wherever we went, people stopped us.

"Ai ya! So cute!" they said, pinching my cheeks. "How plump! What did you feed her?"

And Ba bragged about me shamelessly.

"Nothing special. It's luck! See those little cheeks? Redder than Country Glow apples! Look! Even her hands have dimples! My daughter, she is the plumpest, cutest girl in Beijing! Do you know she weighed eight jin when she was born? Ya! No kidding! Eight jin! And a Dragon Year baby, too!"

Mama tugged his sleeve like a kite string to pull him down to earth, whispering, "Must you say the plumpest and cutest in Beijing? Can't you be a bit humble?"

But Ba only laughed. After we saw *The White-Haired Girl*, a revolutionary ballet about a good daughter named Happy, I became a little Happy ballerina. I rode on Ba's shoulders, giggling and waving my chubby arms while he danced down the sidewalks singing to me the song Happy's baba had sung to her:

> *"Other people's daughters wear the flowers,*
> *that your poor baba has no money to buy.*
> *So I buy two yards of red ribbon,*
> *to put in my Happy's hair."*

Mama, our loyal audience, laughed and cheered our performances. She was happy for me, so safe and loved. Compared to her own refugee childhood, I lived in a honey jar.

I have flashes of memories: white pigeons hopping in the morning sun on the golden eaves of the Forbidden City; Mama feeding me sugar-frosted plums in the crowds of Da Shi La market; flying kites in Tiananmen Square, our own kite lost among colorful thousands; Ba raising me into the branches to smell the sweet jade magnolias in Bei Hei Park; gliding swiftly over North Sea Park Lake in a bamboo basket, Mama and Ba pulling me on a rope, skating ahead like a pair of flying swallows; and National Day Celebration, when the cheering masses waved like crops in the wind and rainbow fireworks painted the night sky.

My best kindergarten friend, Little Curly Hair, was a Rabbit Year girl, a year older than me. Frail, lovely, and shy, she had large eyes with long, curved lashes, and her thick, curly hair floated on her head like a cloud. As I was loved in our yard for my plumpness, she was adored for her lovely, soft curls.

Her parents and grandpa lived down the hall and worked in Mama's Ministry of Culture branch. Her grandpa, a spry, white-haired scholar and prominent intellectual, had a wispy chin beard and walked with a bamboo cane. I loved to go to their home to watch the seven glittering goldfish that swam in a bubbling tank. Her grandpa sprinkled fish powder that fell like snowflakes through the water, and the seven fish swam and ate them gulping. He said they were magic fish who changed into seven golden fairies at night.

Little Curly Hair's grandpa, a king of kids, played our games and told us stories. He taught us to string wooden beads and make a necklace. He took us out to the street vendors to buy red-bean popsicles and almond tofu jelly. He sometimes wore different-colored socks. On Sunday afternoons, he and Little Curly Hair walked in the compound holding hands. I often went with them.

When the flowering yard bloomed in dazzling spring colors, the air filled with sweet perfumes. Then we picked apricots, dates, and plum blossoms, snowy honeysuckles and pink fairy-furs. We chased butterflies and cats and petted rabbits in their cages. We rolled on the spongy green lawns and treasure-hunted for ladybugs under shady umbrella arbors of tangled purple vine.

I loved being at home with Mama and Ba. People visited each other and shared meals. Women shopped, washed, and sewed together, borrowed and loaned communally. Evenings, neighbors gathered to play cards and checkers, talk, laugh, and drink tea. Sunday night, rooms filled with people and chairs and the air turned foggy with cigarette smoke. Feet stamped, elbows wagged, hands gestured and waved. Excited heads, black-haired and white-haired, bobbed and turned like potatoes stirred in a washtub. A wild river of voices joking, arguing, laughing, made the room hum and whirl. And behind it all an amniotic silence, like deep water, warm and still, surrounded and held us.

We children played in a forest of chairs and legs. We crawled among melons on the floor, straddled them like horses, petted their smooth green skins, yearning for their sweet red insides. Cut them up and eat them! Their juice washed our faces and stained our clothes. Our neighbor, "Grandma" Yang, quick-fried the seeds in her wok. We squatted in a half-circle around her, awaiting her sizzling treasures. Crouching eagerly, we contemplated Grandma's sweet, wrinkled face, soothed by her singing, waiting to be fed like her little birds. We cracked the hot seeds open with our teeth, devoured the tiny meats, and made a little hill of empty shells on the floor.

So life tasted at two years old—sweet, joyous, and endlessly satisfying. It swelled inside us, immense, wondrous, unstoppable, like shining bubbles rising up from a dark, fathomless womb to burst in light. We didn't know we lived in the calm before a hurricane revolution that would uproot our peaceful lives, cast our ancient history aside, and change our world forever.

I rode home on the kindergarten bus on a late May afternoon in 1966. Beijing exploded outside my window. Celebrating masses packed the sidewalks, poured in rivers through the dusty streets, singing, chanting, marching, and dancing, waving red banners and flags, holding posters and huge pictures of one man. Red-collared, green-uniformed men and women were everywhere. They chanted and shouted passionately through megaphones with the cheering masses.

"Long live Chairman Mao!"

"Long live our Great Helmsman!"

These living words, painted on huge red banners, were draped across buildings in black characters ten feet high. Corner loudspeakers blared marching music. Posters covered walls and windows. Yellow, green, purple, blue, and red leaflets whirled down like huge snowflakes to cover the ground.

My bus plowed like a ship through a sea of writhing bodies, shouting heads, and waving arms as the masses rushed, churned, and bubbled through the carnival streets. We arrived at dusk before the Ministry of Culture building, where our parents waited to take us home. I looked for Mama, beautiful, almond-eyed, standing on the steps, radiant in her white dress, her skin smooth and fair, and her long shining hair falling down over her shoulders. Then I saw her, changed . . . her hair cut short above her ears, wearing

Jaia at age two in the Ministry of Culture backyard with Ba (above) and with Mama (below).

a dark blue jacket and pants. All of them, mothers and fathers, dressed the same.

"My Little Jaia!" She came and picked me up excitedly. "The revolution has begun!"

A group of children ran by, laughing and shouting through the blanket of fallen leaflets, kicking them up like snow. I didn't know that these leaflets now covered our nation, nor that Chairman Mao had formally declared a Great Proletarian Cultural Revolution. We entered Mama's Ministry of Culture building, and the door closed behind us. As we stood in the huge, quiet lobby, Mama pointed and said softly, "Little Jaia, look. . . ."

A gigantic man, eerily radiant, stood at the center of the hall, hands clasped behind his back. His stern bronze face almost reached the third floor. Glowing white neon bulbs outlined his form in concentric rings, flashing outward from center to periphery. He gazed far off, and his wise, penetrating eyes saw ten thousand li. "Chairman Mao!" Mama whispered in awe.

We were tiny dolls cowering at the feet of a god. I stared up at this blazing deity who had summoned us, fearing he would talk, blink, suddenly look down at me. Soon I would see him everywhere, indoors and out, in his huge pictures, posters, statues, and busts. His noble face would watch me from the walls of every room and stare out at me from the picture buttons everyone would wear on their proletarian uniforms.

I would learn of Chairman Mao, the greatest, most powerful being in the world, a hero-savior, the source of all good and happiness, an immortal who would live ten thousand years. We were all his children. And we would love him, worship him with awe, bow down to him and surrender our lives. I cannot tell the power his universal image held in my mind and in the hearts of my people. No emperor before him ever reached Chairman Mao's glory.

Monday we rose at six in the morning. In the hall, Mama made a breakfast of rice and pork bits left over from last night's dinner. The hallway was our communal kitchen, covered with a thick, ancient residue of grease and smoke. A naked bulb dangled from the ceiling. Mornings hummed with the energy of mothers busy over woks, preparing breakfast for their families. We children ran from wok to wok to see who was eating what. And the mothers laughed, dipping their chopsticks in, teasing us with little tastes.

Out on the crowded street by seven, we scrambled onto the

kindergarten bus. Our parents went to buy us street vendors' sweets to console us on our ride to school. When they handed them to us through the windows, we gobbled them up. What remained when we arrived at kindergarten would be confiscated by Teacher Yi.

We bawled as our bus pulled away from the curb. These one-week separations from our parents were the misery of our little lives. I hated leaving Mama and Ba. And I dreaded kindergarten and stern Teacher Yi, a skinny, short-haired, goat-faced woman who called us "Chairman Mao's little soldiers," spanked us for opening our eyes at nap time, clawed our backs when she bathed us, and often shouted, "You must grow straight and tall and red!"

I never saw any tall red people, and I never knew what she meant or how to please her.

> *"The East is Red and the sun is rising.*
> *In China arose Mao Zedong.*
> *He seeks happiness for all of the people.*
> *He is the savior star for all of the people."*

In kindergarten we woke to "The East Is Red" playing over the indoor speakers on the Party's morning broadcast. After breakfast we solemnly faced Chairman Mao's enormous picture and bowed together, performing Morning Asking.

"I will always be loyal to you, Chairman Mao, until the last drop of my blood! I will always do whatever you say until my last breath! I want to be your best kid! Please guide me through this day! Ten thousand years alive, Chairman Mao! Ten thousand years! Ten thousand years!"

Chairman Mao watched over his people. He heard our every word, knew our every thought. He loved each one of us. His compassion was broader than the sky. His wisdom was deeper than the sea. Every word he spoke was a drumbeat of truth. He liberated the masses and gave them food and homes and families. This was why his name meant "Source from the East."

We lived our lives for Chairman Mao, from morning to evening, in the sight of his heroic image. We would follow him forever, and he would lead us to liberate the dark world from slavery. In our daily lessons, Teacher Yi taught us the Revolutionary Teachings.

"Who is the Reddest Sun of our hearts?" she asked.

"Chairman Mao!" we shouted.

"Right answer!" she praised us. "And who do you love most?"

"Mama!" "Baba!" "Grandpa!" we answered unevenly.

"No! Wrong, wrong, wrong!" she scolded sternly. "You must love Chairman Mao the most! He is your dearest, no one else! Not your mama! Not your baba! Not your grandpa or grandma! Remember this! Now, who do you love the most?"

"Chairman Mao!" we shouted.

"Very good!" said Teacher Yi, satisfied and smiling. "And who is Chairman Mao?"

"Chairman Mao!" we shouted again.

Her smile vanished.

"No! No! No! You must say Red Sun this time! Chairman Mao is Red Sun, Red Sun is Chairman Mao! You must remember!"

We memorized Chairman Mao's poems and words and many political slogans, chanting them daily.

"We all depend on Chairman Mao Thought!"

"Crush the Soviet bear!" And "America is a paper tiger! Death to American imperialism!"

I learned early to fear Russians and Americans, two races of demons who spent their lives plotting our destruction. But we were protected by Chairman Mao, our glorious Party, and our great historical destiny.

I became Chairman Mao's best kid, even on my Sundays at home. To Mama and Ba's pleasure and amusement, I bowed to Chairman Mao again and again, sincerely offering him the wax

mango which everyone kept under his picture. I was devoted to him. Mama and Ba proudly presented me to our neighbors to recite Chairman Mao's poems from memory. When I was done, the neighbors cheered and pinched my cheeks and patted my head. I felt like a hero.

Screams, crashing metal, shrieks in the dark . . . the door of our kindergarten burst open. Black shadows darted howling into the cold room, wild-waving arms banging weapons in the dark.

"Ahhhh! Yahhhh! The American ghosts are here! Grab your sheets! The atom bomb is exploding! Run to the shelter!"

Crash! Crash! Crash! went the pot lids.

Crack! Crack! Crack! the metal spoons hammered on woks.

"Hurry! Hurry! This way! They will kill us all!"

Stumbling out of bed in terror, we grabbed our sheets, covering up, as we had been taught, to protect ourselves from the poison rain that fell from American bombs. We fled into the hall, where hundreds of children covered with bedsheets milled and sobbed and poured through the back door into the schoolyard night. We bleated, stumbled, and bumped into one another, stampeding bare-

Jaia, about three years old, plays in Bei Hai Park.

foot across the cold yard to the shelter. Even the moon and stars hid behind the clouds from the Americans.

"Run to the shelter!" "Be orderly!" "Stay in your groups!"

Our teachers shouted over the din, herding us to the underground bomb shelter in the middle of the playground. An uprooted slide was set in the entrance. One by one, we were yanked, lifted, and stuffed like straw dolls into a yawning chute, to slide down a dark tunnel. I screamed all the way down. Invisible hands grabbed me at the bottom. Demon eyes glittered in the darkness. American ghosts in the shelter! I screamed again. A hand pinched my arm.

"Shut up! Don't resist!" a familiar voice said.

Screaming children dropped one by one down the slide.

"Shut up!" a voice hissed. "They will hear you and find us!"

My classmates cried and whimpered all around me. I soon made out their huddled forms, heard their breathing, felt their warm bodies near me. Then, only sniffles and an eerie silence.

The shelter grew colder. I wrapped myself in my sheet, waiting for the bombs to explode, for howling American ghosts to pour down the slide, shooting their guns. No one came. I drifted off.

"Wake up! Wake up!" Our principal's voice. "The American ghosts have left. We can go back now."

Fog creeping down the slide made the dawn-illumined tunnel a misty pathway to the light. A door opened. Sleepily we climbed from our silent tomb into the pale morning.

In my two years in Beijing kindergarten we had many attacks—sometimes the Americans, sometimes the Russians. Teacher Yi said a Hungry Soviet Bear lived on our northern border, a Greedy American Wolf hid in Vietnam on our southern border, and we were a big Peaceful Panda in the middle, fighting for our lives. When I told Mama how Americans and Russians invaded our kindergarten, she laughed and said they had not really been there.

But they were all too real for me. My terror intensified my love for Chairman Mao, who saved us every time. And it stirred my rage against these Soviet and American demons who tried to destroy our happiness and steal our lives away.

August 18, 1966: Over a million youth attend the first Tiananmen Square Red Guard mass rally. Wearing green PLA uniforms, red armbands, and Chairman Mao picture buttons, they chant his sayings for hours and wave his Little Red Book in the air. When he appears over the Gate of Heavenly Peace, their roar is heard for miles. Cheering, weeping, even fainting at the sight of him, they pledge their loyalty and devotion "to the last drop of blood." Chairman Mao's instructions echo across China, setting tens of millions of youthful hearts on fire.

"We must strike down, smash, and utterly expose the counter-revolutionary revisionists! The bourgeois rightists! And the reactionary bourgeois academics!"

Part of the fuel to be burned is a whole class of people like my parents, the intellectuals whom Chairman Mao has named the "Stinking Ninth Category" in his list of the People's enemies.

Ever since Chairman Mao's disastrous Great Leap Forward in 1958, in which he moved our vast peasant population into communes by decree, resulting in famines costing nearly thirty million lives, the Party—led by Chairman of the Nation Liu Shaoqi—has sought to reduce his power and abandon his fanatical ideological emphasis to chart a new course of economic stability. But Chairman Mao sees this as capitulation to bourgeois materialism, a selling out of the Communist ideal. Now he sees corrupt Party leaders subverting his Cultural Revolution for political gain, while feigning support. He calls it "waving the red flag to oppose the red flag."

Outnumbered by political peers who are slowly reducing him to a figurehead, Chairman Mao takes his case to the people, who revere him. He calls on the children, raised to worship him as a God. From their ranks, he creates his Red Guard. He sets the Revolution on their youthful shoulders and turns them loose on the Party hierarchy that has challenged his hegemony. And he turns them on all his enemies, who are the "enemies of the people," the enemies of mankind. The next morning over a million Red Guard occupy Beijing. Going to work, Mama sees hundreds of uniformed teenage boys and girls holding Chairman Mao's Little Red Book in their hands, their belongings wrapped in blankets and strapped on their backs. They storm her building, shouting slogans and accusations and making wild threats. They cover the halls with political posters, burst into offices, topple furniture, and beat up anyone showing "antirevolutionary resistance."

Eleven mass rallies in the next six months draw over a million Red Guard each. From every province, they pour into Beijing and out again like a red tide, driven by naive passions and a holy cause: to follow Chairman Mao and make revolution; to destroy the old,

backward society and build a new one; to crush all "Black Gang-
members, antirevolutionary rightists, revisionists, Stinking Ninth
Category intellectuals, and enemies of the people."

They become soldiers of an occupying army intoxicated by a
sudden, miraculous victory; the pendulum of history has swung
them from impotence to absolute power in a single stroke. Puffed
up, invincible, burning with inexplicable rage, they become a fire
and a flood, a hurricane force of nature sweeping across our moth-
erland, reducing our prized culture of five millennia to a charred
relic in three short years. And they call it revolution.

"Today is the day of Remembering the Bitterness and Tasting the
Sweetness," Teacher Yi solemnly announced to our class.

We sat erect in our chairs, hands clasped behind our backs, staring hopefully into our empty bowls.

"Everyone rise and bow to our Great Helmsman."

We bowed to Chairman Mao's picture, shouting over and over,
"Never forget the class bitterness! Always remember our hatred
through our blood and tears!"

We sat down. Two teachers came, taking small dark triangles of
bread from their bamboo baskets and placing them in our bowls. I
looked at mine, mouth watering, wishing it were bigger. My first
bite of that bread was a nasty surprise. Coarse, bitter, textured with
stems and chopped hay, and seasoned with foul herbs, it had a re-
pulsive taste. We quickly spit it back into our bowls.

"Swallow!" Teacher Yi shrieked. "Do not spit! How can you
know what your parents and grandparents suffered? How can you
know the sweetness we have now if you don't taste the bitterness
we had before? Every one of you, eat!"

She and her two assistants advanced into our ranks. Children began crying. I picked up my bread again, now wishing it smaller. A
little boy at my table spit his piece out again. Teacher Yi swooped
down on him like a cormorant, forcing it into his mouth and pinch-

ing his lips shut with her bony fingers. After a short, one-sided, tearful struggle, he swallowed. So did I. Our sniffles and sobs made the classroom sound like a disturbed chicken coop.

"This bread is what people ate before our Liberation," Teacher Yi said. "People were so poor that when children cried for food, their parents gave them bread made out of stone powder. Even now, all over the world, especially in Taiwan, Japan, Russia, and America, people can't eat even such bread as this. You children are very lucky."

The other two teachers returned smiling with their baskets. Several children burst into tears again. But now, in each of our bowls they put a plump steamed bun topped with red dates.

"And now," said Teacher Yi brightly, "taste the sweetness our beloved Chairman Mao has brought us. Let us thank him."

And we did, one eye on his picture, the other on his heavenly bun. That black bread was the nastiest food we had ever tasted. But this sweet bun was the best in the world. We gobbled it down like greedy little pigs.

"We should always remember this and be grateful," Teacher Yi droned on.

My mind was on the sweetness, not on Teacher Yi. But I felt grateful to Chairman Mao, who had loaded these delicious buns on the truck and delivered them to our kindergarten. And I felt sorry for the rest of the world, full of poor people who could not even eat the nasty black bread. Following Chairman Mao, we would liberate them all.

Everyone now wore Chairman Mao's picture pin, and his Little Red Book in a red pouch on a shoulder strap. I loved Chairman Mao's pins. I couldn't read, but I loved his Little Red Book. We waved it happily in the air while chanting his sayings. We held it lovingly to our hearts while facing his picture for Morning Asking and Evening Report. We carried it with us wherever we went.

And Teacher Yi warned us never to turn it upside down. This was antirevolutionary!

I never turned Chairman Mao's Little Red Book upside down. I wanted to be his best kid. I would follow him and become a Little Red Soldier and then join the Red Guard when I grew older like my brother, Big Honesty. I wanted to wear a red armband and make revolution like the Red Guard who patrolled Beijing, pushing and shouting at bad people, waving their Little Red Books in the air like flags.

But Teacher Yi said we intellectuals' children were born polluted. We needed discipline and purification in order to become Little Red Soldiers. That we loved the "candy bullets" our parents gave us on Monday mornings showed "bourgeois lust." That some of us still had colorful clothes and blankets showed "bourgeois pride." Teacher Yi even cut the pink plastic buttons off my coat and sewed on wood ones. And she cut out the magical clowns embroidered on my bedsheet. Mama said nothing.

That summer Mama gave me a bottle of alcohol-based perfume to cure my mosquito bites. Teacher Yi's sharp nose smelled it the first day. She snatched it away and held it up to the class.

"Does everyone smell the corrupting stink of this bourgeois poison?" she fumed. "Jaia is a nasty, bourgeois little girl!"

Holding the offensive bottle at arm's length, like a dead rat by its tail, she dropped it with a clang into the garbage can. I didn't know what "bourgeois" was. But I knew it was very bad. And I decided never to be bourgeois again if I could help it.

The Ministry of Culture was occupied by Red Guard and attacked daily in the news. Chairman Mao had called it a bourgeois organization stinking of capitalism and feudalism, a black nest of intellectuals, a graveyard full of dead people, foreigners, and ghosts. Then one morning all Ministry of Culture workers were ordered to Xian Nong Tan sports stadium. Mama arranged for me to live with her aunt in Nanjing if she and Ba didn't return.

Years later she told me about that day, when over fifteen thousand Ministry of Culture workers arrived at Xian Nong Tan stadium. Several thousand soldiers, police, and Red Guard led them in onto the wooden bleachers. Many PLA officers, some from the Party Central Committee, watched them from a stage on the field. Chairman Mao's huge picture sat on a wooden easel between a microphone stand and a red flag.

A Central Committee member went to the microphone. He was smaller than Chairman Mao's picture. A wall of Red Guard rose from the bottom of the bleachers and faced the workers.

The leader shouted in the silent stadium: "We will now sing 'The East Is Red!' "

Fifteen thousand workers leaped up, anxious to show Red Spirit. They sang "The East Is Red," then chanted Chairman Mao's sayings, "A revolution is not a dinner party," "Sweep all cow ghosts and snake spirits thoroughly away," "Let us be tough, strong, and unafraid of death and sacrifice," and "Never forget the class bitterness, always remember our hatred through our blood and tears."

They sat down. The Central Committee member at the microphone wiped his forehead. Thirty thousand eyes watched him. Then he broke the silence with a shriek like a soldier thrusting his bayonet.

"We all know the Ministry of Culture has become a black dying vat! A rotten black nest full of cow ghosts and snake spirits! All you who are in this vat are contaminated! Stained black! Many of you were dyed unknowingly! You are partly innocent! You may be reformed through diligent study of Chairman Mao's teachings and your own revolutionary actions! You must cooperate fully! Examine yourselves thoroughly! Confess your crimes and purge your hearts red! Then you may be reembraced by the people!

"But some of you are black to your bones! You black melons on the black vine have knowingly brought the black dye in and poured it into the vat! You have secretly followed the black line of your evil leader, Liu Shaoqi! You have betrayed the people and the revolution! You have betrayed our Great Helmsman Chairman Mao! Now you must be purged before you stain others black!" (Liu Shaoqi, Chairman of the Nation, was then a prisoner of the Red Guard in his Zhong Nan Hai Compound home.)

"Those of you loyal to Chairman Mao and his Great Proletarian Cultural Revolution must now cast out these black traitors one by one! You must name these cow ghosts! These snake spirits! These capitalist roaders and imperialist walking dogs! You know who they are! Do not hide them! Expose them! Shout their names out bravely! Do not fear them! Let their crimes be known! Let their reign of terror end! Let them face the people's wrath!"

He watched them. Silence hummed like cicadas. Fear howled like a cold wind in the void. Then a man stood up near the bottom and shrieked a curse in the silent stadium.

"XIA YAN!"

It cracked the frozen moment like a hammer's blow. Xia Yan, Ministry of Culture vice minister and one of China's celebrated authors, worked in Mama's building. Novels, plays, movies, and literary criticism had flowed from his pen for over forty years.

Mama didn't recognize the man who called Xia Yan's name. Maybe he was a worker acting out of revolutionary zeal. Maybe he bore a grudge against Xia Yan, resented his fame, saw him as an obvious target. Maybe he was planted to strike the first match. After a pause, hundreds, then thousands of voices joined in until it became a chant of nearly twenty thousand people, screaming, "XIA YAN! XIA YAN! XIA YAN!"

Other voices chimed in, "Kill the black traitor!" "Bring him out!" "Ten thousand feet march on his corpse!"

A few rows down from Mama, people yanked Xia Yan from his seat. Many hands thrust him down, grabbed him, passed him like half a sack of rice to the bottom. The Red Guard took him, dragged him to the center of the dirt field, and left him. Tiny, scared, alone, sixty-seven-year-old Xia Yan wept. At the smell of his blood a sleeping dragon awoke, roared his name with twenty thousand tongues, and cursed him with fire. Xia Yan shook like a puppet in the waves of hate. His frail limbs clattered like dry bamboo. "Traitor Xia Yan!" "Crush the rotten egg!" "Death to Xia Yan!" "Kill the black puppet of Liu Shaoqi!"

"Who else? Who are the others?" the Central Committee official screamed into his microphone.

More names were called out: Hung Mei, Zhou Wei Shi, Situ Hui Min, three artists whose age and fame placed them in Xia Yan's class. My neighbors Grandpa Li and Grandma Yang also were called out. And so was Little Curly Hair's grandpa. It went on and on, each one dragged from the bleachers onto the field. When the official at the microphone brought it to an end, more than a hundred "black melons" stood in a line at the center of the field—scholars, writers, artists, and high-ranking department officials, many famous in their fields.

The Red Guard put black paper dunce caps, vests, and signs on these criminals, who then circled the field as the crowd chanted against them. Many convulsed with sobs. Finally the Red Guard herded them off to the cowshed in our living compound.

When Mama told me this story years later, I asked her how they had chosen these Black Gangmembers. She was silent for a moment, then finally said, "We just knew who they were."

Sounds of footsteps and voices . . . Mama and Ba jerked upright in bed beside me. I woke to moonlight pouring through our window and the little neighbor boy crying to his mama through the wall.

"They are here."

Mama's whisper scraped out like broken glass. A loud pounding rattled our door and a man shouted, "Security Bureau ID check! Open the door!"

The pounding began again. Moonlight illumined Ba's bruised

Two-year-old Jaia in the MOC backyard.

face and half-shaved head: one side a skull flecked with stubble and razor cuts, the other side thick with his tousled hair. Red Guard had occupied and ransacked his Beijing Film Studio, beating up all "Black Gangmembers following Liu Shaoqi's black line." They beat up Ba and gave him his yin-yang head with a dull razor, a special insult reserved for those in the administration, and a mark so they could not hide.

Ba went and opened the door. A crowd of shadows poured into

the room, slashing the air with blades of light. When our bulb lit up, I saw wild men lunging like monkeys in our small room. I peered over the covers, terrified, as they searched our closet, bookshelf, and desk, shining flashlights under our bed and lifting the covers off Mama to see if she was hiding something. They even looked behind Chairman Mao's picture on the wall.

A PLA officer stood in the middle of the room holding a pen and notebook, a calm eye at the center of the monkey storm. Shadow men huddled like mute ghosts in the dim hall. The others finished searching and gathered behind their captain. He spoke to Ba, who retrieved our family papers from the ransacked desk. He took them, paying no attention to Ba's half-shaved head. His sharp eyes scanned our papers, like two straws sucking water from a glass. Then he scribbled in his notebook.

"Where is Big Honesty?" he asked.

"My son lives at his school," Ba said.

My brother, Big Honesty, then twelve years old, came home only one Sunday a month.

"Where is Jaia?" the officer said.

"My daughter is here." Mama put her hand on my head.

He turned his eyes on me and my belly dropped like a falling star. Two black holes in an empty face opened onto a cave of darkness. Something reached out and touched me. I clutched Mama and started crying.

"I love Chairman Mao," I sobbed.

The black holes fastened their beams on Ba.

"Why aren't her papers here?"

"They are at her kindergarten," Ba said.

"She's only here on Sundays," Mama said.

"Who else lives here?" the empty face asked Ba.

"No one," Ba said.

Wu Tang, Mama's political criminal uncle, had spent three

months hiding in our room. Several weeks ago, Ba had sent him away. He endangered us all. Had he been here this night, he, Mama, and Ba would have been arrested and taken away.

"You must immediately report any visitors," the officer warned. "They must bring their papers to the Security Bureau. Failure in this will bring a harsh penalty. We will come again."

The officer left, drawing his men after him on invisible strings. I heard pounding on the door of the next room, and the voice shouting, "Security Bureau ID check! Open the door!"

Surprise ID checks came twice a year till I was twelve, always at night. All homes were thoroughly searched and many things were confiscated: bourgeois photos, clothing, and furniture, relics and books published before Liberation. Plants and flowers, indoors and out, were uprooted as "poisonous weeds to the spirit." Even pets— dogs, cats, and rabbits—were taken and purged. Birds were set free. Most people preferred to kill their own pets. At least then you could have the meat.

All fugitives caught in these searches, and those hiding them, were arrested. People without ID were also taken away. Wu Tang, Mama's uncle, was captured on the train leaving Beijing the day he left our home. He was later hanged by his neck from a tree in his Sichuan cowshed, leaving his wife and eight children behind. The week before his death, he passed his wife a note that she would keep for the rest of her life. It read: "Don't lose hope. I will never leave you."

I went to see Little Curly Hair the morning after the first ID check. A pile of broken glass was swept into a corner. The fish tank was gone. And Little Curly Hair was crying. Seven dead goldfish lay stiff and curled on the table. They must have been caught as fairies and purged when the ID checkers came.

January 1, 1967, New Year's Day Proclamation: Chairman Mao, at war with his adversaries, calls for an attack on the Party and on "all monsters and demons anywhere in society." He calls for "hundreds of millions of people to rise up and attack all enemies of socialism." He calls on all peasants and workers to join the Red Guard in his revolution. Accusing those advocating moderation of trying to "repress the revolution," he warns they will "all be dumped on the rubbish heap by the revolutionary masses."

The masses join in and the revolution explodes. People in the cities stop working. Peasants stop farming. All schools shut down so their bourgeois format can be revolutionized. Countless cities become war zones as hundreds of thousands of soldier, worker, peasant, and Red Guard factions rise in bloody conflict, fighting one another to prove their redness and loyalty to Chairman Mao.

The Red Guard cripple major cities throughout China. In late January, they conquer Shanghai, but they fail to cooperate and the city falls in chaos. The Red Guard terror becomes legendary. First they enjoy free train rides across the country, free food in the markets, and fearful respect shown them by everyone. Now Chairman Mao says antirevolutionaries are hiding among the people and tells the Red Guard to go find them.

They patrol the streets, defending the red flag and smashing antirevolutionary conspirators wherever they find or imagine them. They invade homes and interrogate, abuse, and torture their prisoners. (Liu Shaoqi, Chairman of the Nation, will die in captivity at their hands.) They vandalize museums and destroy priceless treasures. They desecrate graveyards and scatter the bones of venerated ancestors, shouting Chairman Mao's saying, "Let the dead make room for the living!" They raze thousands of ancient temples, burn sacred artifacts, torture, castrate, rape, and murder thousands of monks and nuns. They cripple and capture major cities throughout China, occupying thousands of government buildings, factories, and schools and taking over transport lines and communications systems. And they do all these things under Chairman Mao's authority.

Caught up in the emotions and peculiar logic of the times, every excess is justified. In the heightened climate of fear, goaded by Chairman Mao's provocative slogans, many see antirevolutionary evil hidden in every heart. In a moment, for a wrong word or gesture, anyone can be put in a cowshed as a People's Enemy. And millions are. No place is safe. No one can be fully trusted. And hundreds of thousands will die in battle in our three bloody Years of Chaos.

"Mama's ghost is back! Mama's ghost is back!"

This eerie shriek in our room woke me. Ba leaped out of bed. The light went on. Big Honesty, my Red Guard brother, home from school for his monthly visit, lay writhing half-naked in the middle of our room, kowtowing toward the wall with Chairman Mao's picture. His head pounded muffled thunder on the floor like a pestle pounding garlic in a mortar. Mama held me tightly in her arms, staring at skinny Big Honesty. He looked like a big crazy eel, howling and flopping in terror under the rippling light waves of a naked, vibrating bulb.

I heard people in the hall outside. Our door pushed open and a muddle of neighbors squeezed in. They stood transfixed like wooden chickens, staring at Big Honesty, a boy lost in a realm of ghosts. Eerily, the room suddenly filled with the sweet, grainy smell of fresh soybeans. It came from nowhere and rose inside the room to hover everywhere.

Ba, barefoot and bare shouldered, his shorts like a wheat bag, crouched over Big Honesty. He tried to grab him up. But Big Honesty wriggled from his grasp, his terror-glazed eyes slanted up showing white, unaware of our neighbors' shocked stares. He hit the floor kowtowing again, his thin frame convulsing with his sad, desolate wail.

"Mama's ghost is back . . . to count your debts! All your debts!"

"Hysteria! Wake up!" roared Ba.

He slapped Big Honesty fiercely, as if to snap him back into the

Jaia, age three, does a "loyalty dance to Chairman Mao."

human world. Big Honesty jerked and shrank under Ba's flailing palms, seeming to wake from his fevered ghost-dream.

"To count your debts," he whimpered pitifully. "Mama's back. . . ."

Ba was panting hard and sweating. Big Honesty lay on the floor, curled painfully like an old shrimp, his face covered with one arm. Our murmuring neighbors shook their heads, sobered by Big Honesty's nightmare. Mama held me shivering in her arms.

Years later I would learn Ba had had a first wife before Mama, Big Honesty's real Mama, who got sick when he was a little boy my age. She died slowly, spitting blood, while Big Honesty watched helplessly. He never forgot her. Years later he would go back to meet her family, hoping to settle her affairs in this world and pay his respects. I would go with him.

I sat in the school bus on a spring morning. Mama had gone to buy me a sweet for my ride to kindergarten. I heard shouts and saw people running toward our compound. A noisy crowd of hundreds gathered in the street, shouting, pushing, striving toward something

Ba and three-year-old Jaia at Bei Hai Park.

in their midst. Our parents rushed in to be absorbed. The mass drew and devoured them, surged outward and expanded, buzzing with a fierce hunger. Each person became a unit of life within it, struggling toward its center and out again.

Our bus drove away, cheating us of our Monday sweet. Behind, in the churning crowd, Mama pushed in till she found herself at the center, staring down at the body of what appeared to be an old man. His silver hair was soaked with blood. His face was a red, pulpy mass of flesh. His head, turned at an odd angle, hung half off the curb. His shattered spectacles, wire frames twisted and bent, lay nearby. He was curled up as if death had returned him to the womb.

Mama turned away, pushing out through the press of seekers burrowing in. She reached the front steps of the Ministry of Culture and met a young woman from her office. She told Mama what she had seen. The old man had argued with the Red Guard. They tried to take him, but he fought back. So they beat him with their copper belt buckles. They surrounded him and he couldn't get away. When he fell they kept on swinging, down and down.

"His face . . . " the woman said, her voice choking. "How will his family recognize him?"

People came now from all directions to merge with the swelling mass, drawn to the old man's body like a river of ants to a broken fruit. They threaded their way in and out again with a tale to tell.

When Mama went to the compound cafeteria for lunch, the old man's body was gone. All that remained was glass slivers and his blood on the curb. The slivers would scatter in the wind. The blood would fade in time, discolored by the yellow Siberian dust that swept through the city and hung in the air, thicker than pollen. And all the blood spilled in China's streets in the three Years of Chaos to come would be trampled under the feet of ten thousand workers and washed away in the autumn rains.

Little Curly Hair's grandpa was one of the criminals called out in Xian Nong Tan stadium. And soon after the Xian Nong Tan struggle meeting, Teacher Yi announced this to our class.

"Little Curly Hair's grandpa is a bad Black Gangmember," she said. "But now he has been arrested by the people."

Little Curly Hair shrank in her seat like melted wax. We knew having a Black Gangmember relative made you a bad child. And having a Black Gangmember parent or grandparent made you a Black Rodent, no matter how much you loved Chairman Mao. As the saying went, "A dragon breeds a dragon, a phoenix breeds a phoenix, and a rat's offspring knows how to dig holes." We had more than a few Black Rodents in our class. One morning, Teacher Yi brought Little Curly Hair to the front of the room and sat her down in a chair. Teacher Yi was mad.

"Everyone look at her," she said. "We all know curly hair is very bourgeois. I told her parents to cut off her curls, but they have not done it. Now I must do it."

Little Curly Hair burst into tears as Teacher Yi grabbed her hair like wild weeds and began cutting near the scalp. A *ka-cha, ka-cha* sound, like scaling a dead fish, mixed with her sobs. In Teacher Yi's hand, the scissors became an angry metal bird with slashing beaks. Big clumps of curly hair fell softly to the floor. Stone fingers squeezed my heart. Only when Teacher Yi stopped did they let go. Now Little Curly Hair looked like a scared little boy with a dog-chewed head.

After this incident we nicknamed her Shao Tu Gui, Little Bald Ghost. She became fearful and quiet, a hovering shadow. And even from his cowshed her grandpa caused her trouble. Being a Black Gangmember was much worse than being bourgeois! From time to time in class Teacher Yi would ask her, "Little Curly Hair, who is your grandpa?"

"He is a black bad person," she firmly and obediently replied.

"And what do you do with him?"

"I draw the line with him, and I throw him away."

On our Sundays playing in the compound, other adults asked her about her grandpa. She always gave the same firm response. Then other children began taunting her with it, and even spitting on her. This was often done to Black Rodents. I knew Little Curly Hair missed her grandpa and felt sad inside having to draw the line and throw him away. And she was lonely, for many parents now told their children to avoid her. Even I could not play with her anymore.

In our kindergarten we slept in two rows of beds set against opposite walls. Above us, two large portraits of Chairman Mao faced each other across the room like kings on a chessboard. We were his pawns in the dark. At night I lay missing Mama, chewing my bamboo pillow cover, hearing Little Curly Hair's muffled crying beside me.

Things changed at home. Mama and Ba hardly smiled or laughed. We rarely went outside. Our neighbors no longer visited us, and we avoided them. Women ignored each other in the hall as they cooked, staring silently into their splattering woks. Men no longer came out of their rooms to joke and talk. And everyone ate inside with doors shut.

Joy had fled like the end of summer. There were no more evening gatherings, no card and checker games, no Sunday parties, no more melons or Grandma Yang's quick-fried seeds. All the cats and dogs and rabbits were gone. The city zoo and all the parks had closed. It didn't feel good to be anywhere. I felt an ominous force drawing near, silently gazing at us.

Grandma Yang, Grandpa Li, and several hundred of our former Ministry of Culture neighbors were now Black Gangmembers. I saw them on Sunday afternoons when the Red Guard herded them out of the cowshed to line up at the cafeteria. They stood holding tin bowls, waiting for a ladle of rice porridge. We knew not to talk to them.

With schools shut down, the children everywhere ran wild. Little Red Soldiers hunted Little Black Rodents, who often hid in their rooms, afraid to go out. Many children in our compound gathered at the prisoners' food line, cursing, throwing dirt clods, and firing small stones at them with slingshots. The prisoners awkwardly dodged the missiles, looking guilty and helpless. I saw a young boy shoot an old man's eye out with a stone. The children cheered as the Red Guard led the old man away screaming, his hand clapped over his eye, blood streaming down his cheek.

Leaving Mama on Monday mornings grew more painful. Our Sundays together passed swiftly. Our weeks apart crept by, slow as seasons. I was a jade magnolia bud plucked too soon from her branches. I wanted to bloom in her arms.

That autumn I lay fever-sick in delirium. Teacher Yi called Mama to come get me. Mama's sweet face appeared in a sky blue scarf, looking down at me. She rolled me in a blanket and carried me to the bus, cradled in her arms. I melted like snowflakes in her palm. Wherever her love was, there was my home.

I lay in bed. Mama sat beside me peeling an orange. Her face was a full moon. She fed me juicy slivers with her pearl white fingers. I was her little bird. As I watched her, a blissful, sorrow-love welled up in my heart. My loneliness and fear of losing her haunted me. And I felt a secret guilt for loving her more than I loved Chairman Mao.

Unable to express my love for her, I conceived a childish fantasy. In it, I left home to become a doctor and returned to find Mama lying in bed in our darkened room. She gazed at me, her sad eyes opened wide with love. She could not see me. Her beautiful eyes were blind. So I took them out with my fingers, held them in my palms, touched and kissed them. Then I put them back in, better than before. Mama wept with joy and pride. For now her eyes saw a thousand li away. Now she would always be able to see me. And no matter how far apart we might be, I would know she was watching over me.

Spring 1968: Bloody battles still rage throughout China. Many Red Guard factions have acquired grenades, bombs, and anti-aircraft artillery by raiding military bases and robbing trains with weapons shipments headed for Vietnam. Casualties in some provinces number in the tens of thousands. Thousands die in single battles. Thousands of buildings are leveled by antiaircraft fire and hundreds of thousands of people are left homeless. In big cities like Beijing, trucks go out daily to pick up bodies in the streets and bring them to the crematories where they are piled and burned day and night.

Tens of millions of displaced revolutionaries roam our devastated cities. Like burning embers in a dry wheat field, they ignite in skirmishes and violence. With farmers and workers making revolution, crop yields plummet in the countryside; the social chaos ravages the economy, threatening famine.

In desperation, Chairman Mao turns to the PLA. Tens of millions of soldiers spread out across China to reestablish the col-

Four years old, Jaia stands in Tiananmen Square in front of the Gate of Heavenly Peace.

lapsed social order, to pry our nation from the jaws of chaos and the hands of the Red Guard. Thousands of rebel Red Guard factions are hunted down and killed or captured and sent to prisons and labor camps. Over a million soldiers occupy Beijing.

Chairman Mao finally orders all Red Guard to the countryside to be "reeducated" by the peasants. Armed PLA Mao Zedong Thought Propaganda Teams scour all of China, house-to-house, to enforce this exile. More than twenty million city dwellers will also be sent to countryside camps, many as political criminals. Mama and I will be among the first to go.

In the winter of 1968, Little Curly Hair's grandpa escaped from the Ministry of Culture cowshed. Word of his disappearance went out. Wanted posters went up throughout the city. Teacher Yi announced the news in class one morning. We all felt Little Curly Hair's guilt in her grandpa's great crime.

Soon after, the ten-story Ministry of Culture chimney began to choke. The thick gray smoke gushing from its crown thinned to a trickle. Then it stopped. The workers who went in to unclog the grate found the half-burned body of Little Curly Hair's grandpa.

He had climbed up the ten-story ladder and leaped into the dragon's mouth.

Teacher Yi announced this news in class. But we should not feel sad, she said. Only guilty criminals took their own lives. He had opposed the people's justice, and we should be glad that another enemy of the people was dead. Little Curly Hair sat quiet and still. Teacher Yi's words went through her like lightning through a cloud. Then we shouted the slogan, "Let ten thousand feet march on his corpse! Let him never turn over!"

It was my last week of kindergarten in Beijing. I was almost five years old. Mama appeared in my classroom one morning and said we were going on a trip. She rolled my toothbrush, towel, and clothes in my blanket, and we left my kindergarten.

Dreamlike forms in scarf-wrapped faces filled the sidewalks. Garbage and paper shreds torn from weather-beaten posters littered the streets. We got off the bus and headed home. I held Mama's hand, blowing jets of steam into the winter air. To my left, the chimney tower rose like a dragon's neck and pierced the sky. Its huge maw bellowed rivers of dark smoke into the gray clouds.

I stared in awe at this dragon. It devoured living beings, consumed them in its belly, spit them in glowing cinders over the earth, turned to ash and dust. I gazed up at the glowing orange flakes swirling down from their great height. And I feared their burning touch. For to me, they were the ashes of Little Curly Hair's grandpa, the enemy of our people.

Exile in Paradise

It was two days' journey south by train from Beijing to Hubei Province. Silent people filled the wooden benches, spilling onto the floor, huddling in the aisles for warmth. Windows were shut against the cold, and the heavy air stank of garlic, sweat, and cigarette smoke, soiled diapers, and pickled turnips. I sat and slept on Mama's lap, covered with her overcoat. She held me tight and stared out the window, hardly sleeping. Ba had disappeared.

Twenty million people were exiled to the countryside. All Ministry of Culture workers were sent to labor camps in a desolate southern province to reform their thoughts. Now Cowshed Black Gangmembers sat among their former Small Ghost peers like Mama. The black and the stained; Chairman Mao had shuffled them together again.

Not knowing how long this exile would last or if they would ever return, most sold, abandoned, or gave their belongings to the lucky ones remaining behind. Frail hopes faded and dissolved like coal smoke outside the train window. Today's sky looked dark as a crow. And tomorrow looked bleaker than Hubei's barren fields.

I recall the journey as a blur of coldness, pungent smells, beautiful scenery, and the grim, desolate silence of a people grieving without hope, rushing across China on a crowded train, leaving their futures behind them.

When we arrived in Hubei, soldiers put us children in a small kindergarten lined with cots. They put our parents in a large warehouse across the compound. Early the next morning a truck would take them to their camp. I would see Mama once a month for two nights and a day. Black Gangmembers would see their children once every two months.

That night I left our room and wandered alone down a dark hall. I found a door and went outside looking for Mama. Hearing a sound, I looked back. A shadow pursued me in the dark. I ran in terror as thudding footsteps gained. Two bony hands grabbed me, carried me crying and struggling to a dimly lit room, and set me on a stool. The candle flame illumined the stern, inescapable face of Teacher Yi. She had come with us from Beijing. She looked down at me, hard and thin as the scarecrows I had seen in the fields from the train. Her hair stuck out like black feathers under her cap. Her dark eyes gleamed in the flickering light. I stared up at her, crying, hating her. She had kept me from Mama.

"Go ahead, cry all you want," she said.

And I did, till my salty tears burned my throat. Finally, I stopped, beaten.

"Are you finished?" Teacher Yi asked wearily.

"Can I have water?" I asked.

"No water for you, little troublemaker," she said.

She put me to bed with my classmates, and I lay in the dark with a burning thirst. I saw a bubbling stream and Mama on the other side holding a cup of water. But I could not reach her. My new life had begun.

The old army truck crawled whining down the snowy road on the four-hour ride to Mama's camp, plowing over bumps and through deep ruts. Sparse, bare trees stood out on a vast white silent plain. The narrow river rushing alongside our truck would widen when spring melted the snow. We passed many small communes, mud-straw brick and bamboo huts built around large storage barns. Peasants watched us from the fields like stiff fat dolls in their many layers of winter clothes.

We reached Mama's camp set in a barren field by the river. Her reed-shed barracks, a former grain warehouse, was divided in half for three hundred men and women workers. Forty soldiers slept in a smaller barracks. Latrine trenches dug outside the camp provided night soil to fertilize the fields.

My classmates and I played in the snow till a line of shadow figures trudged up the narrow road into camp. Our parents, returned from irrigation digging, moved slowly on heavy legs, tools on their shoulders. We ran to them shouting "Mama!" "Baba!" When I drew near, Mama dropped her pick and knelt down with open arms.

"My baby!"

She grabbed me and I kissed her mud-smeared face. Big Ghosts walked apart at the back of the line. But several in Mama's Small Ghost gang circled me, my former backyard uncles, aunts, grand-mas, and grandpas. I was their once-fat Dragon baby, now a skinny little monkey. And after their long day's work, I was their enter-tainment.

"Little Jaia, why do you come to camp?" one old grandpa teased.

"To reform my thoughts, Grandpa," I said, as Teacher Yi taught.

"Oh! And where are your thoughts?" teased another.

"In here!" I pointed to my temple.

They laughed and oohed and looked impressed. We children went to the women's barracks. Our mamas came in, carrying small basins of river water heated in the kitchen for their weekly bath. Half naked, they washed themselves with towels. I played on the brick platform beds with my friends while Mama washed. Then I heard a voice calling from above, "Little Jaia! Hello! Up here!"

I looked up and saw her sitting on a top bunk—Auntie Willow, Mama's best friend since college and her former Ministry of Culture office leader. I hadn't seen Auntie Willow since she had been put in the cowshed as a Black Gangmember over a year ago.

"My little dim-sum baby! It's me, Auntie Willow!"

She looked older, thinner, with dark skin and tired eyes. But she smiled and I was happy to see her.

"Jaia, come here!" Mama's shrill voice stopped me.

I looked at Mama, then back at Auntie Willow. She stared at Mama, hurt and surprised. I ran to Mama's bed.

"Mama, can I go play with Auntie Willow?" I pleaded.

"No!" she whispered sharply. "Auntie Willow is a Black Gangmember! You can't play with her!"

"Why?"

"You must never even talk to a Black Gangmember! Not Auntie Willow or Grandma Yang or Grandpa Li. They don't love Chairman Mao! And if you love them, you cannot be Chairman Mao's best kid!"

I didn't understand. I did love Auntie Willow, Grandma Yang, and Grandpa Li. How could they not love Chairman Mao? They had always been so good to me. They loved me. But in all my camp visits for the next three years, I avoided them. And they avoided me. Mama's decision was a political necessity.

For me, they became bad people who did not love Chairman Mao. Chairman Mao and Teacher Yi called them monsters, demons, snake spirits, cow ghosts, and enemies of the people. And like Little Curly Hair with her grandpa, I learned to "draw the line" with them and cut them from my heart.

I had never before seen a river or a rice paddy, a mountain or a field of grain. In Beijing, uniformed masses poured in rivers through paved streets and cobblestone alleys. Ancient mythical structures nestled serenely among modern brick and concrete monoliths plunged like fenceposts into the smoke-filled sky. But here, morning dew shimmered on the grass and fresh air tingled my skin. Redwing blackbirds cut across blue skies over fields of yellow boi choi flowers. Here I wandered golden hills and fields, chasing grasshoppers and painted butterflies. I swam in a river. I visited lotus lakes strung together like pearls, where huge water buffalo, half submerged near the banks, munched green lotus leaves under the exquisite pink and white flowers that towered over the water.

Hubei's mysterious, pungent earth, reeking of mud and cow dung, of grass and ten thousand flowers, crawling with frogs, insects, lizards, turtles, and snakes, became my warm and intimate companion. I was exiled in paradise.

Once a week Teacher Yi and her assistants gave us soldier training in the fields near our school. We ran through the tall, yellow grass looking for enemies. We crawled on our bellies and hid behind trees, spying on passing farmers and shooting imaginary Black Gang members with our stick-rifles. We learned much about our class enemies, especially those hiding among us, pretending to be our comrades and friends.

Early one spring evening I sat in the barracks on Mama's bed, awaiting her return from the rice paddy. Women came in, dirty and muddy from preparing the paddy for planting. Mama came up to me wearing a beautiful new Chairman Mao pin on her jacket. Rays of light shone in a halo around Chairman Mao's golden silhouette. A red sun rose above him, and below him was a sapphire blue ocean. Such a special pin! Chairman Mao's pins were everyone's treasures; we all collected, traded, and wore them proudly. I made such a big fuss over Mama's pin that she took it off her jacket and bent forward to pin it on me.

"You can have it, Little Jaia," she said.

Then something terrible happened. Mama dropped the pin on the muddy dirt floor, facedown! Mama dropped Chairman Mao's face in the mud! I knew you must never do this. Mama knew too. She glanced nervously around like a criminal and quickly picked up the pin. She sneakily wiped Chairman Mao's mud-stained face on her sleeve. Then she pinned it on my jacket. But I was very angry. Teacher Yi had taught us you can drop anything except Chairman Mao's pin and his Little Red Book. This was antirevolutionary! It meant you opposed Chairman Mao in your heart! I looked up at Mama. Word by word, with her comrades nearby, I accused her: "You do not love Chairman Mao!"

Her body froze guiltily; people looked over. Mama couldn't even look me, her five-year-old daughter, in the eye. Luckily, none of her comrades saw her crime. Years later I realized Mama narrowly escaped what might have been a political disaster.

When we reached our parents' camp, we tumbled off the truck and ran crazily up the hill to the cowpen, snatching handfuls of tender grasses on the way. Our best friend, Old Yellow, waited, watching us over the fence. And we raced up to him, shouting, "Hi, Old Yellow!"

"Here's your dinner!"

"Eat mine! Eat mine!"

"Mine, mine, mine!"

Old Yellow was a gentle old bull with arched horns like new moons and soft eyes like two calm lakes. We knew he loved us, for he patiently ate all our grasses. Our cowpen uncle would lift us one by one onto Old Yellow's back and lead him in a circle around the pen while we hugged his strong neck.

"Ja! Ja! Ja!" we shouted proudly, with our heads in the sky.

It seemed we rode on the back of a majestic dragon and circled heaven. Often we stayed with Old Yellow till dusk.

For dinner, we all squatted on the ground near the kitchen with our bowls of rice and preserved turnips. Afterward, One-Arm Grandpa, the camp cook, called us children into the kitchen for a special treat. He took his long spoon, scooped at the bottom of the black camp cooking pot, and turned up a round, flat, golden disk of crispy rice.

"Crispy crust!" we shouted excitedly.

Each of us got a piece of warm golden crispy crust that tasted somehow like every good thing the old pot had ever cooked.

"Thank you, One-Arm Grandpa!" we shouted.

"You kids are too polite." He beamed at us. "It's only burned rice. If this were Beijing, old One-Arm Grandpa would give you sweet buns with big red dates!"

Before Liberation, One-Arm Grandpa had been a famous portrait painter of feudal women and scholars. Then the Party trained him to paint workers, peasants, and soldiers. But just after he arrived in Hubei, when his work group was opening the mountain, some dynamite accidentally exploded and blew his painting arm away.

"My old arm blew right over the mountaintop!" One-Arm Grandpa told us, smiling sadly. "We looked everywhere, but we couldn't find it."

Now he worked in the kitchen and no longer had to break open mountains and sweat in the fields.

Awakened by "The East Is Red" playing on the camp loudspeaker, Mama and her comrades dressed quickly in the dark, ate a hurried porridge, grabbed their tools, and marched with the soldiers to the fields at dawn, chanting sayings from Chairman Mao's Little Red Book.

"We reform our thoughts! We purge our hearts red!"

They worked six days a week, sunrise to sunset, even in storms, to distill impurities from their souls—clearing wild grass, hauling rocks, plowing virgin earth, digging irrigation canals, carrying river water or manure in buckets on shoulder poles, and planting, tending, and harvesting the crops. They turned Hubei's rocky wildlands into rice paddies and wheat fields. In winter they turned soil, built buildings, repaired roads, blasted hills open to carve new roads, put up electrical poles, dug wells, and modernized their camp.

Communication between Big and Small Ghosts, Black and Stained, was forbidden and dangerous. Political contamination was a real, ever-present threat. They worked under constant supervision by the soldiers. Even then, comrades often reported each other's unseen mistakes in the evening struggle meetings. One day, Mama and her work comrade leaned their backs against each other to rest as lunch was being brought to the fields from camp.

"Now we can support each other," Mama joked.

Her comrade reported her in the evening struggle meeting, saying, "The Party and Chairman Mao are the people's only support." Mama's PLA team leader rebuked her, and she had to write a series of self-criticisms.

After autumn harvest, field work lessened and political meetings increased. One afternoon we arrived from our kindergarten to find a huge meeting going on. The whole camp had gathered in the threshing yard before a long table laid out with rare, delicious treats: dried fruits, cans of ham, bags of fried pork rind, cured sausage, milk powder, and sugar. I could not believe my eyes. We were having a feast! The PLA commander stood facing the workers. Then I heard his voice.

"What is a revolution?" he shouted furiously. "What did Chairman Mao teach us? 'A revolution is *not a banquet!*' "

A group of workers stood in the front row, separated from the others, looking like frozen crops after a frost. Mama stood among them, her face white with fear. I was so scared. Had she become a Black Gangmember, too? What would they do to her?

"To reform the old belief system is to purge the exploiting class mentality!" raged the red-faced commander. "Will we raise the next generation on *sugar* and *milk powder?*" He waved angrily at the items on the table. "Or on Chairman Mao's teaching? Which is more nutritious? Will we raise our children to be greenhouse flowers?" He glared at the front-row people. "Or pine trees on the mountaintop? All incoming packages are thoroughly inspected! All such corrosive goods will be confiscated!"

That night I asked Mama about the food on the meeting table. "Ba sent us a little gift. . . ." Her voice choked. She stopped, shaking her head, her eyes moist. "Never mind," she said softly.

On a warm, moist day, late in the season of blooming lotus flowers, I wandered through the fields outside Mama's camp, chewing my crispy crust and watching for poison snakes. I came to a large lotus lake. Clouds of pink and white flowers hovered over a jungle of leaves and stems, like a garden floating on a sea. The heads of lazy water buffalo rose from the lake, munching juicy green leaves near the shore. Suddenly a young spirit maiden in a wooden basin glided from a thicket. She moved toward me on the water, steering her basin with a bamboo pole.

I gaped as she floated gracefully to shore. She had sun-darkened skin and wore a wide-brimmed, pointed straw hat. A long, thick, shining braid hung over one shoulder, and her mysterious black eyes shone like dried lotus seeds.

"Hello, little one," she called in a musical voice. "Where do you come from?"

"Number Six Battalion," I murmured, pointing toward the camp.

"Number Six Battalion?" She giggled. "I've never seen such a cute little 'cow ghost' before."

By her hat and thick accent I knew she was a commune girl. Maybe she told me her name. But I remember her as Lian Jei, Lotus Sister.

"What are you eating?" She puzzled over the brown burned rice in my hand.

"Crispy crust," I said shyly.

I broke off a piece and gave it to her. She bit and scowled.

"It's burned!" she said. "We feed this to pigs in the commune."
I envied the pigs in her commune.

"Do you want to ride on the water?" She held out her hand.

I stepped into her basin without hesitating. She dipped her bamboo pole into the mossy bank and we floated away from shore, sailing into the lotus forest. Gigantic pink and white flowers, some bigger than ripe honey melons, towered over us. Butterflies fluttered among them. Fat carp darted away from our boat as we passed and hid under the floating leaves.

"You think your crispy crust is the best thing in the world, don't you?" asked Lotus Sister.

"Mmm hmm," I said, mouth full.

In my little memory, only Tasting the Sweetness cakes surpassed it. But you had to eat Remember the Bitterness bread to get them.

"Let me show you something," Lotus Sister said.

We stopped near a great pink lotus, its petals mostly fallen. Lotus Sister reached up to the old flower. The top of its trumpet-shaped head, once hidden by a crown of petals, was dotted with thumb-sized holes. Inside each hole sat a round seed, bigger than a peanut and covered in a silky green skin.

One by one, Lotus Sister took them out and peeled them, handing me the milky white seeds. I tasted them. Mmmmm! A sweet, tender, juicy nut fruit! Much better than crispy crust! Greedily, I ate them all.

"Every part of Sister Lotus is a treasure," she said. "Her seeds brighten the sight and make your eyes clear and strong. Oou, her root, calms inner fire and cleanses the heart, bringing peace and healing sorrow. Sister Lotus rises from the mud, but her face is turned to heaven. She is pure and without stain. Her stem is soft, but she stands straight and tall like bamboo and dances with the wind. Whenever you want, come to her lakes and she will feed you. But take from Old Lotus, whose petals have fallen. Her fruit is sweetest. And she loves children, especially little girls."

I didn't understand all my Lotus Sister's words. But I saw she loved these flowers like her own sisters. We sailed on the lake till dusk. A chorus of frogs rose from the water with a cool mist, and it began to rain. Lotus Sister plucked a large lotus leaf and held it over my head. It made a perfect umbrella. Raindrops bounced on its velvet fur and rolled off like silver beads. They splashed endless circles on the water. She walked me to the edge of the camp, holding the lotus umbrella over my head. For a year after that, when I arrived on my bimonthly visits to Mama's camp, Lotus Sister would be waiting for me by the lake with a handful of fresh-picked lotus seeds.

One evening she came into the camp after I had gone to sleep, asking to see me. She told Mama she was moving to another village to live with her new husband's family. She had come to say good-bye. She left me three gifts: a jar of honey-glazed Oou root, a transparent green onion stalk filled with lightning bugs, and a small cotton pouch full of lotus seeds.

I shared the honey-glazed Oou root with Mama the next morning. The onion stalk full of lightning bugs I hid under my kindergarten bed. For several nights I watched their lights grow dimmer in the dark and go out like fading stars. I saved the pouch of lotus seeds. Over time they dried and grew black and shiny. And when I looked at them, I saw my Lotus Sister's sweet black eyes.

"All young men come to the cowpen immediately! We need your help!"

It was New Year's Day in Mama's camp. For twenty minutes the camp loudspeaker broadcast this urgent message. A crowd gathered at the cowpen. People joked and talked excitedly, milling about.

"All you children go wait in the toolshed!" our cowpen uncle called to us cheerfully. "We are eating beef tonight!"

We were going to eat beef for New Year's! Now Teacher Yi

came and herded us to the toolshed. Some boys protested. They wanted to watch the soldiers kill a cow.

"It's too dangerous for you children even to watch," Teacher Yi said sternly. "It's a bull!"

She left us in the shed and hurried back to the pen. She was going to watch! We crowded in the doorway staring out. People rushed by. The killing of a bull was a great event. Many peasants from nearby communes had come to watch, bringing their children with them.

This was too much for us. By ones and twos, we sneaked out of the shed and joined them. Hundreds of people crowded around the large square pen. I squeezed through the forest of legs to the fence. Old Yellow stood warily in the center of the pen. We were going to eat Old Yellow!

He turned his head from side to side, nervously eyeing the crowd. He had never had such an audience before. The PLA commander climbed onto the fence and shouted into his megaphone, "Is everyone ready?"

The soldiers who had come to kill Old Yellow raised their fists and whooped a war cry. The crowd roared. Old Yellow jerked in fright and his eyes widened.

"Where's the knife?" the commander cried. "Who has the knife?"

"Here it is," One-Arm Grandpa yelled, waving a big, shiny knife above his head.

I felt so sad. Old Yellow was our dear friend. We loved him. Now we were going to eat him. Did he know the ugly knife was raised for him? That the soldiers had come to kill him? That we had come to watch him die? He stood motionless in the winter sun. Dried mud smeared his yellow fur. His tail, long and thin as an old man's whiskers, swished nervously from side to side. His eyes were big and wet and scared. I think he knew. The crowd buzzed with a hundred conversations.

"Oh, that Old Yellow, I hope his meat is not too tough."

"Bourgeois! Be grateful if it tastes just a little like meat!"

"You can't eat beef right after you kill it. The meat is sour. You must air it out for at least two days."

"Stop farting nonsense! I never heard such a superstition!"

"All right, Closing the Net Formation!" the commander thundered into his megaphone. *"Let's go!"*

A dozen strong soldiers holding lassos climbed bare-chested into the pen and surrounded Old Yellow. The excited crowd cheered and pressed to the fence. I crouched, peering through the boards. The soldiers began circling Old Yellow in different directions to confuse him. One big soldier held the knife. Old Yellow watched, nervous and confused, as the circle tightened and the net closed around him. Then he raised his head.

"Moooooooooo!" he wailed pitifully into the morning sky.

The sound was shockingly sad. Suddenly the crowd fell silent. Everyone must have remembered they liked Old Yellow.

Whirrrrrr!

The commander's whistle shattered the silence.

"Comrades and Party members! Be strong!" Whirrrrr! he blew again. "Take your positions and throw the traps!" Whirrrrr! "This is a test of our unity!" Whirrrrr! "Remember Chairman Mao says, 'Mercy to the enemy is cruelty to the people!' " Whirrrrr!

He raged into his megaphone, blowing his shrill whistle after each exhortation. The crowd cheered wildly for the soldiers in the pen. Old Yellow snorted and crazily swung his head. He was no longer sad. Rage widened his soft brown eyes, burned his tears dry. He bellowed and charged the men in front of him, kicking up a great cloud of dust. They scattered for their lives. Some leaped onto the fence. People outside screamed and bumped into each other in a panic. Dust stung my eyes and choked my throat.

The soldiers returned and circled Old Yellow again. Finally, one got his rope around Old Yellow's neck. Several more ropes quickly trapped his head and horns, and then a leg. They pulled him between their taut ropes and tripped him to the ground. They piled onto him and twisted his head back by the horns. Then a hand reached in with the glinting knife and thrust its blade into Old Yellow's throat.

A fine spray of blood unfurled from the wound like a sheet of red silk. Then it rained down gently on the soldier's arm as he cut his sharp blade across Old Yellow's throat. When he pulled the knife from the grinning gash, blood gushed and spurted out, forming in seconds a pool into which Old Yellow's dying head sank. Excited by the kill, people cheered and swarmed over the fence. They congratulated the heroes, slapped their backs, and lifted them onto their shoulders. They talked loudly and milled about the crowded pen.

Several of my classmates and I climbed through the fence and ran to Old Yellow. I stood near him. He lay still at my feet, a giant on the dusty field, his head pressed in a wet, red patch of sand. Bubbles of blood hissed from the wound in his big neck, which I had always hugged riding him around the pen. A girl sobbed beside me. Flies as big as hornets crawled across his wound, shining like green emeralds in the sun. I touched his forehead, wondering if his open eyes could see me. But something had left them. Old Yellow was gone. With a shock I started to cry.

That afternoon they chopped Old Yellow into thousands of pieces, and several hundred people swallowed them all for New Year's dinner that night. One-Arm Grandpa nailed Old Yellow's horns on the kitchen wall over the camp pot. I saw them every time we went to get crispy crust.

One night I dreamed I saw Old Yellow in his pen. He blew up a cloud of dust to hide himself. But the soldiers caught him, threw him down, and thrust the ugly knife into his throat again. The red spray unfurled, his bloody eyes rolled at me. And I heard the crowd chanting, "Hao chur! Hao chur!" Good eat! Good eat!

It was the summer evening our whole village looked forward to all year. Tonight we were going to see a movie! Our class followed

Teacher Yi outside as dusk fell, and hundreds of farmers and their families began arriving from the many nearby communes. It seemed all Xian Ning territory ambled down the dirt road heading east toward the river, talking and laughing excitedly. Mama was here visiting from her camp. We walked together, holding hands. Everyone had a bamboo stool, and many people carried unlit torches for the night walk home.

We reached the open field outside town and set our stools by the river before a white cotton sheet, our movie screen, stretched between two posts. Since the image showed through the sheet, people sat on both sides to watch. The summer sun set to a chorus of crickets as we waited for the movie to begin. People gossiped, laughed, and told jokes and stories. The pungent odors of earth and tobacco filled the air.

I sat near the very old people, mysterious, sparkling eyes, all sinew and bone and crinkled rice-paper skin. The old grandpas sat quietly, veiled in pipe smoke, like statues carved of dried ginseng root. I loved the old grandmas' faces and how their fathomless eyes narrowed to slits when they smiled. We all slapped at the huge mosquitoes; three, the joke went, made a meal.

Darkness fell and the round moon rose and hung like a clean mirror in the velvet sky. The projector hummed to life. The reels lurched and turned. A pillar of light lit up the white sheet, and everyone clapped and cheered. We children leaped up, waving our arms to catch the light, casting giant shadows onto the sheet. One of the Eight Revolutionary Example Plays, which we all knew from the first scene, was about to begin.

Suddenly the projector made a strangled noise and fell silent. Shrieks of disappointment filled the air. But a festive mood quickly returned as we sat under the moon, young and old together, talking and laughing, eating dried sunflower and pumpkin seeds, littering the earth with shells.

An hour later the nervous PLA soldier working on the projector announced there would be no movie this year. Some people groaned, but others cheered and clapped again. We had enjoyed our evening together. People lit up their torches in the dark. Mama held my hand and we started home, walking quietly toward Xian Ning. No one wanted to talk.

Soon a gentle humming rose like evening mist over the water, peaceful as a cradle song. More and more people joined in until we were all humming in heartfelt harmony, under the mirror moon and the shimmering stars, along a flowing river of torches.

I lay beside Mama one summer night, drenched with sweat, too hot to sleep. The heavy air buzzed with mosquitoes. All around me, people muttered curses under their nets and clapped their hands in the dark. Mama took her bamboo fan and began fanning me. I drifted off to sleep and woke later to find her still fanning me. A long day's work in the hot sun lay ahead of her. I didn't realize the pain she hid and the sorrow she swallowed, or know of her serious illness these past two years, that a tumor was growing deep in her womb.

"Do you like Hubei, my baby?" Mama asked, still fanning me.

"Mmm hmm," I nodded drowsily.

"What would you think if we had to stay here a long time?"

"I don't mind," I said, "but I want to live in camp with you."

I always wanted to stay with Mama in her camp. But her PLA commander said young children living with their parents weakened their revolutionary wills and eroded their workers' volition.

"Would you miss your ba?" Mama asked. I shook my head. "Would you miss Beijing?"

I shook my head again. She fanned me quietly. These three years, my faraway ba and hazy Beijing had become dream memories. I hardly thought of them. It seemed I was born in this land, between these grassy hills, beside this bamboo river, in this reed shed. Who did I miss but Mama? Perhaps my Lotus Sister, who moved away, or Old Yellow, whom we killed and ate. But wherever Mama lived, there was my home.

That autumn the Party declared Auntie Willow reformed. With her status now changed from Black Gangmember to Reformed Small Ghost, she offered to let me live in Beijing with her sixteen-year-old daughter and a nanny. Auntie Willow, whom Mama and I had shunned these three years for political survival, became our friend again and my way out of the countryside and back to Beijing.

Early one morning on her last visit to my kindergarten camp, Mama borrowed a pair of scissors from Teacher Yi. She cut my hair short, revolutionary style, so it matched hers, and we walked down Anti-Imperialism Road to the center of Xian Ning town.

The broad dirt road was crowded with barefoot farmers in wide-brimmed straw hats, their trousers rolled to their knees and bare legs smeared with mud. Their skin, darker than ours, and leathery from a lifetime spent working in the sun, made them look like another race. Many carried buckets on bamboo shoulder poles and head baskets filled with vegetables and rice to the commune warehouse. Their strides, rhythmic and muscular, sagged their poles like crescent moons, as their heavy buckets bounced up and down with each step.

We stopped and got two bowls of tofu jelly from an old street vendor with white, bushy eyebrows. Mama ate slowly, and when I finished first, she poured half of her tofu jelly into my bowl. "An old woman like me doesn't need much food," she said.

When we finished, we went to the public bathhouse and stood under the hot water for ten cents. Mama washed me sparkling clean and said I smelled like a lavender bud.

From her straw sack, she pulled out my old powder blue linen dress with the rounded collars and frills on the bottom. I hadn't worn it since leaving Beijing three years ago. I hadn't known she had brought it with her. Mama held it up, measuring it against me.

Mama and seven-year-old Jaia at Xian Ning photo studio in Hubei.

"It still fits," she said, apologetic and slightly sad.

I put it on happily. It was my favorite dress. Mama put her Beijing white cotton shirt on and we went across the street to Marching On photo studio. The villagers stared at us in our nice clothes. A few followed us into the studio to watch us have our picture taken. They circled me, twisted my dress between their fingers, and exclaimed how they had never seen anything like it before. Mama smiled proudly at me.

"She's a lucky girl," she told them. "She's going to live in Beijing and go to school."

"Ah! Lucky, lucky!" they responded happily. "Only by Chairman Mao's blessing!"

Mama combed her hair in front of the mirror and smoothed the wrinkles from her shirt. We sat on the bench facing the camera, and I leaned against her warm, thousand-jin-carrying shoulder. The villagers huddled behind the photographer, watching as if it was a significant event. I didn't know this was our good-bye picture.

It was our last evening in the camp. Mama and I sat on our suitcase in the open truck. We would reach Xian Ning town by midnight and catch the early-morning train to Beijing. Mama and her comrades' three years of labor had transformed this primitive bamboo camp. Now it had a wide road, three two-story brick buildings, a pump well, and electrical poles strung with wire. Three curved wooden footbridges spanned the river; their quaint arcs fell into dark green rice paddies chiseled like jade squares in an endless plain.

I thought, as we sailed along the bumpy road, that Mama would stay with me in Beijing. In my mind, we were both going home.

The White-Haired Girl

"Mama, how far is Beijing?"

"Thousands of li, Little Jaia. It will take this train two days and a night to get there, going as fast as it can."

"What will we do there?"

"We will have a new life, better than the old one."

"Will we live in our old home with Ba?"

"Perhaps."

"Will we go to the zoo and the park, and the skating lake?"

"Yes, Little Jaia. And we'll see movies together."

"Tell me the story again, Mama . . . about the White-Haired Girl."

Once upon a time before liberation, a poor old farmer named Bailao lived with his beautiful daughter, Happy. He loved Happy very much. She had pink cheeks, lovely eyes like full moons, and black hair tied in a long, shining braid. Every day Bailao farmed for his landlord from sunrise to sunset. Every year they grew poorer.

One New Year's Day the snow turned the whole world crystal white. In their little straw hut, Happy prepared a New Year's dinner of noodle soup. A New Year's flower in her hair like other girls wore would complete her beauty. But she knew her poor father could not afford it.

That evening, Bailao came home frosted with snow. Happy welcomed him, brushing him off like a good daughter. From his jacket, Bailao took a red ribbon he had bought for her with his last two yuan. This was Happy's New Year's gift. Bailao tied the ribbon in her hair. Now her beauty was perfect. Then he sang Happy the Red Ribbon Song.

> *"Other people's daughters wear the flowers,*
> *that your poor baba has no money to buy.*
> *So I buy two yards of red ribbon,*
> *to put in my Happy's hair."*

Suddenly the door flew open, and the cruel landlord and his hired men leaped in.

"It is the end of the year, Bailao!" shouted the landlord. "Your big debt must be paid tonight!"

"But I have no money," Bailao said.

"There is only one way to clear your big debt," the landlord said. "You must sell Happy to me as a slave."

Bailao knew of the landlord's greedy eyes for Happy. He knew how cruel it would be for Happy to be his slave.

"I will never sell my daughter," he said firmly.

The landlord and his men leaped on Bailao and beat him until he fell bleeding to the floor. Then the landlord dipped Bailao's thumb into his own blood and pressed it onto a Selling Daughter Contract. Now Happy belonged to him.

They bound Happy and dragged her away from her ba. Bailao crawled out the door after them, leaving a trail of red blood in the white snow. Then he died, and the snow buried him soundlessly.

Each day the cruel landlord beat Happy. At night he tortured her in the dark. One winter night, she escaped to the Wild Moun-

tain. The landlord, with his men and dogs, pursued her for days. The snow fell fast and deep. Finally they gave up. Happy was free. But the razor-sharp north wind howled and pierced her flesh. The hungry mountain tiger roared and hunted her day and night. Happy ran and hid, shivering with fear and cold, her belly empty, her clothes torn.

All she found to eat were wild berries, dried and frozen on the branches. Finally she found an abandoned Buddhist temple. She hid behind the altar, where a clay Buddha sat. From time to time, superstitious peasants came to say prayers and leave offerings of cooked rice. Happy ate these offerings after they left.

Years passed. Happy lost her red ribbon. Her pink cheeks faded. Her clothes wore to shreds. From suffering and lack of nourishment, her body became skeletal and her shining black hair turned white as snow. Only rage warmed her. Only hatred kept her alive. They grew strong in her and became like fires shooting out of her wild eyes.

The village people feared her. They fled in terror when they saw her. They said the Wild Mountain belonged to her. And they called her the White-Haired Ghost. . . .

Our blue city bus rushed down the wide avenues between rivers of pedaling cyclists. Beijing shimmered eerily, haunted and beautiful. Everything I saw seemed both familiar and strange. We passed old brick buildings and ancient temples, smoking factories and socialism yards, laundry-draped balconies and zigzag alleys, and bicycles leaning tangled like chains against the walls. The tall trees lining the streets and alleys formed mazes of shaded corridors. Tattered posters marred every wall, window, pole, and fence, and their shreds scattered like autumn leaves.

The masses exiled in the countryside left the streets half empty. Yet a million PLA soldiers patrolled our city. They were everywhere, rifles fixed with bayonets, watching us with eyes of stone.

Sometimes children teased them to life. But the barbed wire decking the walls of the government buildings seemed to wrap around them, silent and invisible, drawing them apart.

We got off the bus in Three Li Village, the foreign embassy district. Shiny foreign cars sped along wide, clean, poplar-lined streets, past modern embassy buildings, huge houses with wrought-iron fences and green lawns watered by automatic sprinklers.

We entered a five-story brick building, climbed the stairs to the top, and knocked at the first door. It opened. An old, tiny, hoop-hipped woman with a toothless smile stood in the doorway, a pear on two legs with her head where the stem should have been.

"You must be Comrade Lin." She shook Mama's hand.

This was Wang Ma, nanny for Auntie Willow's daughter. This was my new home. I knew by Wang Ma's shape she was a little-feet grandma. She led us in, walking in that peculiar, hurried, bound-feet gait.

The two-room apartment was like a palace! It belonged to the work unit of Auntie Willow's land-surveyor husband, who came home only two weeks in a year. Both rooms, one with a balcony, overlooked a tree-filled compound. In the kitchen, Wang Ma turned a dial on the stove and blue-orange tongues of flame leaped up in a circle to dance and lick the bottom of the kettle! The toilet down the hall was no night-soil trench dug in the earth, but a sunken white ceramic basin that cleaned itself with water when you pulled a chain! No more frozen butt in winter! No more night-soil stench, mosquitoes, and buzzing flies in summer!

Though I was only seven, Mama told Wang Ma I would start school now, a year early, to reduce her work burden. Auntie Willow's husband had enrolled me in the local Three Li Village school for children of Party cadre and foreign diplomats. My year-early start in such a good school was luck. Mama had feared my growing up illiterate in Hubei like other camp children.

"Does she wet her bed?" Wang Ma asked over tea with a smile.

"Jaia never wets her bed," Mama said.

So they began bargaining over the fee for my care.

"Twenty yuan a month," Wang Ma said firmly, her smile fading. "Can't be less. I'm old. Now I have two children to watch. The parents are never home. I'm responsible no matter what, day or night. It's too hard. I only do this as a favor to Comrade Willow."

Mama desperately wanted me in Beijing. And I had nowhere else to stay. She was in no position to bargain.

"All right, twenty yuan," she said wearily.

Wang Ma bit her lip; perhaps she should have asked for more. Mama counted over the money Ba had sent her. This trip had been hard on her. Her thin, calloused hands were like brown leaves with protruding veins. Three years' hard labor, small food rations, and excessive bleeding from her mysterious female problem had weakened her body and spirit. Her youth had faded. Wrinkles webbed her face. Her once bright eyes had dulled.

"My family is grateful to you, Comrade Wang." Mama held Wang Ma's hands. "Her ba will pay you at the beginning of each month."

"What?" Wang Ma was shocked. "Her ba lives in Beijing? Why doesn't she stay with him?"

Mama looked down and said softly, "You know how it is in this revolutionary era. His situation is unpredictable. Who knows where he may be tomorrow? We are lucky to have you to take care of her." Mama turned to me. "Come, Little Jaia. Bow to Wang Ma. Always obey her and treat her like your grandma. Be good, and do not shame me."

I bowed to Wang Ma. Then Mama left, saying she would be back that evening. That night, I fell asleep waiting for her return. I woke to find her sitting on the edge of my bed with a package wrapped in her old blue scarf.

"Little Jaia, this is for you. Open it."

I sat up drowsily and unwrapped the gift. It was a child-size PLA uniform. Excited, I got up and put it on. My hands sought the jacket pockets. But there were none.

"I got a big uniform and made it small for you," Mama explained. "I hemmed up the sleeves, jacket bottom, and trouser cuffs. I sewed the pockets up inside. Next year, you can unstitch the seams and have pockets. It will grow with you."

Mama's second gift was a lacquered wooden box with a bamboo thicket painted on its lid in fine brush strokes. Its amber lacquer, cracked with age, made the scene an ancient, golden autumn. It glowed quietly. I opened the lid and found three wooden pencils with red characters engraved on the stem.

"What does it say, Mama?" I hadn't begun learning characters.

"These are Chairman Mao's words and calligraphy," said Mama solemnly. "He says, 'Study hard, grow daily.' Remember always to be Chairman Mao's best student. I must go back to Hubei for a little while."

"No, Mama! You must stay with me!"

Tears came to her eyes. She looked down for a while.

"My baby," she said, "I must go back to harvest the rice for Chairman Mao, or we will have no rice to eat. And you must start your new school here so you can learn to read and write. Use these pencils. Write to me often. And I will write you. Keep my letters in this box. I promise, when it is full, the rice will be harvested, and I will come back to you."

Mama sat watching me till I fell asleep. Next morning when I woke, Wang Ma said Mama had gone to Hubei on the early train.

I now attended one of Beijing's finest schools in a modern brick building with a courtyard garden, grass, and trees. My new classmates, privileged cadre and foreign embassy children, came in all shades of black, brown, yellow, and white skin colors. Some had blue eyes and blond hair. Yet all spoke Chinese and recited Chairman Mao's teachings from memory. We studied Maoism, Marxism, math, Chinese, art, and calligraphy.

We sat together, hands behind our backs, memorizing our lessons through loud repetition. Trained to be polite, diligent, and studious, we greeted important foreign dignitaries at airports and formal ceremonies, offering them flowers and performing songs and dances. Many "foreign eyes" came to our classroom to take pictures and notes. I studied hard and became a top student.

But I missed Mama terribly. Each week I sealed my homework in one of the preaddressed envelopes she had left me and mailed it to her. These pages, many stamped by my teacher with a special merit red flag, were filled with my childish calligraphy.

I learned to write "Long live Chairman Mao and our forever righteous Communist Party!" and "Victory to the revolution!" and "The People's Liberation Army are our friends!" before I learned to write "Mama."

Mama wrote me every week. But I could not read her letters. "Word-blind" Wang Ma could not read either. I feared to ask Bing Mei, Auntie Willow's strange daughter. And I dared not ask my teacher. She would know Mama was a problem person in a labor reform camp. And Ba, whose visit I anxiously awaited, did not come. Months of Mama's letters piled up in my lacquered box. And I burned inside with fever-love, wondering how she was, if she missed me too, and when she would return.

My new roommate, Bing Mei, Auntie Willow's daughter, looked older than her sixteen years. A fierce creature stared out from her brooding eyes, under her wide forehead. Bing Mei had no friends. She rarely spoke or looked at me or Wang Ma. But when she sat on the stool before the shining black wooden monument in the hall between our rooms, she mysteriously came to life. Wang Ma called this thing a piano. She said it played music. And it belonged to Bing Mei.

Every day after school, Bing Mei sat on this stool. She set her secret music books open on the piano and lifted its polished lid. A master preparing for battle, she raised her hands and cracked her fingers. Then they rippled and soared over the black and white keys like two flocks of water birds skimming a lake. Hours passed. Her forehead sweated as she turned page after page. But I never heard the music. Only silence and the strange, panting animal noises Bing Mei made from time to time.

Intrigued, I snuck up to her piano one evening while she studied in her room. Quietly, I lifted the lid to touch the long row of black and white teeth, cool and smooth as polished jade. I pressed down. Bright, clear, bell-like tones sang out of nowhere, followed by a shriek and pounding feet. Bing Mei leaped out of her room at me, a mad tiger. She flung away my hand and slammed the lid. It banged and the wounded piano hummed and growled.

"Don't you ever! Ever! Touch my piano!" she screamed.

Bing Mei was crazy. I never touched her piano again.

Bing Mei, drawn to her mama's piano when she was only three, was recognized as a prodigy by the age of five. At seven, she performed publicly to packed crowds in the Ministry of Culture auditorium. All who heard her play knew she would reach greatness.

When Bing Mei was ten, the Cultural Revolution began. The piano became a Western, antirevolutionary artifact. For safety, Auntie Willow warned Bing Mei to play very softly. Then she told her to touch the keys gently, but never press them down. Any sounds coming from this bourgeois instrument endangered their family. In the end, even a silent piano was dangerous. The Red Guards accused Auntie Willow of playing her piano while the peasants starved. Her neighbors and coworkers testified against her, and she

Eight-year-old Jaia and a school-mate.

was thrown in the cowshed. This is how Auntie Willow became a Black Gangmember.

When I moved into Auntie Willow's apartment, Bing Mei, a high school senior, had played silent piano for six years. She practiced with heroic intensity. She perspired and groaned in frustration. Sometimes she wept, locked in her room. Wang Ma and I hid while she practiced. Wang Ma called Bing Mei crazy for her silent music and her strange noises. But how much strength Bing Mei had, to play all those years, never pressing down the keys to hear the singing, bell-like notes.

My best school friend, Round Round, lived down the hall. Her father, a PLA captain, was our district's Security Bureau chief. Round Round was the first child I knew who lived with her parents. Her name fit her perfectly. She had bright round eyes and a round red face. Her round, short twin ponytails, tied up at the sides of her head, looked like a panda's ears.

"What's it like to live with your own parents?" I would ask her greedily. "What do you do? What do you talk about?"

I felt like a cold person trying to squeeze next to someone else's stove. But her answers always seemed evasive.

"It's okay." "We don't do anything." "We don't talk much."

I couldn't believe it! Was she too stingy to share her happy life with me? Or was she a spoiled girl who didn't appreciate her own family? We were friends for several months before she invited me to her home to study.

"We must be very quiet," she told me outside her apartment. "My father is reading."

I quietly followed her in. Her home was even bigger and nicer than Auntie Willow's. A blue wool carpet covered the cement floor, and white cotton drapes covered the windows. A large, gold-framed picture of Chairman Mao on one wall dominated the room. Under it, on a wooden altar, sat a golden wax mango in a glass case. Years ago the people had given Chairman Mao a shipment of mangoes as a gift, and he had distributed them back to the people. It made national news, and after that everyone kept a wax mango under his picture as a way to share both this gift to him and the reception of his blessing.

Captain Chen sat at his desk, absorbed in a hefty red volume of Chairman Mao's collected works. He had a thin mustache on his serious face and short hair graying at the temples. His PLA uniform and red collar completed the portrait of a noble hero. I stood respectfully behind Round Round.

"Don't be formal," he said, looking up. "Come in. You must be our new neighbor, Jaia."

"Yes, Captain Chen," I said.

I glanced away nervously. My eyes fastened on the golden mango with the engraved bronze plaque at the bottom of its glass case.

"Do you see that plaque?" said Captain Chen proudly. "That's Vice Chairman Lin Biao's calligraphy! It says, 'To Chairman Mao's Best Student,' and is signed, 'Lin Biao.' "

I stared in awe. Vice Chairman and Long March General Lin Biao, Chairman Mao's best friend and hand-picked successor, stood next to Chairman Mao on the front page of his Little Red Book and had written its introduction, which we often recited. Every morning, after wishing Chairman Mao "Ten thousand years alive!" we ended by chanting, "And good health to Vice Chairman Lin! Good health! Good health!"

Captain Chen opened a pouch, pinched a twist of tobacco leaf, spread it on a strip of paper, and rolled a cigarette with his stained yellow fingers. He licked the edge, sealed it, and lit it up with a match. Two smoke jets streamed out of his nose, enveloping him in a gray cloud. He stared at me quietly, examining me up and down like an old bird.

"How is your mama in Hubei?" he asked matter-of-factly.

I froze and looked at the floor in shame. He knew everything about me. Even Mama's stain was no secret to him.

"Don't worry," he reassured me. "It's my duty to know about everyone in my district. She is a very good mama to write you so often. Is she doing okay?"

Tears came to my eyes. Mama had been gone for months, writing every week, and I didn't know how she was at all.

"I don't know, Uncle," I said. "I can't read her letters yet."

"No one has read them to you?" He looked surprised. I shook my head. "Go bring them here," he said. "I'll read them to you."

I flew home and came back in no time with my lacquered box. It was nearly full; Mama would be coming home soon. Captain Chen sat me beside him and read me all Mama's letters, written in large, precise characters for a child's eyes.

"My dear daughter. Mama misses you so much. You are so good and you make me so proud. Your lessons deserve teacher's excellence red flags. You are Chairman Mao's good student. And your calligraphy is so pretty! Please send me all your homework. I read it every day. Is your health good? Have you caught any colds? Are you eating enough? Tell me everything as soon as you can. Do not miss me. Mama."

I was so happy sitting beside Captain Chen, hearing Mama's sweet words coming out of his mouth. I wished Round Round were my sister and Captain Chen were my father, too. He invited me to dinner that night, and I met Round Round's mother, a sweet, short-haired woman with Round Round's eyes. She managed the day shift in a bicycle factory. Round Round was very quiet around her parents.

Captain Chen asked me many questions. Did I like school? How was my home life? Was I happy? How often did I see Ba? And why didn't I live with him? He was surprised to hear I had not yet seen Ba, who instead of bringing Wang Ma her money each month, mailed it to her.

"Come back often, Little Jaia" were Captain Chen's parting words that happy evening. "And bring your mama's letters."

I took him at his word. I had found a new father.

"My dear daughter. Do you have enough pencils and notebooks? How about erasers? Today, my comrade goes to Beijing. I thought all week about what to give you. I gave her this handkerchief and a pretty postage stamp for you. Do you like them? Yesterday One-Arm Grandpa asked me if you remember his crispy crust. He says you must be eating sweet buns every day in Chairman Mao's Beijing town. I miss you. Take care of your health. Mama."

"Attention for an urgent Party bulletin!"

Our principal's voice thundered over the school intercom on a mid-September morning in 1971. Something terrible had happened! Was it war at last? The Russians invading? America crossing the Vietnam border with their atomic bombs?

The Party news now blared into the class in mid-broadcast as an outraged, breathless announcer spoke of treachery and betrayal! A traitor and a devil! A vicious plot against Chairman Mao! An enemy of China had crept into the Red Army as a spy to destroy our Precious Red Mountain! A Kuomintang human time bomb was planted in the heart of the Communist Party to assassinate our beloved Chairman Mao!

This was stunning, terrifying blasphemy! Who wanted to betray and kill our Great Helmsman? The announcer's next words sent lightning bolts through my heart.

"Big Traitor Lin Biao will be forever cursed by the people! His stinking corpse will rot on the rubbish heap of history!"

Had I heard right? Vice Party Chairman and Long March General Lin Biao? Chairman Mao's "Best Student and Most Intimate Friend" a traitor? The announcer ended with a last terrible confirmation.

"Big Traitor Lin Biao's plane was shot down as he fled across the Soviet border! The People's Enemy, Lin Biao, is dead!"

My ears rang. This was strange, unreal. Lin Biao, a People's Hero for forty years, had fought the Kuomintang and the Japanese to save our motherland. The Party's spokesman for years, his voice was heard more than any Party leader except Chairman Mao.

Yet all this time he was plotting to destroy the Party and kill Chairman Mao! Now he was dead, his voice silenced forever. The moon had tried to kill the sun who gave him light. There had been war in heaven for forty years. Nothing was what it seemed. My bewilderment was immense. The shock of this would be with us all for months.

That hour we tore out Lin Biao's introduction to Chairman Mao's Little Red Book. And we passed around our teacher's knife and carved him carefully out of the frontispiece, leaving his blank silhouette standing like a ghost beside Chairman Mao. This was done to every Little Red Book in China. All pictures of Big Traitor Lin Biao were taken down and destroyed. In group photos, Big Traitor Lin Biao's image was cut or airbrushed out, leaving an empty gap where he had stood with other Party members. When I next visited Round Round, her father's plastic mango with Lin Biao's engraved plaque was gone.

The anti–Big Traitor Lin Biao campaign lasted over a year. I wrote hundreds of posters in class attacking this traitor I was raised to love most after Chairman Mao. And his true history was revealed. He had sneaked into the Party as an evil worm burrows into the heart of a red apple and waved the red flag higher than anyone to hide his evil intentions. His speeches and articles, praised in their time, were brought out and exposed as ancient treachery.

We heard many stories of his rotten life. He had slept every night in a bourgeois vibrating goosefeather bed. He had lived behind three layers of curtains, blocking the light, hiding from the Red Sun, proving his heart shadowy and dark. And he had secretly called himself the Flying Horse. What arrogance! Everyone knew there was only room in the sky for the Red Sun!

We also learned that our eternally wise Chairman Mao knew of Lin Biao's evil plans from the very beginning, even before the Long March. He was never deceived for even one moment. I puzzled much over this. Chairman Mao knew Lin Biao was an evil spy, yet wrote his name into the constitution as future Chairman, making him the second most beloved leader of our nation. Why? But the Party told us we could not hope to understand the length, subtlety, and complexity of class struggle, especially as it applied to this situation. But Chairman Mao's great mind encompassed and resolved all the apparent contradictions. We could only trust in him.

Each day, Round Round and I walked to and from school together. Inside our building near the front door, a short stairwell led down to a basement room. Posted on its door was a large sign which we could not read. We puzzled over what it said. As we learned more characters in school, we began, day by day, to decode this mysterious sign. It became our project together. And with each character we learned, our pride grew.

First we deciphered the characters "away" and "under." Then "keep" and "black." But with most of the sign figured out, it still didn't make sense. We were tantalized. When we recognized "member," and finally the last two elusive characters, "arrest" and "gang," the message on the door was revealed:

KEEP AWAY! BLACK GANGMEMBER
UNDER ARREST!

We asked Uncle Chen, as I now called Round Round's father, about this Black Gangmember. He exploded.

"Stay away from that door! Both of you!" His thin frame tensed, and his eyes flashed. "This evil Black Gangmember has rejected all help and has refused to embrace the masses! They must not see or talk to anyone!"

His fury startled me. This Black Gangmember in our basement must have committed terrible crimes to be arrested and make Captain Chen so mad. After that, when Round Round and I came home from school, we sometimes tiptoed down the stairs and pounded on the door.

"This is your punishment, Black Ghost!" we shouted.

And we ran laughing up the stairs. I never heard a sound from the other side of the door.

One summer morning, Round Round came to my room. Mysteriously, she said she had something to show me. She took me to the back of our building where a small section of fence blocked the wall. She crept up to it low and peered down through a crack between two boards. Then she motioned me over. I crept up beside her.

"Shh," she whispered. "Look."

I peered down through the crack. A ground-level window blocked with iron bars opened on a tiny basement room. A woman in black sat on a narrow bed staring at the floor. Her long, tangled hair hung down, covering the sides of her face. Suddenly, I realized she was the Black Gangmember behind the warning sign posted on the basement door! The criminal in our basement was a woman!

Something about her fascinated us. We snuck back several times to spy on her. Once she lay on her bed, eyes open. Another time she stood below her window, staring up at the patch of blue sky over the fence top. Once she paced restlessly back and forth in her tiny room. She seemed desperate.

Early one Saturday morning, Round Round and I carried two wash buckets of water downstairs, around to the back fence. We peered down through the crack into the open window. Our Black Gangmember slept in her bed, well within range. On a whispered count of three, we flung the water over the fence down through the window. A loud splash was followed by a shriek. For the first time, we stuck our heads boldly over the fence top. She stood under the window, clutching the rusty bars, shaking with rage, her clothes and hair drenched. We had made a direct hit.

"This is your punishment, Black Ghost!" we shouted gleefully.

This was the clearest I had seen her. She was Mama's age, gaunt, hard, and spare as bone. And she was mad, insane. Her piercing eyes, sunk in her head, were ringed with dark patches, like twin caves dropping into two shining pools at night. She stared up at us, her look naked and unashamed. And she was screaming, "I have done nothing wrong!"

She was transparent—no mask, nothing left to hide. Her "face" was gone, eaten from within. Suffering and apocalyptic rage had seared away all familiar human expression. Her skin hung on her bones like a wet garment, clinging to their varied shapes. Her body was a furnace, her organs burning coals, her lungs a bellows. Her heart pumped liquid fire through her veins. And every scream, every breath, sent flames roaring into her head. She was a creature of fire that fed on itself, that she herself could not put out.

Jaia, age
eight, stands
behind a
marble lion
at Heavenly
Temple
Park.

"I have done nothing wrong!" she screamed. Her eyes burned
through us. Lightning danced in her skull. "I have done nothing
wrong!"

Even her voice was a terrifying weapon. In that moment, I felt
she could have torn us apart like rice-paper dolls. She was the
snake spirit, the cow-headed demon who lived in the realm of lost,
tormented souls. Now I knew why Uncle Chen had locked her
away. Who could make her confess, or silence her? Who could meet
her burning eyes or quench her rage?

Gripping our buckets, we fled in terror, around through the

front entrance, past her basement door, up five flights of stairs, and into our separate apartments. For days I lived in awful, sickening fear. She would escape and come find me for revenge. What room could hold her? She would press her body against the wall and burn a doorway out. I never went back. Weeks later, Round Round did. The Black Gangmember was still there. But her window was closed forever.

I never learned who she was, nor what her crimes had been. I don't know if she stayed when I moved away, if she lived or died. I wondered if she had a daughter like me, awaiting her letters, wondering where she was. I never forgot her. In time, my fear turned to guilt and ripened into shame.

Years later, in my mind, I finally went back and opened her window, to let in some fresh air and a little light, a little hope, a little peace. And I whispered to her through the bars, "Mama, forgive me."

"My dear daughter. Every day I miss you. Every night I take out your picture and look at you under the kerosene lamp. Have you grown taller? Has Ba taken a new picture of you lately? Please ask him to send me one. Even the one-inch size will be good. We just finished tonight's Reforming Thoughts meeting and are waiting for lights-out. I am on my bed knitting you a sweater. Only two sleeves to go. I hope to have it ready before autumn's chill. Take care of your health. Mama."

Round Round excelled as a teller of dark, chilling tales that often left me anxious for days. She told me how our snake spirit demon had called my name through her basement door. She said a ghost with a long pink tongue slept under the demon's bed; it was her servant, and obeyed her orders. Sometimes Round Round saw it hiding in dark corners or heard it wandering in our hall at night. Once, when it was hungry, it chased her up the stairs. But she escaped to her home with her parents. Round Round said the ghost with the long pink tongue only ate children our size whose parents weren't home.

It had eaten a little girl downstairs the year before I moved in. When it came for you, it was unstoppable. It pressed up to your door, slipped its long, pink tongue through the keyhole into your ear, and sucked out your brain while you slept in your bed. Because of the ghost with the long, pink tongue, I feared going onto the stairs alone. I dreaded dark corners in my room at night. Even in my bed, hiding under my covers, I knew I was not safe, because my parents were never home.

That winter a shocking story circulated through Beijing. Two young sisters had been found abandoned in one of the beacon towers along the Great Wall, frozen to death. Round Round soon came to me with her own colorful version of this story.

"Did you hear about those two frozen sisters? My father saw them with his own eyes when they dragged them out of the tower! Their father wanted to get remarried because his Old Wife suicided. But New Wife didn't like his two daughters because they had Old Wife's suicide blood in them. So she made him choose between her and his daughters. Of course, he chose her!

"He took his daughters to the Great Wall, to the top of the highest beacon tower, and told them to wait there while he went to buy some bean cake. Then he went and married New Wife. The next day the Security Bureau found the sisters holding each other, frozen dead. They even had frozen teardrops the size of ripe litchis stuck on their faces."

"Did your father catch him?" I asked, horrified by his crime.

"Of course! No one escapes the Public Security Bureau!" Round Round bragged. "And they gave that nasty demon two choices.

" 'There are two ways you can die,' they told him. 'Standing up or sitting down. Which way do you prefer?' " Round Round stared at me intensely. "Which would you choose?" she demanded.

I considered it uneasily, prodded by her look.

"Ahh . . . mmm . . . how about sitting?"

Round Round scoffed at my stupidity.

"Ha! You're as stupid as that dummy father! That's what he said, too. So they tore off all his clothes, even his triangle pants, and tied him sitting naked on a fancy toilet over a black hole. Then they left him there. He thought his last choice wasn't too bad. But guess what?" Round Round's eyes grew rounder and she leaned forward. "A huge snake thicker than Chairman Mao's right arm crawled out of that black hole, right up into his stomach through his asshole, and ate him from the inside out! That's how stupid you are!" she hissed. "Just remember, when they ask you how you want to die, make sure you beg them to shoot you standing up. That way is so much nicer."

Round Round and I played with the neighborhood kids. In our favorite game, struggle meeting, we took turns standing on the "chopping demon stage" where criminals and class enemies were struggled against, our heads bowed, a piece of cardboard on a wire hanging around our necks like a criminal label board. Our "chopping stage" was the neighborhood's outdoor cement Ping-Pong table.

"Confess your crime!" we yelled at the one cowering on the stage. "Tell us what you did!"

"I'm a walking dog, Black Roader, despotic landlord, Russian spy?" the criminal guessed, pretending innocence, throwing in multiple titles to confuse us and hide his real crime.

"Crafty! You are an American spy! Don't try to hide! The masses' eyes are snow-bright. Isn't it so?"

"Yes! American spy! Isn't it so?" we echoed gleefully.

Someone jumped onto the chopping stage to twist the criminal's arms back over his head in the "airplane," forcing him to bend low the way soldiers and Red Guard did to real Black Gangmembers.

"I confess! I confess! I'm an American spy!"

Our "criminal" started shaking his body and quivering his legs intentionally, looking pathetic, pretending to cry, but making absurd facial expressions.

"Be serious!"

"Be obedient!"

"Don't be a brazen-faced toad!"

"Shameless!"

"Loathsome!"

"Tell us where you hid the transmitter your owner sent!"

"I don't have none!" The criminal rolled his guilty eyes.

"You know our Party's policy! Leniency to those who confess and severity to those who hide!"

"Don't be stupid! Confess!"

"Maybe you would like to taste a revolutionary's iron fist!"

"Where is the transmitter? In your pocket?"

"Under your pillow?"

"Buried in the floor?"

"We are coming to your house to dig your earth three feet down for every inch around till we find it!"

"Smash his body!"

"Shatter his bones!"

"This guy's a born walnut! We must crack him to get the meat!"

We imitated the adults in their "tiring strategy." Our shouts were tossed hand grenades, wearing the criminal down till he could not hold out any longer.

"I confess, I'll tell you . . . I hid it . . . I hid it in my . . . my . . ."

"Where did you hide it!" we shouted like thunder.

The criminal, rolling his toad-eyes, confessed the ugly truth.

"In my asshole!"

We could not hold back after that. We grabbed each other and fell in a pile under the table, laughing till our stomachs ached.

For half a year, I had been going to study in Round Round's home after school. Uncle Chen encouraged me to visit often. I rarely saw his wife. She always came home late from her factory. He now treated me with an affection he didn't even show his own daughter, Round Round. They seemed somehow distant from each other. One afternoon he picked me up and set me on his lap.

"Come, Little Jaia," he said. "You are like my own daughter."

I had never seen Round Round sit on his lap. Then his hand began struggling under me like a trapped animal inside his trousers. His other arm firmly gripped my waist. His strong tobacco odor breathed hard on the back of my neck. And he made awkward conversation. It chilled me, made my heart a knot on a rope. It felt frightening and strange.

When the wild creature under me ceased its desperate struggle, Uncle Chen pushed me off his lap without a word and left the room. He repeated this ritual with me often. At times I tried to leave his lap, but could not break his fierce grip. Round Round sat rigid on her stool, silent as snow, ignoring us, seeming absorbed in study. I knew she felt the strangeness of these moments, so charged with unbearable tension. But we never spoke of it.

I soon grew so anxious and afraid of Uncle Chen that I stopped visiting. He began coming to get me, asking Wang Ma if I could help Round Round with her homework. Of course she sent me. And I obediently went. Who could refuse a PLA captain, chief of the Security Bureau? I was only a stained "intellectual's child" whose Small Ghost mama lived in a Hubei reeducation camp, and whose absent ba seemed to have forgotten her.

Uncle Chen filled me with a strange terror I didn't understand. Finally, perhaps fearing discovery, he stopped coming to get me. I lived next door to him for more than a year after that. And Round Round was still my best friend. But I never went into their home again.

Bing Mei graduated from high school and had to find a job. Still dreaming of being a great pianist, she applied to Beijing Radio Broadcasting Station. They needed pianists to play revolutionary background music. She planned to practice her forbidden music secretly in the studio at night. But a preliminary review of her personal record revealed her mama as a former Black Gangmember, still in a labor reeducation camp in Hubei. Bing Mei's rejection devastated her.

Now Wang Ma began a campaign criticizing her impractical ways and foolish love of imaginary music. All Bing Mei needed, said Wang Ma, was proletarian work. In any case, she must find a job or take whatever the work office assigned her. One day Bing Mei came into the apartment holding a letter.

"They assigned me to work in Green Willow butcher shop," she told Wang Ma numbly.

She started work in the butcher shop, an hour away by bus. She left home early each morning, came home late at night, and spent her days learning her new trade: skinning, scaling, chopping, and cutting slabs of meat with her butcher's tools.

Months passed. Her fingers lost their slender suppleness, becoming red, thick, and coarse as carrots. Her right hand grew calloused from wielding heavy knives. She grew duller, gloomier, more withdrawn. Her face darkened, as if to hide, and her eyes narrowed, as if to shut out the sight of the world. All that second year, Bing Mei never sat at her piano again. Wang Ma said her strange sickness had finally healed.

Wang Ma had gnarled hands, thin bamboo fingers curled like chicken claws, bones like loose firewood stuffed in an old rice sack. Brown patches stretched in continents across her aged body. Her head sprouted sparse silver hair and sat like an overripe melon on her thin neck. Her narrow eyes appeared alternately vigilant, suspicious, or remote. She reminded me of a broken doll.

Yet each morning as we listened to the Party radio announcer reciting Chairman Mao's "Prominent Instructions," a dim light shone in her eyes and her lips moved over her toothless mouth in silent repetition as she struggled earnestly to memorize Chairman

Mao's precious words. When the announcer finished, military music began and she sat repeating what she could remember. Wang Ma made me listen and recite Chairman Mao's words with her every day.

" 'Every word we learn is an extra red heart dedicated to Him and an extra bullet shooting toward the enemy,' " she quoted. "Chairman Mao's books, though not gold, are more precious than gold; though not steel, they are stronger than steel. Ten thousand rivers return to the sea, but all truth comes from Chairman Mao."

When I drank water from our tap, she would say, "Jaia, remember the well driller with every swallow!" as she had heard the announcer say on the radio.

Wang Ma talked like, lived through, and drew all her thoughts and ideas from the radio that played everywhere from morning till night. She was word-blind and could only read her own name.

When she heard on the radio how Guizhou Province commune workers shaved a "loyalty" character within a heart on their hogs' foreheads to show their love for Chairman Mao, Wang Ma grew inspired. She also wanted to make some heroic gesture and be noticed by the Party. Maybe she would hear about herself on the radio. But we didn't have a hog.

Wang Ma grew frustrated. She desperately wanted to be on the Neighborhood Committee Senior Group and have authority to watch over the neighborhood with revolutionary vigilance and keep people on the straight red path. But there was so much competition, so many old men and women striving for a few committee spots. You had to stand out and be noticed. So Wang Ma began a campaign. As we stood in the market line waiting to buy vegetables, Wang Ma clutched her multicolored straw basket and sang songs she had learned from the radio, in a voice worse than a chicken getting its head twisted off.

"Raising my head, I see the Big Dipper.
My heart is missing Mao Zedong,

missing Mao Zedong.
I think about You when I am lost,
and find my direction.
I think of You in the darkness,
and Your Light brightens up my journey,
brightens up my journey . . ."

Her face turned rosy; her glassy eyes gazed into the blurry winter sky, where fluffy gray dumplings swirled in a steaming pot. She sang passionately, with peaks and valleys, as if she saw the Big Dipper in broad daylight through the clouds. People stopped and stared, amazed, and whispered back and forth about her. But no one dared laugh. When she finished, Wang Ma smiled serenely and quoted dialogue from a radio story.

" 'Don't laugh at this old grandma! Although I am tone-deaf, it is the real feeling for Chairman Mao in my heart! The more I sing, the younger I get!' May I have ten jin of cabbage, comrade? Remember Chairman Mao says, 'Dig tunnels deep! Store grain everywhere! Never seek hegemony!' "

I was embarrassed to be with her in public. I wanted to crawl inside my own shoe. Wang Ma's favorite quote for a while was "Sophistry cannot alter history!"

But what did this mean? Wang Ma didn't know. Neither did Bing Mei or I. Finally Wang Ma asked a neighbor, who said it meant that the evil words of a ghost could not change the truth. Wang Ma proudly used this word at neighborhood struggle meetings and came home bragging, "I told that Black Ghost to stop his sophistry!"

During one "Reaching into the Soul and Attacking the Heart" meeting, our Neighborhood Committee accused a former teacher of being a spy. The committee said a typewriter found in her room was really a telegraph used to send secret messages to America. After several more meetings, the woman, in her thirties, jumped from her fifth-floor building across the street and hit the dirt alley facedown. Some of my classmates went to see the spot where she landed. They claimed it was indented in a human shape and stained with blood. I didn't dare go look. After that, I walked around the alley on my way to school instead of taking the shortcut through it. The woman's neighbors said that as she fell to her death she shouted, "Long live Chairman Mao!"

"Who is she to say Chairman Mao's name?" Wang Ma said sourly. "She jumped from her guilt. Suicide is an antirevolutionary act! It's only a pity because we have lost another negative teacher to struggle against. Chairman Mao says, 'In class society, no human is necessary outside the class structure. Counterrevolutionary suicides are unavoidable.' Chairman Mao says, 'We must have no humanity, justice, mercy, or virtue relations toward them.' He says, 'A death for the people weighs more than Taishan Mountain. But a death for exploiters and oppressors is lighter than a feather.' Remember, Jaia, tigers and wolves are stalking among us. We must sharpen our revolutionary vigilance."

Chairman Mao gave a purpose to our lives, turned chaos into order, and awakened awe in our hearts. He was the only thread connecting me to Wang Ma. But I was miserable in her home. She screamed that I was too much work for her, and not enough money. She underfed me. She ignored me. She hit me in anger. I hated her back and desperately missed Mama and Ba.

One day, I decided to run away to find Ba. And if I couldn't find Ba, I would take a train to find Mama. I packed my bag with schoolbooks, notepad, pencil, a towel, socks, underwear, and my lacquered box with Mama's letters. Then I sat on my bed, waiting.

Wang Ma fussed in the kitchen, preparing to go to her other, secret housecleaning job which Auntie Willow and Mama knew nothing about. I waited, feeling more and more hopeless. How would I find Ba? Wang Ma didn't even know where he was. He always sent her salary in an envelope with no return address.

How would I find Mama? Which bus went to the train station?

Which train went to Hubei? How would I pay for my tickets? The first soldier who saw me with my bag would take me back to Wang Ma. She would be furious and beat me, and further reduce my food rations. I was always hungry now. The front door opened and closed. Wang Ma was gone. I sat on the bed a long time, thinking. Then I slowly unpacked my things and put them away.

"My dear daughter. New Year's is next week. We will have beef again in camp. Everyone is very excited. Is Ba taking you home for dinner? Maybe you can go ice skating in North Sea Park Lake. Do you remember when you were a baby how we pulled you behind us in your little basket? Maybe next October for National Day we will go watch the fireworks in Tiananmen Square. Take care of your health. Mama."

New Year's Day, almost a year in Beijing without Mama. The rice was harvested. Mama's letters, which I could now read, had long ago filled my lacquered box. But she was not coming home.

Ba was coming today, his second visit. I hardly remembered his first visit four months ago. I had lain ill in bed for three days, delirious with fever, unable to eat. Wang Ma, worried, had tracked Ba down through the Security Bureau and told him I was dying. He had come, bringing me a fresh pineapple. I had felt such comfort when I looked up from my dream and saw Ba standing over me. The next morning my fever was gone. So was Ba. So was my pineapple. Wang Ma and Bing Mei had eaten it for breakfast.

"Jaia! Your father is here!"

Wang Ma stood in my doorway. I looked through her.

"What are you staring at, empty eyes? Come! You make your father wait!" She walked away angry, muttering, "Girl small, ghost big!"

I came out. Ba stood at the front door in a blue proletarian uniform. His handsome face looked tired. But his eyes were bright. Seeing him gave me sudden hope.

"Ba!"

I walked toward him uncertainly. He smiled.

"Hello, Jaia. Are you ready?"

"Yes, Ba."

I watched him, searching for his warmth. I didn't know if I should hug him or not. He watched me, cautious and aloof. I stood, arms hanging down, a useless scarecrow in a winter field.

"Let's go," he said.

He turned and started down the hall. Obediently I followed him downstairs and outside. He unlocked his bicycle.

"Get on the pack rack," he said. "If I see a cop I'll squeeze my brakes twice. You jump right off and meet me at the corner."

Riding tandem was illegal. We navigated half-empty streets slick with ice and fragrant with New Year's dinner smells. A sharp wind blew snow needles into my cheeks. Twenty minutes later we stopped before a large red-brick apartment building.

"We're home," said Ba.

I followed him to the fifth floor and down the hall to a door.

"Here we are," said Ba.

The heavenly smell of roast duck leaked from inside. Mama was back! I pushed open the door and ran in shouting, "Mama! Mama!"

A beautiful young woman stood in the kitchen looking awkwardly into my hopeful face—not Mama, but a folktale river goddess with large eyes, a proud nose, and high cheekbones. I stared at her, bewildered. She smiled like a sudden crack on a vase.

"You must be Jaia," she said.

I looked at Ba.

"Where is Mama?"

He seemed genuinely surprised.

"You know where she is! Now be polite!" He seemed annoyed at my bad manners. "This is your Auntie Shang."

I stood mute, disappointed.

"Call her Auntie Shang!" Ba said sharply. "Call her!"

"Hello, Auntie Shang," I said, but my eyes returned to seek an answer in Ba's stern face.

"Where is Mama?" I asked again, near tears.

"In a Hubei labor reform camp where Chairman Mao put her!" Ba seemed perplexed and angry.

"When is she coming back?"

"Pah!" he snapped, exasperated. "How would I know? Ask Chairman Mao! He will keep her there as long as he likes. Maybe forever! Besides, she didn't want you anymore, so she sent you back. Now I've found you a new mama, Auntie Shang. I did this for you! So treat her as your mama, with respect! Chairman Mao rejected your old mama. She is gone. There's nothing we can do."

"Mama is coming back!" I cried.

Ba's mouth opened as if he would swallow me whole.

"You! Daughter! Never contradict your father! Without me you would not be born! Are you Chairman Mao's best kid or not?" I stared at the floor. "Hasn't he said only cow ghosts and snake spirits need reforming? Hasn't he said, 'Intimate or not depends on the class'? These are Chairman Mao's words. What do they teach you in school? Your Mama is Stinking Ninth Category! You'd better draw the line with her if you want a future. Do you want to spend your life in re-form camp like her? Now stop crying! Be strong, not weak!"

"Come, come, come, dinner is ready," Auntie Shang interrupted, trying to sound cheerful.

She brought in a big, steaming pot from the kitchen and set it on the table.

"And don't teach her during dinner," she said coyly to Ba. "You'll spoil my special Five-Spice Roast Duck!"

Pa! Bang! Pop! Firecrackers exploded in the street below. It was New Year's, 1972, and I would soon be eight years old.

"My dear daughter. Spring is here. Wildflowers are blooming in the fields. Our camp's pig mother just had ten piglets. They are black

and white like little pandas. So cute! Old Yellow's grandson, Little Yellow, is full-size now. He helps us plow the paddies. I wish you were here with me. Spring is the farmer's best season. We must work hard for a good autumn harvest. You are in the spring of life now and must work hard for your own harvest. Do you understand? You must listen to Chairman Mao and study his teaching. You must be his best kid. Take care of your health. Mama."

In my second year in Beijing, I saw Ba every few months. After dinner, he and Auntie Shang would walk me to a nearby theater. Then they'd leave arm in arm while I went in to watch one of the Eight Revolutionary Example Plays. These tales from our haunted past before Liberation, the only movies shown for nearly ten years, cast a spell over my childhood. I memorized them all, word for word, song for song.

In the theaters of my childhood, I watched my Red Army heroes liberate the people, heal them, and set them free, leading them from the dark night into the splendid morning of Liberation. Happy, the White-Haired Girl, found on the Wild Mountain by the Red Army, became a soldier. Her thirst for revenge became hunger for justice and a burning desire to serve the people. Her dark night over, a Red Sun rising over the mountaintop, she danced ecstatically, embracing her Liberation.

Happy's regeneration touched me deeply, filled me with hope. My own troubles lacked the dimensions of her epic drama, and were nothing beside the suffering of the masses. I had never seen war or famine. Unlike the White-Haired Girl, I had smooth skin, shining black hair, and my parents lived.

Happy's scarred heart was a furrowed field. My heart's little scars were etched in like fine calligraphy. Yet one day I would be fearless like the White-Haired Girl dancing on a mountaintop. My Liberation would shine from my face like a Red Sun. Glorious music would celebrate my triumph.

Always the Revolutionary Example Plays ended in victory. Saved and Liberated, the White-Haired Girl led her comrades to capture the evil landlord who tortured her and murdered her father. Faced by her power, the wicked man fell trembling at her feet, and the soldiers dragged him away to be bulleted. Happy's triumph was the People's Justice.

After the movie, I waited outside. Passing shadow people with scarf-wrapped faces wandered through the dusty dream streets. Finally Ba appeared on his bicycle.

"Get on," he'd say. "Wang Ma is waiting."

And we'd ride to Auntie Willow's house, watching for policemen all the way.

After the Rice Harvest

If autumn is the season of the harvest, spring is the season of hope. On a spring day when I was nine, Mama returned north with the swallows to Beijing. Happiness overwhelmed me. Memories of rice harvest celebrations echoed in my ears, cheering Hubei villagers dancing down the dusty roads, banging their gongs and drums and blowing sweet, haunting tones on their brass suonas.

China, allowed into the United Nations after twenty-five years of isolation, needed trained intellectuals to work in Beijing Library's U.N. Information Center. With her excellent work record, political reliability, and English skills, Mama was the one lucky candidate chosen among all her camp comrades.

So often in my dreams I had run to her, wanting to touch her, to be held by her. But I could never reach her. She watched me and floated away like a kite with the string cut. So many times I woke up crying. Now I ran toward Mama, and she opened her arms. I reached her and she held me tight. It was real!

"Mama!"

"My treasure! Mama has missed you!"

I curled in her arms like a little shrimp and squeezed her neck.

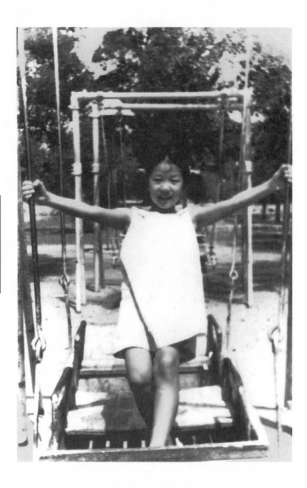

Ten-year-old Jaia in Heavenly Temple Park.

I didn't want to let her go, to ever lose her again. The rice was harvested! Mama was home! Her loving smile, her familiar smell, her heavenly warmth. Our sorrows were salt grains melting in a sweet-water well. Now we would all live in Ba's new apartment, eat at one table, go to the park and the zoo! We would never be separated again. Life would be sweet beyond imagining.

* * *

Ten-year-old Jaia, wearing the scarf of the Little Red Soldier, stands on Facing the Sun Avenue with Mama, who had returned from Hubei.

"Shaaarrr-pen scissors! Shaaarrr-pen knives!"

The scissor man's yowl arched over the neighborhood, advertising his arrival. He pushed his tilted cart in the shade of the sentinel poplar trees, his dangling iron plates clattering like wind chimes with each turn of the wheels.

The spring air rang with the hum of cicadas, which had taken over Beijing after all the birds were killed in Chairman Mao's antipest campaign. They filled the poplar trees and bowed the branches. Their buzzing had sawed my ears for days till I grew used to it. Now I never noticed it.

I loved standing on our balcony, watching Facing the Sun Avenue, listening to the symphony of neighborhood life. Ten donkeys pulled ten wagons piled high with ten mountains of bricks, scrap metal, and old wire. Ten drivers cracked their whips onto their donkeys' twitching backs.

"Der-jia-woo-luuuu! Der-jia-woo-luuu!" they sang in a ragged chorus, slicing trails of echoes down the dusty alleys.

Honking cars, lumbering buses, and chiming bicycles filled the streets. Produce-laden commune tractors spewed thick black smoke into the spring air. Children screamed. Neighbors argued. Electrical saws whined in a nearby furniture factory. A flock of singing hammers pounded steel in a casting workshop. And Mama hummed happily in the kitchen, a delicious dumpling aroma rising from her wok. These things were sunshine in my heart. What a great Facing the Sun new home! What a wonderful new life!

Mama looked smaller, and I had grown. The top of my head almost reached her chin. Now that she was home, she took care of me. No more messy hair or dirty and unmended clothes. Every day she combed my hair and tied it in two pigtails with pink fiberglass threads. She put away my outgrown, worn-to-patches, proletarian uniform, and made me two pretty new outfits: two ruffle-collared blouses—one white, one pink—and two accordion-pleated skirts—one black and one lavender floral print. She had wanted to make me something special after our two years apart. People in their proletarian uniforms stared at me when I went out in my new clothes.

But soon Mama began finding things belonging to other women: a scarf slipped off a hanger in a closet corner, an intimate letter torn in the garbage, pictures of Auntie Shang in Ba's dresser, his expense book showing many large restaurant bills. On a day not long after her return, Mama came to me.

"Little Jaia," she said, "only the truth can help Mama now. Tell me everything you remember about Ba while I was gone."

From Mama's sad eyes, I knew it was serious. I told her what I remembered from Ba's few visits: dinners with Auntie Shang; me watching movies alone; Ba telling me Mama would never come home, saying Auntie Shang was my new mama. Each thing I told Mama carved a wound. Her face clenched in pain, tears glistened in her eyes.

"Traitor," she finally hissed. "Traitor . . ."

The word stunned me—the name for enemies of the people. A

stone stuck in my throat. I could not swallow. When Ba came home, Mama accused him, her voice choking, binding me at her side as her eyewitness. Ba seemed shocked and hurt.

"Where did you hear that? Someone spread these stupid rumors! You know everyone has many enemies in this Cultural Revolution!"

He looked innocent as a Red Army hero in a revolutionary movie. Mama produced her evidence; Ba explained it all away. The intimate letter was movie-script work. The silk scarf was a studio prop. Antie Shang's pictures were given to him by her husband, who wanted his wife to be a movie star. Ba was smooth, convincing. His voice was patient, reasonable. I began to doubt my own memories.

Then Mama made me repeat all I had told her that afternoon. I didn't want to. But she said I had to be Chairman Mao's honest kid. Guilt churned my belly as Ba stared at me in horror, his face twisted in pain, an innocent man falsely betrayed by a trusted comrade. But his eyes were polished jade.

"Jaia! What are you saying? You imagined these things!"

His look made ice inside my bones. I could not see him through my tears. Ba was a stranger and I felt sick to death. Mama believed me. But I had put a curse on my family, and a bitter fight began.

They screamed and grabbed each other. I begged them to stop, but they did not hear me.

"Only verbal struggle! No violence! Contradictions should be resolved peacefully among the people!" I cried desperately.

But Chairman Mao's magical words, which could stop a falling mountain, failed to stop them. They fought like hungry wolves on a deserted hill, grabbing, punching, kicking, tearing at each other. I tried to protect Mama, but they kept pushing me away. I finally fell sobbing against the wall.

They had passed beyond my reach. A war had begun that would last for years—a war of two opposing wills, of two red-eyed wolves mad with thirst for each other's blood. When they fought, Ba, the stronger, beat Mama, who tried to hurt him before she fell. I often tried to defend her. Sometimes Ba beat me in his rage. And he made wild threats.

"I'll kick you to death!"

"I'll smash your bones!"

"I'll kill you both!"

During one fight, Mama and I fled to my room and locked ourselves in. Ba pounded on the door and we dragged my bed against it to keep him from bursting in. He got on a chair, opened the lattice above the door, and tried to climb in after us. His mad-red face and one flailing arm popped through the small frame as he struggled to squeeze through. But he stuck there, cursing and howling.

"Why did you come back?" he almost sobbed at Mama in his rage. "Why did Chairman Mao let you go?"

When he left, Mama and I held each other and cried. Tears streamed out of her burning red eyes and mixed with mine. What was happening? I didn't understand. But two fears began to haunt me. Ba would kill us both; or else he would kill Mama, and I would be left alone with him. Neighborhood stories of family homicides, of secret poisonings, planted a fear in my mind; Ba would poison us. In his rages, he seemed capable of any crime. I watched our food for signs of tampering. After I heard that poison turned silver black, I put our only silver spoon in every meal and checked it before we ate.

Finally, to my relief, Ba moved into his movie studio. He came home only once a week, if at all. I thought his leaving would help Mama get well. For the last five years, she had labored six days a week, rain, snow, or shine, underfed, attending study and self-criticism meetings nightly. These last three years she had suffered a mysterious woman sickness, bleeding two weeks of every month. Then it became three.

I watched her dry up like broken husk in the sun. Dark pouches swelled under her desert eyes. Death spots and creased lines spread across her face. As her illness devoured her and her life seeped away, her face became porcelain, yellow-gray with age, spiderwebbed with cracks. She often sat by the lamp late at night, looking shattered and sad, waiting for Ba to come home. All we had now was each other. Our love grew deeper.

"We must leave Ba!" I pleaded with Mama one day. "You must divorce him!"

"No, we need him," Mama said firmly.

"You can marry someone else . . . someone better."

"Ah, how do you know he will be better?" Mama looked sad. "Ba seemed better before I married him."

"No one could be worse," I insisted.

"Jaia, do you remember Lan from my old office? When her husband died, she married a high cadre. She thought he was a hero. Now he beats her and does nasty things to her sixteen-year-old daughter. I can't take that chance with you!"

I felt guilty being the reason Mama was trapped with Ba.

"Then don't marry. We'll live alone. Other women divorce."

"Yes." Mama gave me a patronizing look. "But what kind of women? And who respects them afterward? Stained paper! A broken shoe! What face would I have, with everyone talking behind my back and pointing me out on the street? And I can't let him go free. Why should he be happy and get what he wants? I couldn't bear it! He must pay for what he's done! Besides," she concluded, "I don't want you to grow up without a father."

My new school was a row of old, dilapidated dirt-floor shacks vandalized by students in the three Years of Chaos when schools had all closed. The broken windows were covered with oiled paper. The walls and ceilings were leopard-skinned with firecracker marks. The cracked doors hung twisted on their hinges, and the broken light fixtures dangled without bulbs. Desks sagged and chairs staggered, screws loose or missing, carved with graffiti. Mine read, "Death to Teacher Wong!" and "Smash Principal Guan's dog head!"

My new classmates talked loudly in class, spit noisily on the dirt floor, and rubbed it with their shoes. On morning break, instead of lining up at the faucet with cups, they struggled and fought to drink first, laughing, turning their heads upside down, sucking the water out of the faucet. They were wild and alive.

Influenced by Chairman Mao's sayings against intellectuals and book knowledge, these factory working-class proletarians with their bright red backgrounds could barely read or write and had vigorous contempt for books, teachers, and school. I read and wrote well, had strong, disciplined study habits, and was now learning English from Mama at home. But I was a daughter of Stinking Ninth Category Intellectuals, a Little Gray Ghost, not red at all.

The first morning, I entered my new schoolroom and forty-five pairs of eyes turned on me like flashlights. I knew I was in trouble. In my new clothes, I stood out like a pigeon in a flock of blue jays. All that first day the girls avoided me, watching me with cool, critical eyes. The boys called me names. Some even threw rocks at me after school on my way home, shouting, "Stinky bourgeois thoughts!"

I came home in tears and asked Mama for a new proletarian uniform.

"I used up our year's cloth ration to make these!" Mama said. "You can't just throw away new clothes! Besides, they're very nice. I'll get you a new PLA uniform with next year's ration."

A week passed. At recess I watched other girls laugh and play together, envying their proletarian uniforms, their unity. I felt criminal, set apart, unable to bridge a gulf of estrangement. One morning a girl tripped on a jump rope, skinning her knees, and began to cry. Instead of helping, her friends laughed and jeered.

"Little crying baby!"

"Does it help your knees to water your eyes?"

Shocked, I stared at the class lone wolf, a tough tomboy, who had laughed loudest at the injured girl. She saw me and came over, glaring and tossing her bangs aside.

"What's your problem, Single Flower?" she said loudly.

It was a slap on the face. "Single Flower" implied bourgeois, dirty-minded individualism. Chairman Mao said individualism was a sickness. And everyone hated flowers. We called them poison weeds. No one grew them anymore. Grabbing my ruffled collar, the girl enviously rubbed the soft new cotton between her fingers. Her faded blue proletarian uniform was a hand-me-down landscape of patches. Yet her high cheekbones, snowflake skin, and willow-leaf eyebrows didn't fit her tough act. She was pretty. Her peers didn't like her any more than they liked me, but she didn't care. Her name was Shao Mei, Little Plum. Now another girl came over from the group, glaring at me.

"How modern!" she said. "Are you Western or Chinese?"

Her comrades watched intently, looking for cues, ready to join in. I had feared such a moment all week. To my surprise, Little Plum whirled on the girl.

"You shut up!" she said fiercely. The startled girl backed off. Little Plum faced down the others. "What a pack of common dogs," she sneered. "One follows the other."

She swaggered off, and the girls sheepishly resumed their game. Single Flower, the name she gave me that day, stuck like a bad smell. I was an intellectual's child, born polluted. My clothes and manner confirmed it. Little Plum had named my stain.

The Party's biannual "Learn from Uncle Lei Feng" campaign had begun. For two weeks of every six months, our masses became an army of janitors armed with buckets, mops, brooms, scrapers, and garbage pails. We had celebrated Uncle Lei Feng's greatness ever since I could remember. But these cleaning campaigns had started in the spring of 1972.

That was when our American enemies had sent their king, President Niko Song, into the heart of China, with a batallion of his journalist spies. We had spent weeks before that visit scouring Beijing, because, our teacher told us, these spies were like flies; their job was to look for dirt and spread germs. Then Niko Song came and appeared on our TV screens. Chairman Mao even smiled at him and shook his hand. He looked as scary as I had imagined him to be. But Chairman Mao was not afraid of anything, not even the "King of the Imperialist Demons."

Now in every Uncle Lei Feng Campaign, we spent hours each day cleaning in shifts, supervised by soldiers, scraping thick masses of posters from every wall, window, fence, and pole, washing the nation clean. We swept every street and sidewalk, pulled every weed and blade of grass from every crack. We put new paint over old, replaced broken windows, and repaired old fences. We scrubbed, polished, and shined our motherland as Uncle Lei Feng speeches, stories, and songs blared over the public loudspeakers.

In school we read Uncle Lei Feng biographies, wrote Uncle Lei Feng posters, sang Uncle Lei Feng songs, and studied his legendary journal. I wanted to be like loyal Uncle Lei Feng, Chairman Mao's Best Soldier and the People's Best Son, tirelessly serving the masses with every breath.

Every moment of Uncle Lei Feng's glorious, inspiring life had been spent serving others: washing his comrades' laundry, reading revolutionary stories to Little Red Scarf League members, returning lost children to their parents, putting out factory fires, building houses, erecting electricity poles, digging wells, and donating all his money to flooded communes when the dams he had built for them finally collapsed.

When Uncle Lei Feng took a train, he never sat down. He bought tickets for little old ladies, helped load the passengers' luggage, served everyone hot tea, organized and led revolutionary sing-alongs, gave his food to the hungry, swept the floors, washed the train windows, shoveled coal into the furnace for the conductor, helped unload the passengers' luggage when they arrived in the station, swept the train after they disembarked, and helped elderly passengers home in the dark.

And every night, when he wasn't out in his PLA compound cleaning night soil from the trenches, planting trees to stabilize the soil, growing vegetables for his battalion, fixing broken-down trucks and tractors, and practicing throwing hand grenades, he stayed up late studying Chairman Mao's teachings and writing the immortal slogans that filled his pious legendary journal. And he did all this selflessly, anonymously, with no thought of reward. Whenever someone asked him his name, wanting to thank him for his kindness, he replied humbly, "Call me PLA."

It's a wonder he was ever discovered. Before a falling telephone pole ended his short life at the age of twenty-one, Uncle Lei Feng had written in his journal, "To serve the Party and the People, I would willingly enter an ocean of fire, a mountain of knives, or the deepest abyss. Even with my head chopped off and my bones ground to powder, my heart shall remain red and never be changed."

And his most famous quote of all was "I only want to be a screw for the Party. And wherever the Party puts me, I will shine on that spot."

This, too, was my highest aspiration. In class, to bring Uncle Lei Feng's "Screw Spirit" into action, Teacher Su had us choose "Red Pairs Helping Each Other Study Partners." I chose Little Plum.

"You really want to study with me?" Little Plum asked me after school.

"Of course I do," I told her sincerely.

She seemed skeptical. She thought I didn't like her. But as Uncle Lei Feng had said:

"Treat comrades as warm as spring.
Treat work as passionate as summer.

Treat individualism as the cold autumn wind sweeps the fallen leaves.
Treat enemies as cruel as a severe winter."

I wanted to treat Little Plum as warm as spring and work as pas-sionate as summer to help her study and change. She was two years older than I and a poor student, "twice cooked," meaning held back a year. I was the top student, a year or two younger than my classmates. But I admired her strength and toughness, how she didn't care what anyone thought. And she had an inner brightness that intrigued me. Maybe we could be comrades. Little Plum was so pleased she invited me to her home.

"I'll make boi choi soup and we can study together," she said. As we walked home, Little Plum asked me shyly, "Do you want to know a secret?"

"What is it?"

"Don't tell anyone," she said softly. "But I wish I could be a good student, too."

Her face turned red. I felt so happy that she trusted me.

Little Plum lived in the socialism yard across the street from my building. Our district was one of Beijing's oldest. Some people traced their ancestors back hundreds of years to this same neigh-borhood. Little Plum bragged that five generations of her family were born there, and her ancestors before that had migrated from the railway-station neighborhood five blocks away.

It took me a minute to adjust to the darkness in Little Plum's home. The room smelled of mold, old food, and soy sauce mixed with lard. It had a coal stove for cooking and heating. Two double bunk beds sat end to end against one wall. Little Plum, her brother, and her parents slept there. The plaster walls, full of cracks sealed with old newspaper, were yellow with age and greasy with cooking smoke. A small window cut in the plaster was covered with an oiled

People's Daily. The packed-dirt floor was bumpy, black, and slightly damp. Chairman Mao's huge picture hung alone on the main wall.

"Let's turn on the light, Little Plum," I suggested.

"Has the sun gone down?" She raised her eyebrows. "Don't be spoiled. You know electricity costs seven cents per degree."

I didn't know. Little Plum lifted the stove lid and dropped chunks of coal from a pail onto the ready embers. She prodded them with a metal poker and blew till they started to glow. Then she handed me a kettle.

"Go catch some water," she said.

I went out. The medium-sized yard housed two or three hundred people, with fifty rooms just like Little Plum's honeycombed together. I wandered through the maze of narrow zigzag alleys, ducking clotheslines sagging with damp uniforms, underwear, and socks. Finally, I found the water spigot. Ten people stood in line holding pots, kettles, and basins. After filling the kettle, I returned to find Little Plum cutting boi choi leaves with swift, efficient strokes. She was faster than Mama.

"Sorry it took so long," I said. "There was a line."

"How many people?"

"About ten."

"Since when is ten people a line?" asked Little Plum.

Behind one wall, a radio blared a popular song. A soprano sang how Chairman Mao had healed her. Before she couldn't speak, but now she shrieked as shrill and easy as a bird.

"Miraculous, thousand-year-old iron tree bursts into bloom. . . .
A ten-thousand-year hopeless root grows new shoots. . . .
Today, our mutes can finally speak again. . . .
Thanks to Chairman Mao, our great savior star!
Ah-, ah-, ah-, aaahhhhhhhh . . ."

Her last ethereal, passionate note soared higher and higher into the clouds. It became a dramatic screech, a speeding car on a breaking curve, a knife scratching a blackboard. It sent chills up my spine. Little Plum hummed along wholeheartedly, dropping boi choi leaves into the pot.

"Do they always play the radio so loud?" I asked her.

"It's not so loud," she said. "The walls are thin. When they don't whisper you can hear every word. Heyo, Uncle Zuk," she called through the wall, just raising her voice.

"Heyo, Little Plum," a man's voice bounced back.

I jumped. It almost sounded as if he were in the room with us. Little Plum smiled and stirred the soup. Her relatives lived in rooms behind three of her family's four walls.

Soon the green smell of boi choi soup filled the room. For my sake, Little Plum pulled a string on a naked bulb dangling by a cord from the ceiling. A faint halo flickered on. We squatted on the dirt floor eating boi choi soup seasoned with soy sauce. Little Plum's family had no table.

"Where do you do your homework?" I asked.

"I don't," she said matter-of-factly. "Who needs to study? Chairman Mao says too much book learning makes you stupid."

"He also says, 'Study hard, grow daily,' " I countered.

"He says everything," said Little Plum matter-of-factly. "You just have to choose the saying you like."

"But you must learn enough to read Chairman Mao's teachings yourself," I reasoned. She nodded. "We can study at my place tomorrow, if you want," I added.

Little Plum smiled excitedly.

"In that tall building? Shake!" she said. "I've never been off the ground floor!"

Our home amazed Little Plum. She wandered through our rooms, enthralled, pointing at drawers, shelves, and closets, asking, "What's this for? What's inside that?"

Many things impressed her. We owned more clothes than we could wear at one time, and more dishes than we could use at one meal. We had two rooms and a kitchen, two tables and closets. We had a water spigot and a toilet, a balcony and glass windows. And we lived higher than a tree.

Our kitchen was Little Plum's biggest thrill, with its gas stove and running-water sink. She was a master of recycled cooking materials: a little flour, some old dried mushrooms, some peanuts from a cracked jar, seaweed shreds and crusty date pieces lying in back of the cabinet, a dash of vinegar and soy sauce. Little Plum the alchemist cut, chopped, mixed, and transmuted the abandoned remains into unexpécted delicacies. In fifteen minutes our sunny kitchen filled with the delicious aroma of peanut-date-mushroom dumplings floating like fat little pigs in a tasty seaweed broth. When I admired her proletarian skills, Little Plum proudly quoted from *The Red Lantern,* her favorite Revolutionary Example Play, about an orphan girl named Iron Plum: " 'The poor people's child becomes independent early,' " she said.

When she found an old movie script in Ba's trash, she couldn't believe he had thrown it away. She asked if she could take it home, earnestly explaining, "Thick paper like this makes windows for the whole winter."

When she found our old-clothes rag pile in the closet, her eyes blazed indignantly.

"Your ma uses these for rags? Bring me a needle and thread!"

I got out our sewing kit with three needles and four colors of thread, and she frowned as if we'd been hiding it from the masses. Then she began mending a hole in my outgrown PLA jacket.

"These aren't rags yet," she said. " 'New for three years, old for three years, mending and fixing for another three years,' " she quoted, adding, "Who throws away clothes because of a few holes? Stinky Ninth Category devils who don't know Chairman Mao's teaching!"

But Little Plum had no mean spirit. When she left, she took our rag-pile clothes with her. Two days later she returned them, tears mended, missing buttons replaced by homemade ones, and a neat patch sewn over each hole. She had even torn the worst rags into strips and tied them on a stick to make a new floor mop.

" 'Thrifty is revolutionary,' huh?" she smiled proudly, quoting Chairman Mao.

Little Plum was a proletarian wizard.

She was also a tough little rebel. At school, she called our classmates "butt-following bugs" who marched in a circle, each one thinking the one in front knew where he was going. And their dirtiness offended her.

"Look how dirty they are!" she would say. "They can grow potatoes on their necks!"

Little Plum kept herself meticulously clean, washing herself daily with a rag and pail of water. She also kept a rock in her pocket and pulled it out ready whenever we crossed a street. Hit-and-run accidents were common, and drivers rarely stopped to help those they had run over. When I asked what her rock was for, she told me, "If I get run over, I'm at least going to put this rock through the bastard's windshield."

Beneath her rebel exterior, Little Plum was proletarian to the bone. She kept house for her parents and older brother, who worked forty-eight hours a week in a metal-pipe factory. She cleaned her house, swept the dirt floor, shopped for food, scrubbed the wok and tin bowls, took out the garbage, greased and papered the window, washed her family's clothes, and cooked them two meals a day. She was almost as busy as Uncle Lei Feng. Her example inspired me.

And our study partnership was a great success. At first, she had doubted herself. She was twice cooked and feared being cooked again. But I told her, "If you study hard, you won't fail."

"Are you sure?"

"I swear to Chairman Mao," I promised.

The idea intrigued her. She studied with me every afternoon and made progress in all her subjects. She began enjoying school. She even asked me to write a sign in my best calligraphy, which she put on her desk. It was Chairman Mao's quote, "Study hard, grow daily."

"From now on, if you see me talking in class, just look at me, and I'll shut up," she told me earnestly.

And she did. She even became polite to Teacher Su. Most of our classmates challenged Teacher Su disrespectfully to show their red contempt for intellectuals and their useless book-knowledge games. The anti-intellectual sentiment encouraged by Chairman Mao still ran very high. My classmates often taunted Teacher Su with Chairman Mao's sayings.

"Teacher Su, Chairman Mao says, 'To be the people's teacher, you must be the people's student.' So you are our student!"

"Teacher Su, Chairman Mao says, 'The more book learning one has, the stupider one becomes.' How many books did you read?"

She always backed down. When we took our tests, my classmates called out one by one, "Teacher Su, is the answer to the first question three or four?"

"You're very close," she'd say, "but it's one number higher."

"Is it five?"

"Yes! Very good!"

The class guessed every question until Teacher Su told them the answers, which they scribbled onto their test sheets. I worked out all the problems on my own. I knew they missed something, getting answers this way, even if they did get high scores.

"Why is Teacher Su afraid of us?" I asked Little Plum one day.

"Don't you know?" She looked surprised. "The Red Guard beat her husband to death in the cowshed. They were both teachers here. But they got put in the cowshed for being 'bourgeois gardeners raising imperialist shoots.' She got back from labor reform camp last year.

"You know what the older kids did to the teachers last year?" Little Plum smirked. "They'd call the crematory and say, 'Comrade Su died. Send a truck over to pick her up.' Then the cremation truck would go to Teacher Su's house and the driver would tell her he had come to take Comrade Su to the crematory. They did it to all the teachers, even Principal Guan. Now the cremation truck won't go to a teacher's house anymore. Their families will have to bring their bodies there!"

Little Plum almost fell over laughing.

Ba had been gone for weeks. And one night Mama did not come home. I stood on the balcony as the sun sank in a haze of dust and factory fumes. The stream of bicycles thinned to a trickle. The streets became dry riverbeds. Smoky darkness filled the city, and the lights along Facing the Sun Avenue flickered on like a string of glass beads.

I waited anxiously for Mama, hearing the commune delivery tractors scattered across Beijing chugging home in the dark. Comforting neighborhood sounds hung in the air and turned lonely. People chattered, dishes clattered, oil splattered in woks. "Getting cool people," palm fans and bamboo stools tucked under their arms, sauntered into their yards, home to bed. Beijing slept, a vast, silent shadow under the quiet stars. And Mama still didn't come.

I don't know how long I stood there, anxiety building. Then I was sobbing. Something terrible had happened to Mama! She had been run over in the street! The Party had sent her back to her camp! She had died from her illness and been taken to the crematory! I would never see her again!

A solitary bike chime rang down the broad, empty street, and Mama appeared. With a shout, I ran downstairs through the front door. She pedaled up and got off her bike. She looked frightened when she saw my tear-stained face and red, swollen eyes.

"Jaia! What happened?"

"I didn't know where you were!"

"What's wrong with you?" Mama asked. "I stayed late at work to talk to my comrades. Don't stand here crying all night! Tomorrow you'll look like a big swollen peach!"

I felt stupid and ashamed. How could I tell Mama that every time we separated I feared she would die or be sent away and I would never see her again? Even when she went one block to stand in the food lines at the market, I could not stop my fears.

"Did Ba come home?" Mama asked hopefully.

I shook my head. Tears circled the edges of her eyes. I knew she and her work friends had been discussing strategy about Ba.

"Come upstairs," Mama said softly. "You haven't eaten. We'll make dinner together."

After dinner, we sat at the table and Mama examined my face. She ran her callused fingers softly over my cheeks and felt in gentle circles around my eyes.

"You'll have a good life," she pronounced, trying to make me feel better. "More luck than me. You don't have any unlucky moles. See this?" She pointed to the sesame-sized mole just below her left eye. "It's called a tear mole. It's bad luck. It sits under the eye like a black teardrop that never goes away. It means your tears will wash your face your whole life. You don't have any, so you will have a happy life."

I wanted to argue for Mama's happiness. But her words seemed final and profound. And her tears did wash her face too often. Now she touched the small mole to the right of her mouth.

"This one is called a rice mole," she said. "Its meaning is determined by its distance from your tongue. If your tongue can touch it, your life will be easy and abundant. Mine is too far away. See? My tongue cannot reach it. So my life is bitter and poor. You have a little rice mole there, see? So close! Your tongue can't miss it! You will always have enough. Before I married Ba, I tried to change my luck. I bought acid mixed with herbs from a healer who said it would burn my bad luck away. But it didn't work."

Mama's words hurt my heart. I did not want happiness if she could have none. Her life was bitter. Her mama had died when she was three and her own father had sent her away. The Party she loved had exiled her and stained her personal record with black marks. She was sick for years and couldn't get well. Now Ba had passed beyond her reach, floating away, like a kite with the string cut.

Mama spoke often of Ba when he disappeared, her voice sad with longing.

"Your Ba wasn't like this before. But people change." She sighed. "Ai, people change."

"What was he like?"

I wanted to know. Mama needed to remember. Ba's changing was a painful mystery. Only memories held his place in our hearts. So Mama told me many stories of Ba. Talking slowly, her voice full of feeling, she built his legend in our minds. And together we remembered who Ba had been, so that we could still love him.

Ba was born in Shandong Province, at the foot of Taishan Mountain, where the Yellow River once emptied into the Yellow Sea. Ba's family lived in poverty, laboring four seasons a year for their landlord to earn their food. Grandpa farmed. Grandma served in the landlord's house and worked in the fields with Grandpa at planting and harvest times. Ba and his younger sister were born in the family's thatched-roof hut while Grandpa worked like a horse in the sweat-soaked fields.

"A lucky son! Thank heaven and earth!" was Grandma's grateful prayer when she had Ba. "Now we won't have to buy a horse!"

They named Ba Lucky. When he was eight years old, the great monsoons came to Shandong. For weeks, falling rain filled the sky and covered the earth, blowing and swinging in the howling winds like bead strands strung from heaven. The Yellow River choked on the yellow sands swept into her belly from the Mongolian Desert. And our Yellow Mother became the Mad Yellow Dragon who devours her own children.

Ba and his family fled to the hills. Devastated, they watched the river rise, engulfing their farmland, their crops, and their whole village, sweeping away the life they had known. Thousands of villages and vast tracts of farmland in several provinces were swallowed up. Tens of thousands of peasants drowned. Human and animal corpses, uprooted houses, crops, and trees floated along for hundreds of miles in the muddy torrent and were swept into the Yellow Sea. The land was ruined and millions died in the resulting famines.

With only a water gourd, a begging bowl, and their patched clothes, Ba and his family joined the survivors in a mass exodus northeast, begging their way along the coast. Starvation drove them up through Beijing, fallen capital of the Qing dynasty, into Japanese-occupied Manchuria. They walked fifteen hundred miles in half a year and settled in Hei Long Jiang, Black Dragon River Province, in a tiny lumber town along Xing An Forest. There they built a one-room home of wood scraps foraged from the lumberyard.

Grandpa became a lumberjack for a Japanese mill. Grandma worked as a farmhand for a Japanese landowner. Life got better. Hardworking and thrifty, they began saving pennies in their water gourd. A family saying, treasured for generations, advised, "Save a mouthful a day, buy a horse in seven years."

It seemed this might come true. Grandpa and Grandma managed to send Ba and his sister to the local school that trained Chinese children to become loyal Japanese subjects. Ba and his sister studied hard. Under their Japanese teachers, they became convinced of their glorious Japanese ancestry and heritage.

"I am a Japanese!" they shouted daily. "I will always be loyal to His Majesty, the Supreme Emperor of Japan!"

In my childhood, Ba still recited this teaching in flawless Japanese, and occasionally boasted of being "at least half Japanese." His confusion about his nationality grew deeply rooted. Years later, as a young Communist soldier, he had night dreams of being Japanese and living in Japan, of tea gardens strewn with white cherry blossoms, of serving the emperor as a samurai warrior. And in spite of our intense hatred of the Japanese for their invasion and brutal slaughter of eight million Chinese, Ba could murmur wistfully, "If the Japanese had not left China, today we would be as advanced as any country in the world."

But Ba's family life was suddenly changed one cool summer morning. The long warning shout, "Mountain Falling!" echoed through the misty pines. The cut tree groaned, cracked, and fell in the wrong direction, shattering Grandpa's skull and breaking his back. Lying under a trunk thicker than his chest, he choked out a mouthful of blood and departed open-eyed to the land of his ancestors. Grandma spent the family's horse money on his coffin. She and Ba dug Grandpa's grave and buried him.

Grandpa's death plunged the family into poverty and grief. Ba, eleven years old, was forced to drop out of school and find work tending yards and cleaning houses for rich Japanese. But he wanted to be someone bigger than his lifelong struggling father, whose biggest dream had been to one day own a horse and plow.

Ba decided to become a man. He swore to his mama if she let him return to school and become educated, he would work to support his family and bring them all a better life. He swore to himself he would become a true samurai and cultivate a warrior's virtues. He would eat bitter and grow strong. So he returned to school, and went to work before and after.

Each morning, he rose while the stars twinkled in the black sky. He ran through the dark, silent forest and jumped into the lake. He ran even in winter, testing his spirit against the north wind's blade and his naked flesh in the icy waters. Afterward, he stood on the bank rubbing snow over his body, reciting a samurai mantra his teacher had taught him: "Issho Kenmei! Issho Kenmei!" Risk one's life! Risk one's life!

Eating bitter was samurai virtue. When his teacher gave him a New Year's candy, he stared at it the next morning till his mouth water ran, then took it on his run and threw it into the lake. When he pierced his leg with a scythe at work cutting grass for his Japanese employer, he bound his wound with a strip of cloth and finished the job. At night, weary from work and school, he forced his mind clear and studied before going to sleep. So he turned flesh to iron, bones to steel, and sharpened his will and his mind like tempered swords. An inner fire awoke in Ba.

Some mornings, he rose and knelt in the dark on the slanted floor. He raised the family cutting knife aiming its blade at his belly. In his mind, he plunged it in, imagining seppuku, cold steel cutting through his entrails, to feel terror in his guts without flinching. Ba knew he was born to be a warrior.

The year Ba turned eighteen, as the world united to defeat the Nazis, the Chinese allies joined together for the final battle to drive out the Japanese. Two days after the mushroom clouds rose over Hiroshima and Nagasaki, the Japanese invaders surrendered unconditionally to the Chinese allies. They spent the next thirty years as war criminals in Chinese prisons.

With the Japanese gone, Ba wandered across northeast China, stalking fate. He found the Red Army, whose impeccable discipline and code of honor resembled the samurai path he most admired. Their declared mission to liberate the poor, oppressed Chinese masses and all oppressed peoples of the world awakened his youthful idealism and gave a new, heroic purpose to his life.

Ba spent four years with the Red Army Number Eight Troop, fighting the Kuomintang across northeast China. In hand-to-hand combat in the "forest of guns and the rain of bullets," he saw his own blood run and his comrades killed in battle. He slept in caves,

Ba as a young man.

cellars, trees, bushes, in dry ditches under the stars. He starved and ate cooked leather belts, boiled tree bark, and grass roots. He caught rats and shot wild pigs. But no suffering or bitterness could turn him back from the vision of his people's liberation. And Liberation came.

In 1949, the people finally stood up and drove the Kuomintang out of China. Ba went to the countryside in the Land Reform move-

Mama at age twenty-five.

ment. When the sun rose, the farmers put on new, warm clothes and went to work in the same fields. But now they planted hope and reaped a harvest of freedom, prosperity, and a better life. The people worshiped the Party. The Party served the people. And Ba knew he would serve them both for the rest of his life.

After five years of working with the peasants and serving on his county committee, Ba was promoted and sent to Beijing's Diplomatic Institute, the training ground of future Party leaders. What a prize for this peasant warrior of twenty-eight, to live in Beijing, the heart of China, and be near Chairman Mao. Ba was already a tiger, and now the Party was giving him wings!

Ba was a top student; his sharp mind and his years of "eating bitter" disciplines made mere study an effortless pleasure. Beloved by his classmates, he became student union leader and captain of the basketball team. Everyone admired this tall, handsome cadre with the Northeast accent from the most noble poor peasant family background. He had brilliance, tremendous energy, endless enthusiasm. He had humility, generosity, charm. Mama said their fellow students gossiped before graduation that Ba would become a high-ranking cadre, an ambassador, a foreign minister, and maybe find a place on the Party Central Committee. And Ba, whose roots were straight and red, fell in love with Mama, an exploiting-class daughter who spoke an Imperialist language. They were worlds apart. But after graduation they were married and began their ascent. Nine years later I was born.

Then the Cultural Revolution came.

Little Plum was puzzled by all the secrets in my house: the box in Mama's closet bound with string, the locked suitcase under Ba's bed, Mama's and Ba's locked dresser drawers. They hid everything from each other. And from me. But I found where Mama hid her keys and explored her secret treasures. And when Ba went out one day and forgot to lock his dresser, I seized the opportunity to discover his secrets. I found his old white shirt, its back torn and stained with rusty stripes of blood. I found love letters, pictures of women, and a picture of a young girl who looked very much like me but was not me. I found a twenty-three-year-old marriage license signed by Ba, and the wife's name on it was not Mama's.

"Why are so many locks in your house?" Little Plum asked me.

Little Plum's home had no secrets. Her family had nothing to hide and no place to hide it. Their only privacy was in their pockets.

One afternoon I took Little Plum into Mama's room to show her what I had found in Mama's locked dresser drawer—a white embroidered silk gown, wrapped in an old sheet. When Little Plum saw it, she shrieked, her willow-leaf eyebrows shot halfway up her forehead. She grabbed it eagerly, held it to her body, then ran and stood before Mama's mirror admiring her beautiful reflection.

Next I took out a pair of beautiful gold earrings with red, sparkling stones; a round silver case with an elegant mirror, pink chalk disk, and pad inside; an oblong ivory tube carved with flowers; and a crystal bottle filled with golden perfume.

Little Plum opened the silver case and gazed into the mirror. I pulled the top off the ivory tube and touched the crayon inside. My fingertip came out red.

"Ooohhh! Let me show you!" squealed Little Plum.

She grabbed the tube, twisted the bottom, and the red crayon rose above the rim.

"What is it?" I asked.

I didn't know what Mama's treasures were. Little Plum did.

"You put it on your lips to color them red," she said. "All women wore this on their lips before the Cultural Revolution."

Next Little Plum picked up the bottle of golden liquid with foreign words engraved in the crystal glass. She opened it and a painfully celestial smell invaded the room, pore penetrating, making us nostalgic for a past that didn't belong to us.

"Foreign mosquito water! It's *sooo* bourgeois!" Little Plum was too excited. "Your mama should have turned these in," she said.

Mama's treasures from her years as a foreign diplomat were antirevolutionary bourgeois artifacts. If Little Plum told anyone, it would get back to the Neighborhood Committee, which would tell the Security Bureau, which would send Mama back to her Hubei camp. I would lose her again. I put my hand on Little Plum's arm.

"You can't tell anyone about this, Little Plum," I said firmly. "You'll get Mama in big trouble."

"What kind of friend do you think I am?" Little Plum looked hurt. "I think your mama is real shake! I love this bourgeois stuff! I wish it was all mine!"

I was surprised. Little Plum's opinion of my "Stinky Ninth Category" mama had suddenly changed. These bourgeois treasures made Mama "shake" in Little Plum's eyes and brought out a side of Little Plum I hadn't seen before. She picked up the dress again.

"Before our Cultural Revolution era, all women wore these dresses," she said, smoothing the silk against her body. Next she looked in Mama's mirror and rubbed the red crayon on her lips. "They put this on their lips and the pink powder on their cheeks and curled their hair. Their shoe heels were long, like thick chopsticks. They had pretty purses the size of a dog's ear, too tiny to hold anything. And they always wore mosquito water. Maybe someday we'll dress this way and boys will look at us!"

We both giggled. Now she rubbed the chalk on her cheeks with the pad and turned them pink.

"How do you know all this?" I asked.

"From my ger mer's magazines," she said casually.

I was shocked. "Ger mer" was hooligan slang for "gang brother." Was Little Plum a hooligan? Our classmates said so. But I didn't believe it.

She smoothed her hair back, admiring her reflection, her red lips and pink cheeks. And her eyes sparkled.

"Look!" she sighed. "Now I am so beautiful!" She looked at me hopefully. "Don't you think?"

"Shake!" I said.

Little Plum smiled. She was in bourgeois heaven.

I had been so happy being Little Plum's friend. She had taught me to cook, clean, and be thrifty-proletarian. And I felt a sense of accomplishment from our study partnership, seeing her grow in self-confidence as she became smarter in school. Her parents were very grateful to me.

But something changed in our second semester. She came over less to study. She made mysterious new friends who weren't in our school. She began acting up in class again, talking, making loud jokes, and spitting carelessly on the floor. She no longer stopped talking when I looked at her. Her mind was somewhere else. I felt her drifting away. And I didn't know how to get her back.

One day she came to school with strange hair; she had curled it with a hot coal poker. It looked burned and unevenly chewed. Even worse, she had shaved off her eyebrows and painted them on again with charcoal. She looked like a ghost. I asked her what happened. She said it was her new style.

"It's too out of control," I told her in her own slang.

But she seemed pleased. Teacher Su said nothing. I worried Little Plum would get in trouble with the Neighborhood Committee. That day, she invited me to her home for the first time in weeks.

"If you think my new style is out of control," she bragged, "let me show you something really dangerous."

Intrigued, I went with her. Little Plum lifted up her bed mat. A thin, newspaper-wrapped package lay underneath on the board. She always kept boxes of dried orange peels, live beetles, lizards, and other strange things under her bed. She collected and sold them to a nearby herbal medicine shop.

But now I could not believe my eyes. The package under her mat contained moldy magazines with loose pages and cover dates from the 1930s, the Japanese-invasion era. The women on the covers looked "womanly" in the bad way, with curly hair and bare-shoulder dresses with rips up the thighs. They had jade-smooth skin, cat-whisker eyelashes, red lips, pink cheeks, and charcoal eyebrows. This was how Little Plum was trying to look!

These were the nasty, illegal Kuomintang "yellow magazines"! People went to prison for having them! Little Plum opened one. The inside pictures were worse than the covers. Some of the women wore clothes that barely covered them! Their body parts showed!

"Are they out of control?" Little Plum smiled bravely. "Look how bourgeois they can get!"

She sighed over them, turning the pages for me, past photos of half-naked men and women kissing, all twisted together. *Yai!* Little Plum and I were criminals for looking! What would Mama think? I had thought I was brave for reading banned foreign books in Beijing Library like *The Little Mermaid Girl* and *The Beautiful Sleeping Princess.* But these magazines terrified me.

"Like it?" asked Little Plum in a bragging tone.

"Where did you get them?"

"From my gang brothers. They say I can be pretty like these women, because I've got 'the look.' " She seemed proud. "You can borrow them for one day, if you want. You could join us, too," she added hopefully.

Her gang brothers! Little Plum was going too far!

"I can't," I told her. "Mama wouldn't let me."

Little Plum seemed disappointed. I went home that afternoon, afraid for her. She had been dragged into the water. And I didn't know how to save her.

Individualistic, antirevolutionary hooligan gangs had arisen in our streets the last few years. Big hooligans had guns, sold drugs, stole, robbed, and killed people. But the hooligans in most neighborhoods were little rebels who smoked cigarettes, wore their jackets unbuttoned, and grew "hang-bangs" slanting over one eye. They made slingshots and broke windows and streetlights and killed birds. They called each other numbers instead of names, hung out on corners, talked strange slang, and communicated late into the night in an eerie code of whistles. I often fell asleep with their atonal whistles rising up through my fifth-floor window.

Hooligan boys loved to scare girls. They followed us, making nasty remarks and animal noises, whistling, and sometimes exposing themselves. I'd heard hooligan boys and girls did dirty things together. Most people hated them: I did too. I couldn't understand Little Plum's interest in them.

Principal Guan had criticized Little Plum for her "messy bird-nest hairstyle." She skipped school often now and hardly ever studied with me anymore. She bragged to me about staying out all night with her gang brothers. And her tobacco breath told me she was smoking. Yet she still managed her home, cleaning, hauling coal, shopping, and cooking meals for her family. I marveled how she could be a hooligan and a good proletarian daughter at the same time.

One day after school our neighborhood police chief, Captain Wei, came to my home. He had been here a month ago with his men on a midnight ID check. Now he stood in the doorway looking serious. Short gray stubble covered his head like rust. I thought he had come to see my parents, that some neighbor had reported their violent fights. He watched me sternly.

"Jaia," he said, "you are friends with Little Plum."

"Yes, Uncle Wei," I answered softly.

"How often do you see her?"

"Not much anymore."

"What do you do when you are together?"

His unexpected questions puzzled me.

"Homework," I said. "We are a Red Study Pair in school."

"What else?"

"We cook," I said. "She taught me to sew."

"Did she ever steal things from your house?" he asked.

"No, Uncle Wei."

Little Plum had pride. She never took a dumpling from our wok, and even asked before taking papers and orange peels from our garbage. It hurt me that people misunderstood our friendship. "Only a rotten fish seeks a smelly shrimp's company," they said. Even Uncle Wei seemed to think so.

"Your teacher says you are a good student who behaves well in class. We don't understand your friendship with Little Plum. She is a bad egg, a hooligan who disobeys her parents and stays out all night. Who knows what she does? You must stay away from her. You can't help her now. Leave her in the Party's good hands."

"Yes, Uncle Wei," I answered obediently, my heart pounding.

Uncle Wei left. I shut the door after him. And I shut a door on Little Plum, who had wandered beyond my reach. I felt relieved now that she was safe in the Party's hands.

All that week, I avoided Little Plum at school as Uncle Wei had instructed. I looked busy, in a hurry. After school I rushed home. Little Plum knew I was dodging her. She finally cornered me on the playground one morning.

"Hello, Jaia," she said.

Anger bent her voice. Her eyes stuck in me like two nails pressed through a board.

"Hello, Little Plum. How are you?"

My words came out dry as husk. I was a fish gasping on a rock. She enjoyed my discomfort. It was like our first encounter on the playground almost a year ago.

"Hypocrite!" She spat the word in my face. "What do you care? You've been avoiding me all week."

Stung, I lashed back, "Why do you become the hooligans' walking dog and shame your family?"

Little Plum's eyes widened in a fierce, wounded look. She stared at her new enemy. Suddenly she slapped me hard in the face, turned, and left the schoolyard.

At seven o'clock next evening, my Little Red Soldiers Patrol Team stood in formation on the school playground facing Captain Wei. We wore Little Red Scarf League insignia: a bright red scarf and green PLA belt with copper buckle. Each of us held a tall, red-tasseled wooden spear bought at Hundred Goods toy counter. There were nine of us tonight. One was missing—Little Plum. She had not come to school that day. We began chanting with Uncle Wei, "Chairman Mao has told us! 'Never forget the class bitterness! Always remember our hatred through our blood and tears!' "

Four old women flanked us wearing PLA belts and red scarves

and holding wooden spears—our Neighborhood Committee Senior Group. Everyone called them the Little Feet Patrol. Infamous meddlers and passionate gossips with a fierce Party loyalty, they found power and purpose in their roles as neighborhood watchdogs and spies. And each had earned a special, behind-the-back name.

Old Eyes led her three worthy lieutenants, Old Tongue, Old Ears, and Old Feet; all bound-foot feudalism victims whose belts sat like bucket hoops on their pear-shaped bodies. In Little Red Soldier scarves they looked like penguins with red bow ties.

Though unpopular in the neighborhoods for their aggressive, "sticking their noses in everywhere" spirit, Little Feet Patrols were treated with slavish politeness and respect. As liaisons with the local Security Bureaus, their words changed lives. The Little Feet Patrols ruled their neighborhoods, as head eunuchs had once ruled the emperor's court. Only hooligans, with no face to lose and reckless with fate, treated them disrespectfully.

Our chanting finished, Uncle Wei prepared us for our evening's patrol with an inspiring speech.

"You Little Red Soldiers must always honor your duty," he began gravely. "For Chairman Mao has placed his trust in each one of you. Beware! Our class enemies seek revenge! Their evil is tireless! And you must tirelessly oppose them! Be vigilant! Laziness, a weak will, a poor attitude, serve only our enemies. Be brave, loyal, and strong! If you yawn, if you blink, if your mind wanders one moment, our enemies may seize that one moment out of ten thousand to destroy our precious Red Mountain!"

Captain Wei stood stiffly erect, hands clasped behind his back. His voice rose in urgency. Before sending us off with our Red Guardians, Captain Wei, to inspire us and sharpen our vigilance, always told a true story of youthful heroism. Such events regularly occurred just prior to our patrol evenings.

"Only three days ago," he began, "a Kuomintang spy was caught in South Beijing burying his antirevolutionary notebook. A young boy your age taking out his family's garbage saw this spy digging suspiciously in a trash pile. He quickly ran to his Neighborhood Committee head, who immediately ran to his PLA captain, who ran right out with our people's soldiers to arrest the traitor.

"Thanks to this Little Red Soldier's vigilance, an efficient Neighborhood Committee head, and the brave, quick response of our police, this Kuomintang spy no longer hides behind our red flag, a living time bomb plotting against us and sending Party secrets to his cousin in Taiwan. But even now others like him are living among us, posing as our loyal comrades.

"Remember this on your patrol tonight, and at all times. Learn from this young hero's example. Always keep your eyes open. Watch everyone! Suspect everyone! Be fooled by no one! Strive hard, work together, be courageous and loyal, and victory will be ours. You can make the difference. Chairman Mao has called your young, red generation the hope of China, our morning's rising sun. Be his best kids! Never sleep! Never rest! Never give up his struggle! Carry his red flag forward to the end!"

Uncle Wei's speeches always stirred up our heroic fantasies of catching class enemies. We saw their black shadows lurking behind every garbage pile, fence, and electrical pole. But the only bad eggs we encountered on our patrol evenings were hooligans who came out to whistle, make nasty remarks, and joke sarcastically about our spears as we passed by.

Uncle Wei left and Old Eyes glanced sternly through our ranks.

"Who has seen Little Plum?" she asked. "I know she was not in school today." No one spoke. Old Eyes looked at me. "You are her comrade," she said. "Where is she?"

"I haven't seen her, Grandma," I reported firmly.

I hadn't seen Little Plum since she slapped me yesterday.

"Then we must find her," Old Eyes said. "When our comrades are in trouble, we must go look for them. March!"

Old Eyes and her three lieutenants started off in a strenuous, foot-bound gallop. We followed them like ducklings, gripping our spears. Their rapid, quick walking pace made them seem to run. With each step their heads wagged, their elbows pumped like pistons, and their bodies shimmied and writhed from their ankles up through their shoulders.

"Look at us," Old Eyes loved to say. "We walk like ducks on hot coals. You girls are so lucky to have your Liberation feet."

"So lucky!" Old Feet sadly agreed.

They loved to describe the years of agony they had suffered as footbound children. They hated their "lotus feet."

"Our feet were crushed short as they grew," Old Feet explained. "You can't imagine the pain. Cutting them off would have hurt less. I was older than you before mine stopped growing. Each step was in fire as I learned to walk in a new way. I fell often and my clumsiness shamed me. Finally my feet healed and I walked the way feudal men desired and women with no lotus feet envied. But after Liberation I burned in shame again, for each step marked me a feudal slave. I cannot change my feet. So I have learned to accept them. Now I walk proudly for the Party."

Old Ears nodded wisely, interrupting, "Yes, we walk proudly today to remind your red generation of your good fortune. Every day you should thank the Red Army, the Party, and our Liberator Chairman Mao, to have been raised in his revolutionary cradle."

Old Tongue pointed at our feet, concluding triumphantly, "Look, there is your Liberation! March on!"

We reached the entrance to Little Plum's socialism yard and followed the Four Olds in. We cut through narrow alleys under tangled clotheslines draped with underwear and proletarian uniforms, marching straight for Little Plum's door.

Old Eyes arrived on Old Feet's heels and hammered the flimsy door with her fist. It rattled on its hinges. A moment later, it creaked open and Little Plum's mama peered nervously through the gap. Her gray-streaked hair, pinned behind her two large ears, exposed her thin, tired face. She had the full, broad, sloping lucky nose that people said brought good fortune. But somehow, her nose had betrayed her.

" 'We must always struggle against inner selfishness,' Comrade Tu!" Old Eyes thundered Chairman Mao's quotation in a formal opening, her shrill voice echoing through the yard. She glared at Tu, one hand on her hip, the other gripping her erect spear. "We have come to see Little Plum!"

" 'Never take a needle and thread from the masses,' Committee Chairman," Tu responded meekly. "Little Plum is not at home."

"Comrade Tu!" Old Eyes blustered, giving Tu no breathing time. "She was not in school today, and she did not show up for patrol duty tonight!" She clucked in irritation. "This is not the first time, as you well know."

"As we all well know," Old Ears added disapprovingly.

"Something must be done!" Old Tongue pointedly declared.

Old Feet, who could think of nothing to add, shifted from one tiny stump to the other, shook her head, and "Hmmm'd" ominously. The many heads stuck out through half-open doors and windows pleased the Four Olds immensely. The center stage delighted their hearts. And they knew an audience witnessing their authority increased it. "Beat one monkey and frighten the whole pack" was wisdom they readily applied.

Old Eyes firmly pushed the door back, and Tu with it. In the dim room, looking trapped against the far wall by the coal stove, stood Yu, Little Plum's father. Skinny, like his wife, Yu had a wary, beaten look. His pinched, poor man's nose must have canceled out Tu's lucky one. I edged to the back of the group. I liked this old couple and didn't want them to see me here. Little Plum might think I had kindled these sparks for revenge.

"We don't know where she is," Tu pleaded in a subdued voice. "We haven't seen her since last night."

"Last night!" Old Eyes shrieked in outrage. "Comrades! Why didn't you report this to me?"

"You know the proper procedure!" Old Ears accused. "Don't you care for your daughter?"

Tu looked down. Behind her, Yu squatted by the stove, shrinking himself, and began stirring the ashes with the same metal poker Little Plum had curled her hair with.

"She is a stinky hooligan! And whose fault is it? Are you not shamed?" Old Eyes pronounced their guilt to the whole yard.

"Comrade Yu! Control your daughter!" Old Tongue shouted into the house at Little Plum's father.

Yu looked up warily from his crouch, more angry than shamed. But he said nothing. I felt sad for them. Who could control a daughter like Little Plum?

"Our Senior Group will come visit you at noon tomorrow with a regular committee member," said Old Eyes sternly. "Make sure Little Plum is here."

Tu and Yu would have Little Plum there at the hour or risk a greater consequence. Old Eyes turned to scan her audience in the yard. A door banged shut. A few heads ducked in from their windows. This event was for everyone's benefit, the Senior Group's warning crack of the whip. Their message was clear; nothing could be hidden from the Little Feet Patrol.

Puffed up with victory, the Four Olds took off at a ferocious waddle. Heads held high, they cut through our patrol team and marched staccato-step across the yard, planting their spears in the earth with swinging strides. We scrambled into formation and trailed them through the alleys, ducking wet jackets, bras, trousers, diapers, and underwear all the way to the front gate.

Little Plum was not in school all the next week. One morning, on my way to class, I saw her come out of the school nurse's office. She looked down miserably as we walked by. I guiltily hurried past her, relieved that she did not look up. In the last few weeks of school, Little Plum did not return.

Summer spread out, long, wide, and hot as pan bread on a stove. Poplar leaves withered in the sun's searing glare. Trees cast ink-black paper-cut shadows in the bright orange sun. The humid air hung over the sweating crowds rolling down the blistering sidewalks, glistening like dumplings in a boiling pot. Road tar cracked, bubbled, and turned to black pudding. And all night, the torrential summer rains fell, howling winds blew, and lightning crackled and flashed, washing the heat away till morning. Little Plum always said this was the best season to die of a heart attack.

Other kids' fathers lived at home, took them to parks or the zoo, played with them, and told stories. My Ba was mercurial, an angle in motion, an elusive shadow hovering out of range. Wrestling demons, stalking life with hair-trigger intent, he was born for freedom but bound to us by fate. At home, he was a prowling tiger. And Mama and I hid like prey. His bristling intensity unnerved us. His predator's awareness invaded our thoughts, penetrated our bones like heat. The walls echoed with his silent force.

Ba wore a key chain on his belt with twenty-some jangling keys and always carried a padlocked black leather bag. I never saw him open it. Before going out, he locked his cabinet, desk, and dresser drawers and tested every lock. Even when he left, he was never completely gone. Minutes or hours later, he might rush up the stairs in his jangling strides, burst through the door, recheck everything, then leave again without a word. And at night before going to sleep, he shined his flashlight under his bed, behind the curtains, and inside the closets looking for something, someone. . . .

Sometimes I imagined he was a spy on a secret mission for the Party. But I knew Ba was haunted. And I wondered what he had done. I feared his strangeness. And his emptiness stirred a deep sadness in me. He was a dark well down which my heart dropped stones, longing to hear a splash, an echo, that never came.

Ba was vain and temperamental about his good looks. People often thought he was a movie star. He ironed his proletarian uniform daily, even his bedsheets and underwear. Morning and evening, he rubbed special creams on his face, slapped his skin one hundred times in front of the mirror, tugged his thick hair to increase the blood flow to the scalp. He had me search his head for white hairs and pluck them out with tweezers.

"White bandits!" he cursed each one passionately. "Tombstones!"

I felt guilty for finding them. I never plucked them all. Leave a few in back, I thought. Later, he criticized me for the white hairs I had missed in the places his eyes could not see.

Yet for all his vanity, Ba had an iron will and a soldier's discipline. He rose each morning at five and ran for an hour in the streets, rain, snow, or shine, to keep his athletic condition. At his studio, he lifted barbells, trained in martial arts and gymnastics. One day, he took me into his gym to watch him spin and fly on the pommel horse and parallel bars. He was fifty then, but looked thirty-five. And in skill and power he matched the young gymnasts with whom he trained. Amazed, I asked him as we walked back to his office how he had learned these abilities.

"It's nothing," Ba said casually. "I taught myself. Watch."

And he cartwheeled into back-handsprings down the narrow hall.

A jack of all trades, Ba learned many skills: producer, cameraman, makeup artist, tailor, gymnast, electrician, locksmith, cook, herbalist, carpenter, gardener, mechanic, martial artist, plumber, barber, farmer, jeweler, appliance repairman, weather predictor, conman, forger, spy, and thief. He could even knit a sweater. With one eyebrow raised, Ba did everything better than best, and improved on perfection. Even the illegal chicken he raised laid two eggs a day, or one with double yolks.

Inconceivably busy, Ba lived from purpose to purpose. At home, he performed obscure, meticulous labors in his room with small, special tools. A jeweler's magnifying glass sucked in one eye, a penknife pressed between thumb and forefinger, he altered official documents and ID, forged official rubber stamps, scraped purchase ink marks off our food-ration book to buy extra pork, tofu, peanut butter, cooking oil, and dried mushrooms. Ba got us extras of every rationed food. We ate minority rations of beef when he changed our ethnic status from Han to Hui. Then he made us Muslims and we ate lamb. Then he changed us back to Han so we could have pork again.

Once when we went shopping, a suspicious sales clerk held our ration book to the sun and asked why our stamp looked so thin. I was so scared I almost started crying. Ba was not even ruffled.

"Don't ask me," he barked, annoyed. "Ask the Security Bureau!"

We got our illegal food effortlessly. Ba was always going into battle. Even going to buy tofu, he cut knifelike at military speed through the crowds. I was his little soldier, always bringing up the rear, admiring his muscular, swinging arms, his explosive legs, his spectacular, crowd-passing strides. I trotted after him, wondering if I would be able to keep up with him when I grew older. And he called to me over his shoulder, teaching me: "Move like the wind! Strike like lightning! Never show weakness! Never look away from the enemy! Quick! Go grab a place in the soy-sauce line!"

And off I ran.

My Ba was a wild man, a natural genius, an unexplainable phenomenon. Eternally capable and forever self-assured, endless possibilities and perfect solutions arose where he appeared. His mind-like-water penetrated every crack, conformed to every shape, discovered every weakness, and found its way through.

Jaia and Ba pose in front of Beijing Fine Art Museum.

I never saw Ba read a book. But he read the newspaper every day, front to back and between the lines. And he knew what it all meant: the changing order of high cadre's names on any list; who was mentioned how often, and who not at all; whose picture was moved from front page to third; who stood beside Chairman Mao, who was moved three people away, and who had disappeared; and why certain ideas or historical figures were criticized or praised. From these clues, Ba foresaw vital shifts in power, new political waves. And when the wave came, he knew how to act, what to say or not to say, whether to lie low or stand up, laugh or frown, condemn or praise.

"You've got to keep up," Ba told me. "Never get caught in the changing tide. The right information is better than a bullet. With it, you can't lose. Without it, you won't survive."

Sometimes Ba simply vanished for days, weeks, even months. Then, strangely, I missed him painfully and wanted him back in my life. I thought of him often then, how he sometimes called me "Kitten" and told me I was carved for success. "You're not like your mama," he said. "You're like me. Nothing can stop you!" His studio makeup lady told me he bragged about me often and said I was a one-in-a-million child. I wanted to believe her words. But I searched my whole life with Ba and felt confused. I ached then, because I knew I loved him. And I feared he did not love me.

One winter day, a telegram came from Ba's sister in Northeast China. His mama, Nai Nai, was dead. Ba took the next train home for the ceremony. He was gone two weeks. All that time I thought of his sadness—Ba, orphaned without his mama, unhappy at home with us. Maybe he loved Mama and me but could not tell us. Maybe we misunderstood him. Maybe if we forgave him, his heart would wander home and we could be a family again. I decided I would try to be a good daughter again and give him a new chance.

The night he came back, Mama and I were ready. I brought him his warm slippers, a towel, and a basin of hot water for him to wash his face. Mama brought him a bowl of egg noodles. We sat next to him, full of sympathy, wanting to comfort his broken heart. Two weeks of grief had not changed his face. His eyes were not red from crying. He had even gained weight. The two-day train ride home had left him robust, vigorous, even cheerful.

His suitcase, which he had refrigerated by tying it outside the train window, was full of the funeral gifts his relatives had brought Old Nai Nai: packs of dried mushroom and fragrant fungus, pearl rice, a frozen wild chicken, a hind dog's leg, a jar of salmon eggs, a bottle of fiery white Ar Guo Tou liquor with a dried toad in the bottom. Ba was immensely pleased with his grim harvest.

"Look! Can you believe all these treasures came from that poor little mountain? My stingy old ma never saw such a feast!" He had the grin of a mountain bandit counting booty from an easy raid. "These are just leftovers! We feasted for three days! I'm set for winter." He proudly patted his rounded belly. His face beamed. Mama and I looked at each other. His behavior puzzled us. Perhaps in his grief he had lost his mind.

"How was Nai Nai's ceremony?" Mama asked carefully.

Ba sat up in his chair, a light came into his eyes, a huge grin spread across his face.

"Ha! Ha! Ha!" He burst out laughing and slapped his huge thigh. "Can you believe it!" he exclaimed. "That old scarecrow Nai Nai got what she wanted! She got buried in the earth! In the earth! Even Chairman Mao and Premier Zhou will burn like the rest of us! But my old mama is lying in the ground right now back in Black Dragon River, pissing off the Party! Ha! Ha! Ha!"

Mama and I were shocked speechless. The thought of my grandma lying in the cold, dark earth sent an eerie current up my spine.

"You know what?" Ba was gleeful. "That stubborn old Shandong lady was Buddhist all this time since Liberation! We found a Kuan Yin goddess statue behind Chairman Mao's picture on the altar! What a rebel!" he exulted. "When I got there, my sister and our three uncles told me they had promised Old Nai Nai to bury her on the hill behind the sorghum grove. She didn't want to be burned!

" 'You know it's illegal!' I told them. 'We can't do it! We have to bring her to the crematory tomorrow morning!'

"My uncles are such superstitious peasants! They ganged up on me, all yelling, 'She'll curse us if we burn her! She is our sister, and we must keep our words. Our ancestors are watching!'

" 'But you are Party members!' I said. 'How can you believe in ancestors? This is feudalism!'

"But they were more afraid of Nai Nai lying there frozen on the bed than they were of the Party and Chairman Mao. The whole family fought against me. What could I do? So we snuck Nai Nai out of the house at midnight. Two uncles and I put her on our shoulders. I was in the middle, holding up her waist. Old Uncle walked ahead with the shovels and picks.

"We crossed a big field and started uphill to the sorghum grove. What a scary night! A full moon, a hooting owl, and our footsteps crunching snow. Old Nai Nai had a bumpy ride. Uncle behind me kept stumbling and complaining the whole time.

" 'Watch where you're going! Can't you avoid those rocks? How much farther is it?'

"When we reached the top of the hill, he tripped and fell. I squeezed Nai Nai's waist and pushed my shoulder in her back to keep her head up. But instead of falling back, she sat right up on my shoulder!"

BANG!

Ba smacked his palm on the table, as a traditional talk-story master uses his thunder stick to shock his audience before delivering his heart-stopping, hair-raising punchline. With wide, frightened eyes, Ba shouted, *"Nai Nai's ghost came back!"*

I screamed. Mama stared at Ba in shocked disbelief.

"It's true! I swear it!" Ba protested. "Old Nai Nai sat right up on my shoulder!"

"Go to bed, Jaia," Mama said firmly. "You mustn't hear this."

I didn't want to be alone right then. I didn't want to hear the rest of Ba's story either. Ba decided it himself.

"No, no! The scary part is over. She can stay. The rest is funny. So we dropped Old Nai Nai in the snow and ran screaming down the hill as fast as we could go. Old Uncle was so scared he wet his pants. He had turned around just when Nai Nai sat up on my shoulder in the moonlight.

"He screamed at his little brother all the way down the hill.

" 'You offended our dead sister and our ancestors with your complaining! We are cursed because of you!'

"When we got to the bottom, Young Uncle kowtowed in the field, weeping and begging Nai Nai and our ancestors for forgiveness. We had to go back. Old Uncle said her ghost would wander the hills and haunt us if we didn't bury her.

"We climbed back up the hill and found Nai Nai lying on her side, bent at the waist. She was cold as a winter brick and twice as stiff. Old Uncle made us all kowtow and beg Nai Nai and our ancestors for forgiveness. Even me! Then we straightened her out like a rusty hinge and buried her in the old sorghum grove.

"When we got home, Old Uncle put Nai Nai's picture on the altar next to Chairman Mao. He said she had a powerful ghost to sit up the way she did. He even left her Kuan Yin behind the altar. My sister and her husband told him it was only rigor mortis muscle spasms. They should know, since they're both doctors. But my uncles wouldn't believe it.

"Next morning, the local Party Committee head came demanding Nai Nai's body for cremation. We told him she had disappeared. He got so angry. He knew what we had done, but he couldn't prove it. We stuck to our story. He said there would be an investigation. He was trying to frighten me, a Beijing cadre! So I told him, 'If you want her that much, go look for her yourself! If we find her we'll cremate her. If you find her, you can keep her.'

"Ha, ha, ha!"

Ba slapped his thighs and roared till tears came out. His mama's death was a comedy to him. He didn't notice Mama and me staring at him.

"Attention! Attention! Beijing Security Bureau's file number seven criminals are here!"

Uncle Wei's shrill, amplified voice sliced the hot air one lazy summer afternoon. I ran to the balcony and looked down Facing the Sun Avenue. The familiar green army flatbed approached at a snail's pace. Half a dozen manacled men and women stood huddled on the truck bed under the burning midday sun. Captain Wei leaned out the window with his megaphone.

"Come out, comrades!" he called urgently. "Come learn from our Beijing Security Bureau's educational tour!"

Hundreds of men, women, and children flooded toward him out of their homes and yards, from every direction, to converge on the truck and its fascinating cargo, trudging alongside it as it rolled down the dusty street. It crawled to a stop near my building, and the gawking crowd quickly surrounded it, with streams of people still pouring in.

"Come learn from the mistakes of these evil criminals!" Captain Wei cried into his megaphone as he stepped out onto the street. "They have opposed the people and must pay the price! Come witness the people's justice!"

Several times a year, Uncle Wei's Security Bureau prison truck drove through our neighborhood to "instruct the people." He drew us in, a circus ringmaster promising dark thrills and the high drama of good and evil. The local criminals he carried would soon be sent to prisons and countryside labor camps, or maybe executed. I hurried out the door and down the stairs.

Criminals fascinated me. I had gone with tens of thousands to the outdoor struggle meetings on our local high school soccer field. I had watched criminals tried for their crimes. I had seen men and women collapse weeping as their death sentences were pronounced and be dragged off like straw dolls by the soldiers. I saw their mothers, wives, and sisters wailing and shouting "Injustice!" before they, too, were taken away by the soldiers. The executions always followed immediately at nearby locations. The families of the executed men and women had to drag their bulleted bodies from the field to the crematory.

The Party encouraged everyone to attend the executions, even children. It was patriotic, and thousands went to see traditional Party justice done, one pistol bullet fired point-blank to the back of the head. I never went. The thought of an execution made me sick. Many of my classmates did go watch these criminals "bulleted." They came to class next day talking of nothing else.

"These criminals have contaminated our clean air with their foul smell!" Captain Wei's muffled voice sounded in the crowded stairwell over the chatter of my neighbors. "Posing as our comrades while they sabotaged the harmony of our socialist order! Anarchists and hooligans, they've opposed the dictatorship of the proletariat! Denied the will of the people! Rejected unity with the masses!"

"Hurry! I want to see their faces!"

Grandma Chao, from down the hall, impatiently pushed her husband into the slower neighbors ahead of them on the stairs. With her poor eyesight, she needed to be near the truck to see well. Her four grandchildren, each a year apart, followed her single-file down the stairs like baby ducks.

Over a thousand people had surrounded the truck by the time we got outside. I hurried past my neighbors and pushed into the densely packed crowd. Captain Wei stood before the prisoners, his PLA driver beside him. Each wore a pistol in a leather holster strapped around his waist. The driver's fierce gaze at the prisoners warned them not to speak or misbehave.

I remembered the political prisoners I had seen chained in the back of another prison truck on the way to their executions. Their jaws and shoulders hung slack, dislocated by prison doctors so they couldn't say antirevolutionary words or make rebellious gestures before they died. They had looked like sad, dumb birds with broken wings.

But today's truck carried only hooligans and petty criminals in handcuffs. Heavy boards, on which their names and crimes were written, hung around their necks on thin wire that cut into their flesh and drew blood.

"Ma! Look!" A woman near me pointed excitedly at a young man on the flatbed. "It's Little Du from our factory!"

"He was always puffed up," her ma said. "I never trusted him."

On the truck bed, sweating in the sun in their long sleeves, stood five men with shaved heads and two women with short-cropped hair. One stared sullenly into the crowd. The others looked down guiltily, trying to hide their faces. Several trembled, their faces contorted with silent weeping. The hair of the two women was badly cut by the PLA's scissors. People in the crowd shouted angrily at the prisoners.

"You rotten eggs!"

"We have troubles enough without you pissing in the water!"

"You deserve your punishment!"

People near the truck spit on them to show their contempt. Some children threw clouds of dirt. I was reading the boards around their necks when the woman near me said, "Aai! Isn't that Comrade Yu's daughter?"

"Ah, those poor gray mice," her mother sighed. "Raised a Little Plum for this."

I looked at the girl weeping on the truck in her patched blue uniform and recognized Little Plum with her bangs and curls cut away. My heart tilted and sank. Seeing Little Plum cry was like seeing a tiger weep. It hurt in a strange, shocking way. I had never imagined she could be broken. Squinting in the sun's glare, I read the characters on the board around her neck.

"Little Plum. Fourteen years old. Selfish anarchist. Dirty bourgeois lifestyle. Pregnant by ghost-mixing with hooligans."

"Criminal Cheng, step forward!" Captain Wei shouted.

The sullen hooligan stepped to the edge of the platform. People shouted more curses and spit at him. My eyes sought Little Plum. Iron claws gripped my throat. My tears welled up. It would be bad to cry here. I pushed back out of the crowd and ran home. I shut myself in my room and sat at my desk, wiping my tears, desperately searching my mind. I had failed Little Plum, betrayed her, tempted her to this fall with Mama's bourgeois artifacts, to act out secret longings hidden in my own heart.

I hadn't defended her to Uncle Wei when he visited my home. I had held my words back and sold her out. I was the first one to see her dragged into the water. And I had backed away and watched her sink. I could have helped her. Yet Uncle Wei had told me to stay away. I had only followed his instructions, obeyed our ever-righteous Party. Uncle Lei Feng had written, "Treat individualism as the cold autumn wind sweeps the fallen leaves. Treat enemies as cruel as a severe winter."

But I felt guilty. I never saw Little Plum again. Days later, I read the Public Security Bureau bulletin posted at Hundred Goods department store listing the people arrested in our district, with a paragraph beside each name. Half a dozen names were stamped with red X's. These "crossed-off" people were big criminals, already executed. I scanned the poster and found Little Plum's name. Her paragraph read:

"Little Plum: Fourteen years old. Corrupted by rotten Western lifestyle. Has refused the Party's friendly help and instruction. Has indulged bourgeois appetites, shamed her family, rejected unity with the masses, and lost all moral conscience. Has chosen the hooligan path and become pregnant by ghost-mixing with these rotten elements. Little Plum will be confined to a youth work camp until her full rehabilitation is accomplished."

It was the summer of 1975, and I was eleven years old. Later that year, I heard of a new baby in Little Plum's home. People knew it was Little Plum's child. I lived in that neighborhood for nine more years. In all that time, Little Plum never returned.

Five years later, I would walk down Facing the Sun Avenue in a pretty dress, my hair long and shining, past young women with curled hair, in beautiful silk clothes, on their boyfriends' arms. I would think of Little Plum, and what she had wanted too soon. And how for her crime she had her green youth stolen, and her bright future buried in the countryside earth.

The autumn rains came, cooling the air, patting the windows like loose sand. Beijing shimmered in a soothing twilight. With Little Plum gone, I stayed alone most of the time, reading in my room. Ba came home often now. He and Mama seemed calmer, relieved from a season of bitterness. One afternoon, I came out to find Ba sitting at the window, staring into the rain, singing a simple song from his red army soldier days.

> *"From this corner to that corner,*
> *the tongue is near the tooth.*
> *The People's Army loves the people.*
> *We are all one family."*

His beautiful face looked so innocent. And his sad eyes looked so far away, as far away as he was from those days, and from the man he had once been.

The Long March

The year I was ten, we began keeping a Following Chairman Mao Journal in class. Teacher Su corrected it each week, underlining in red our Best Red Thoughts and underlining in black those that were not red enough. When I was twelve, I began wanting a secret journal of my own, to be read by no one but me, in which I could write whatever I chose. I told Mama. And one evening she handed me a brand-new journal with a deep blue plastic cover. Ba stared at her with a look of outraged disbelief.

"How dare you give her this troublemaking thing!" he yelled.

Startled, I clutched my journal tightly in both hands. Ba glared at me, then back at Mama again.

"Are you both stupid? Our Cultural Revolution is about getting rid of such things! She only knows a handful of words anyway. Don't encourage her! Who keeps a diary of secret thoughts but antirevolutionary spies and Stinking Ninth Category intellectuals? Look at Dry Bread, living like a widow the last eight years because her idiot husband wrote down clever thoughts he shouldn't have whispered to a dog!"

Ba had nicknamed the shy, withered woman who lived next door

Dry Bread. Her husband was former Education Department leader of Mama's old Ministry of Culture branch. Our whole neighborhood knew he was locked in a rubber cell in Beijing Prison for writing "antirevolutionary secret thoughts" in his diary. Dry Bread had no friends and couldn't go out without being glared at, gossiped about, and criticized by our finger-pointing neighbors.

"Do you know why the Party keeps him in a rubber cell?" asked Ba, looking ominously at me. I shook my head. "So he can't crack his head open on the wall like an egg and chicken out!"

"Stop scaring your daughter!" Mama snapped. "Prison or not depends on what you write! She won't write antirevolutionary thoughts." She looked at me intensely. "Will you, Jaia?"

"No!"

"You can't always tell what's antirevolutionary," warned Ba. "The Party decides that."

"What your Ba says is true," Mama said, watching me uneasily. "Do you still want this journal?" I nodded firmly. "Then remember . . . be careful. Be careful! Never write what you really think or feel. That is the most dangerous! Just write like Uncle Lei Feng. You know your old mama could not live without you. Promise me you will only write revolutionary things."

"I promise, Mama."

"Ya!" Ba spat, looking at Mama. "Intellectuals are too tart for their own good! Even reform camps can't cure them!"

He left the room shaking his head. Ba identified with his peasant-proletarian roots even though he held a university degree and also had a Stinking Ninth Category label in his personal record.

I didn't know why I shouldn't keep my own journal, just like Chairman Mao's Best Student and Revolutionary Son, Uncle Lei Feng. I took it into my room and sat at my desk, feeling its smooth cover, drinking up its deep-sea blue with my thirsty eyes.

That year I had read an old folktale about a frog who lived at the bottom of a well. One day a swallow landed on the edge of his well and began to sing. The startled frog called up, asking who she was and where she had come from. The swallow told the frog she was a bird who had come from far away, through the vast sky, across an ocean, over thousands of rivers and mountains and fields. The frog could not understand what she was talking about.

"You are crazy!" he shouted. "Everyone knows the world is only as large and wide as my big well!"

I had wondered then if I was like that frog, thinking the world was only as big and deep and the sky as high and wide as my little well. Now I sat, pen in hand, my new journal opened on the table in front of me. I felt myself growing swallow's wings as a vast, uncharted sky opened above me.

In these clean, white pages I would record noble thoughts and feelings, heroic dreams and goals. I would fly out of my little well and explore the wide world and blue sky of my imagination.

As I pondered my first entry, I realized my great obligations. I could not just write whatever I wanted. I had to be careful for Mama, loyal to the Party, a Little Red Soldier with every word. To do this, I had to solve a riddle: What exactly was an antirevolutionary thought? Was it saying bad things about the Party or Chairman Mao? I would never do that!

"You can't always tell what's antirevolutionary," Ba had warned. "The Party decides that."

Could I write an antirevolutionary thought accidentally? And if it was an accident, was I still a criminal?

"Never write down what you really think or feel," Mama had warned. "That is the most dangerous!"

Why were my real thoughts and feelings dangerous? Weren't some of them good? Suddenly, I wasn't sure what I could write. And I was afraid to ask Mama. She might lose confidence in me and take back my journal. I would be vigilant and watch my thoughts with suspicion whenever I wrote in my journal. Even innocent thoughts might hold small, hidden crimes. Who would care for Mama if I got locked in a rubber cell? I took out Uncle Lei Feng's famous journal and carefully read his first few entries. Then, in my best calligraphy, I wrote, "Learn from Revolutionary Uncle Lei Feng!" I looked up at Chairman Mao's huge picture on the wall over my table, then wrote confidently, "Long live Chairman Mao!" and then, "Long live our forever righteous Communist Party!"

Then I couldn't think of anything else. Enough for today, I decided. I wondered how I would fill the whole journal. But each evening I took it out and wrote at least a few lines. In time, it got easier. My calligraphy and writing skills improved. Mama regularly checked my journal and was pleased by my entries. I only wrote revolutionary thoughts.

To make my journal more interesting, I recorded the Proletarian Hero and Good Example stories I heard in school on the Party's Little Red Soldier radio show, or read in our schoolbooks and the class copy of *Little Red Soldier* magazine. And I wrote how these examples inspired me and made me feel grateful; how I loved Chairman Mao and the Party; how I would live in a village commune and plant trees to stabilize the soil; how I would be a revolutionary soldier and fight for the people's freedom and selflessly serve the masses for the rest of my life.

I wrote many vigilant self-criticism entries; how vain I was for desiring bourgeois things like a ribbon for my hair or a little round mirror to carry with me; how I was weak-willed, lacking in discipline, and not proletarian enough; how I should try harder to be Chairman Mao's Little Red Soldier and study his teaching more diligently because of my Black family background. I wrote these things sincerely and felt them deeply, even though we had been taught to write this way in our Following Chairman Mao Journal and in our weekly classroom self-criticism reports. Anyone reading my journal would have thought I was redder than the monkey's butt in Beijing zoo. And Mama was proud of me.

But keeping a daily journal over time made me aware of feelings and thoughts I dared not write: how I wondered what Dry Bread's husband wrote in his journal to make the Party lock him up in a rubber cell, and if he wrote it accidentally; how I sometimes hated my neighbors, even the Neighborhood Committee, who never came when Mama and Ba tore each other apart and I was screaming for help; why Captain Chen locked the Snake Spirit Demon in his basement; how Mama seemed unhappier and more afraid now that she was reformed; how I feared the Party would take her away and put her back in her camp. Secret thoughts and feelings like these showed a hidden darkness in me. And I knew I must never write them down.

"We mustn't give my father's name," Mama said. "Just write: 'My grandpa was a farmer in Jiangsu Province. My grandma died in a famine before Liberation.' We'll emphasize Ba's family. They have the best poor peasant-farmer background—'red roots, straight shoots.' "

We sat at my table one evening going over my Red Guard application, which, at twelve, I was now eligible to join. I had never heard Mama speak about her father before.

"Was your father really a farmer?" I asked.

"He owned a house and only eight mu of land, but this made him an exploiting class landlord riding on the people's backs," Mama said. "And he went to Japanese university, which made him a soul-selling traitor and Japanese spy. His personal record cannot be cleansed. He is a black wok on our family's back. Telling the truth about him is a death sentence on your political future. But they won't check my Personal Record for your Red Guard application."

I desperately wanted to be a Red Guard and wear Chairman Mao's red banner on my arm. To be on his Revolutionary Honor Roll and gain the acceptance of my classmates was an important step on the climb to success: Red Guard, then Youth League member, and after that the highest honor, which few who sought attained, Communist Party member. I knew it was wrong to hide my family background from my teacher. But I could not let my black-wok relatives bullet my future.

The next day, I read my Red Guard Self-Expression Essay aloud to the class. I wore the new PLA uniform Mama had bought me at the start of the school year. I beamed confidently around the room. My daily writing practice had paid off. I had hit just the right note—a kind of humble bragging in which I displayed my worthy character, using specific examples, while giving all credit for my noble actions to Chairman Mao and the Party. I identified myself with Ba and his poor peasant-farmer parents, refugees from flood, famine, and cruel Kuomintang landlords. My essay made me seem bright red with proletarian roots. Perhaps today my Stinking Ninth Category background would be overlooked.

"Does anyone have any comments on Jaia's Self-Expression Essay?" asked Teacher Hua.

My new teacher, Hua, a former Red Guard in her mid-twenties, was a daughter of Stone Village coal miners, with short-cropped hair and intimidating eyes. Teacher Hua's job, as the Party's gardener, was to pull all poisonous weeds from our minds, straighten our tilted rows, then water, fertilize, prune, and tend us to ensure a fruitful harvest for the Party.

Now, to my huge relief, my new friend and study partner, Li Sing, raised her hand first.

"Yes, Li Sing?" Teacher Hua called on her.

Li Sing rose shyly, staring awkwardly at the floor, looking like a chubby panda in our pack of thin monkeys. Just moved from Shanghai, her thick southern accent and thyroid weight problem had made her an instant pariah. Our classmates, convinced her excessive weight was due to a secret diet of forbidden bourgeois delicacies, had ostracized her as they had me two years ago for my bourgeois clothes. Li Sing and I quickly became friends. I hoped her speaking in my favor now would help. In my essay I had mentioned helping her with her homework. This showed my Screw Spirit actions in daily life. Now, with all eyes on her, she blurted, "Jaia never helped me with my homework. She is lying!"

Li Sing sat down. Silence drowned the room, broken by the ringing in my ears. Everyone turned to look at me. My face prickled and burned. I was so stunned I couldn't speak. I just sat there looking guilty.

"If no one else has any remarks," Teacher Hua said, breaking the silence, "we'll vote on Jaia's application. Who thinks Jaia should become a Red Guard?" Her hawk eyes scanned the room. No hands went up. "Who thinks Jaia shouldn't be a Red Guard?" Everyone raised a hand but me. "Would anyone like to say why?"

"She's not uniting with other students," said Tractor.

"Last year she always wore bourgeois clothes to show her superiority," said Red Flag.

"She tells dirty man-and-woman stories," said Shy Fart, nicknamed for her sneaky, behind-the-back attacks.

Two years ago I had told Shy Fart the story of the Little Mermaid. She had reported me to Teacher Su when I was home sick. Now here she was, two years later, reporting me again for the same crime. This time in front of my face. From now on, I should call her Courageous Fart. More criticisms followed.

"She is too proud of her high marks in school."

"She was close friends with that hooligan Little Plum."

"She irons the wrinkles out of her PLA uniform."

I stared at my desk, wounded by every word, humiliated and determined not to cry. Teacher Hua regarded me sternly.

"Jaia, you should be grateful for your comrade's precious criticisms," she said. "You are puffed up with bourgeois pride, not at all proletarian in spirit. Everything about you is bourgeois. You study far too much. All your book knowledge only makes you a book idiot, a stupid imperialist shoot. Your high marks only show your polluted mind. They are nothing. Screw Spirit and uniting with your comrades are everything. To be a Red Guard, you must make many sacrifices. To be Chairman Mao's Red Soldier, you must love the masses more than yourself. Remember Uncle Lei Feng. He lived only to serve the Party and the people. Learn from his example, Jaia. You have much work to do."

That day Li Sing, my assassin, was accepted into the Red Guard. She had stepped on my bones and climbed up the ladder. I went home after school, devastated, and confided to my journal, "Li Sing has betrayed me. My Red Guard application was rejected. My heart is broken."

Several days later, I returned from the market to find Mama at the dining table, my journal lying open in front of her.

"Your heart is broken?" she asked brusquely. "Let me see the pieces." I looked down. "What nonsense! Grow up, Jaia! If a little thing like this breaks your heart, how will you survive in this world? Worse things will happen in your life, much worse. For your own good, you'd better harden your heart."

I took my journal and went to my room.

"Harden your heart. Harden your heart."

I wrote these words in my journal. Mama was right. Everyone talked about Uncle Lei Feng. But who really learned from him to love and serve the people? Who was really selfless or kind? Who really wanted to be a screw for the Party?

Not my classmates, who taunted and tripped the old coal woman in the schoolyard as she carried her buckets of coal; who fought and laughed at each other's playground injuries and made secret deals to vote for each other's Red Guard memberships. Not me, competing against my classmates to be smarter, cleaner, and better than them. Not Mama and Ba, who often tore at each other in their rage like red-eyed wolves. Not the Neighborhood Committee, who knew of their terrible fights, yet never once came to help them resolve their contradictions. Not the Little Feet Patrol, whose biggest joy was to intimidate the whole neighborhood and get people into trouble.

Not even the masses. Twice a year, for two weeks at a time, we all went out to clean, scrub, and sweep the city during Uncle Lei Feng Screw Spirit Campaigns. I watched my neighbors, plenty of Red Guard, Youth League, and Party members among them, complain, argue, and fight each other to get the easiest cleaning jobs, then curse, grumble, and shout if they didn't get their way. And it seemed the higher one's rank or status, the more selfish and demanding the person became.

These Uncle Lei Feng Screw Spirit Campaigns changed nothing. They came and went, and everyone still struggled, scratched, and fought to get on and off the buses. No one gave a seat to an old or crippled person, a pregnant woman, or a mama holding a baby. Every day was war at the vegetable market, people pushing and fighting in line, cursing the merchants and their sickly vegetables, and even fistfighting over a few pennies or a bruised fruit. Hit-and-run accidents remained common. The drivers never stopped; sometimes they ran over a second person in their hurry to get away. And there were the frequent public executions, where thousands cheered, whistled, and celebrated the crack of the bullet through the back of the head.

Who had ever been selfless besides ever-serving Uncle Lei Feng, happily crushed by a falling electrical pole, dying for the Party at the age of twenty-one? Did I now see things others did not see? Were my forbidden thoughts and perceptions real? Or had I grown blind to a great, noble vision? I felt miserable, lost. I needed a new hero, an ideal, something to believe in. Then Revolutionary Mother Han Wei briefly entered my life.

Our whole school filed onto the playground. We carried stools, which we set in rows before the wooden platform on which Principal Guan stood. He beamed down at us from behind a microphone stand, quietly waiting. When all fifteen hundred of us were seated, he began.

"Comrades! Today we are honored by a visit from a great hero. Revolutionary Mother Han Wei has come to tell us her story of the Long March. This is the best revolutionary education! Her story is a precious gem from our history's rich mine of revolutionary experience. And she and all her Long March comrades are among our greatest national treasures.

"Listen with full attention! Do not let your minds wander! Her words today can change your life! Observe her closely. Learn from her example. When we all become like Revolutionary Mother Han Wei, then Chairman Mao's great vision of our Communist Party as the World's Liberator will be fulfilled! Everyone, give your warmest welcome to Revolutionary Mother Han Wei!"

Raised to venerate our Long March veterans, we enthusiastically applauded. All my life I had revered these great heroes with iron bones, steel veins, and thunder voices, who could climb a mountain of knives and swim across a sea of fire. Their giant, heroic statues, erected everywhere, had bulging muscles and tree-trunk legs.

I now expected to see a Long March giant in the flesh. But instead, a small, old woman in a PLA uniform rose and briskly mounted the platform, a short steel sword with white hair and sparkling eyes. She looked at us, smiling as we applauded.

"Dear children," she began when our applause died down. "I am Han Wei, here to tell you my story of following Chairman Mao. Mine is the story of our past, of the time of bitterness before Liberation.

"I was born into the poverty of Hunan peasant farmers sixty-three years ago, when crops were small, taxes were high, and cruel landlords ruled the countryside. The poorest families in many villages, called 'night farmers,' owned only one suit of clothes. By day, the fathers wore them to work in the fields while the others hid in their homes, unable to come out. But at night, they crept like naked ghosts into the fields to work in the dark. And when it began to grow light, they hurried home in shame.

"Famines occurred in every province. In one Hunan famine, most of the trees in our area died when our starving peasants stripped their bark for food. My family and I also ate bark, pounding, shredding, and boiling it like cabbage into bitter soup.

"In my childhood, tens of millions of peasants starved to death. Many died from eating mud balls mixed with grass and small stones to deaden their hunger. Their burning bellies drove them mad, made them sell their children, made them eat stones and wood and dirt—and even each other. When you are held underwater you think only of air. When you are starving you think only of food. And you fear death. To escape death, ordinary people, good people, ate the dead, starved bodies of their family, friends, and neighbors.

"These things happened all over China under the Kuomintang. We owed everything to our landlords then. And the longer we lived, the more we owed. Greedy landlords took from their tenants the food that might have saved them, knowing they would die without it. Such greed was a sickness of the times.

"My sister starved to death before my birth when my parents fed her food to my brother, knowing only one child could live. A daughter was called 'spilled water' then, because whatever you poured into her was wasted, like water poured onto the ground. Whatever you gave her only benefited her future husband's family.

"Our mothers measured everything they gave us, even their love. From the day we were born, they prepared themselves to lose us. They suffered our births and sold us in the marketplace for a few yards of cloth, a few jin of salt, a sack of rice. Some gave their daughters away at birth to anyone who would take them.

"Many poor parents drowned their infant girls rather than suffer the burden of raising them until they could be sold. For the price of the selling never repaid the cost of the raising. Daughter drownings were common. And if soon after the birth of a daughter the child disappeared, everyone understood. These drownings created shortages of women everywhere. Many men could find no wives.

Scarcity drove prices up. Some families bought brides early for their sons, often arranging marriages at the birth of a girl child.

"My family sold me as a child bride when I was eight years old to a family in the next village. My father was going blind and had to pay a local herbalist for his cure. My family got a decent price and spent it all on his treatment. But he went blind anyway. And from shame that he could no longer work, he stopped eating and died. My father never lived to see the hope of Liberation.

"My new husband was six years old, two years younger than I was. My new family treated me as a servant. My mother-in-law worked me to exhaustion each day to get her money's worth out of me and make me pay for the food I ate. When I made a mistake, she heated the iron in the fire and burned my arm so I would not make the same mistake twice. I still carry the scars."

Revolutionary Mother Han Wei pulled up her jacket sleeves. Her forearms were covered with numerous pale scar lines inches long.

"This was common. If not for Chairman Mao and the Party, many of you girls would have these scars today. Eight years of bitterness passed in my new home. When I was sixteen, we began hearing stories of a new gang of bandits. The Kuomintang called them Red Bandits and said they stole from people and raped women and young girls. But we knew this is what the Kuomintang soldiers did. The mountain bandits, the Kuomintang armies, and our own landlords all took from us in one way or another: our land, our food, our women, our children, our lives. We feared these Red Bandits as one more warlord curse added to our sufferings.

"But we began hearing other stories about these Red Bandits. They called themselves the Red Army; they helped people in trouble; they opened warehouses of grain hoarded by greedy landlords and fed starving villagers; they had women in their ranks who carried guns and were treated as equals by men. These were hard things to believe. No army had ever done such things.

"One day a band of these Red Army soldiers came to our village.

Their leader, a peasant like us, stood in our threshing square and called out to us.

" 'Brothers and sisters! Gather round! I am Comrade Song! I am one of you, and I have news to tell! A new sun is rising in China! And today it shines on you! Till now your lives have been worth less than the dirt you scrape your food from. You are slaves to your landlords and the Kuomintang, who live and profit by your labor. Who has not seen their pigs and chickens living better than you? Who here is worth less than a chicken or pig?

" 'We are the Communist Party's Red Army soldiers! We say that for a few men to live and grow rich on the labor of many without working themselves is a crime against the people! For people to starve to death, indebted to landlords who hoard more food than they can eat, is a crime that must be punished! A system that allows such things is corrupt and evil and must be destroyed! And this is what the Communist Party's Red Army has come to do!'

"These words shocked and frightened us. How could a man say such things and not fear for his life? Some people quickly fled, expecting the landlord who owned our village to come with his gunmen. But Comrade Song and his soldiers were fearless. They went to the landlord's house instead and took him prisoner. They opened his grain warehouse, and distributed everything among the villagers according to their needs.

"They called a meeting in the threshing square for us to 'pour out the bitterness.' All who had suffered under the landlord were told to accuse him without fear. Many victims told stories of his terrible cruelty. In the end, he had nothing to say for himself. For the lives he had taken and the suffering he had caused, our whole village decided our landlord should die. Comrade Song led him shaking into his own empty warehouse.

" 'Look around you, old landlord,' he said. 'This is what you have gained from your evil life.'

"Comrade Song made him kneel, with the whole village watching, and fired one bullet into the back of his head. Everyone cheered. Heaven had opened up and rained justice into our lives.

"Day after day, these Red Army soldiers lived with us. They never took from us, but asked for everything and paid with silver, or by exchange of labor. Their leader, Comrade Mao Zedong, told them, 'Treat the people with honor and respect. Buy from them with fair value. Never take even a needle or thread from the masses.'

"Every day in the village square they made speeches, put on plays and skits, sang songs, and told jokes and stories. By all these means they taught us, educated us, showed us how we had been exploited and who the true criminals were. They revealed the truth to our minds.

"Starving farmers who owed more than they could pay, who stole food to feed their families, were not the criminals. Women driven to prostitution through poverty were not the criminals. Opium addicts driven by suffering to a dream world, sold into addiction by foreign profiteers and their Kuomintang collaborators who profited from their ruined lives, were not the criminals.

"The true criminals were those who stole the fruits of the people's labor; who forced farmers to grow opium instead of rice which they could eat, then sold it in every province, creating over seventy million opium slaves. These criminals who called themselves the people's guardians were like corrupt emperors, hoarding the people's treasures in their gaudy palaces while the people labored, suffered, and died in wretched poverty.

"Little by little, our eyes were opened. But these Red Army soldiers did not only educate us. They helped us repair roofs, build houses, till fields, and plant rice, millet, boi choi, and cabbage. They carried water and night soil like the rest of us. They treated us with respect, as their equals. They gave our night farmers new clothes. Many came out into the sunlight for the first time in years to work in the fields. Slowly, we saw everything being made equal. These soldiers became our heroes. Yet they were like us: humble farmers with callused hands.

"One day Comrade Song called a meeting for the whole village.

" 'Brothers and sisters, we are leaving,' he said. 'But we want as many of you who will to join us. You have seen in your own village what our revolution means. The starving will be fed. The naked will be clothed. The oppressed will be liberated. And all of China will be made equal.

" 'A Red Army soldier is willing to endure any suffering, any hardship, is even prepared to die in the struggle for these goals. We call you to join us. Help us liberate our people from slavery! Help us free our suffering motherland from tyranny! Do not wait for your liberation like prisoners. Fight for it like heroes! Join us! Help us carry the Red Spark to every village and light the fire of revolution in every heart! Our path is hard. Our lot is struggle and sacrifice. But we are the people's only hope!'

"Many men and women in our village came forward to join, as I did. I knew then I did not belong to my husband's family. I was a daughter of the revolution. That night I became a Red Army soldier. It was the spring of 1929 and I was sixteen years old.

"I had found a new life and a new family. My Red Army comrades became my fathers and mothers, brothers and sisters. With my new comrades, I learned to read and write, to march and shoot a gun. We studied the revolutionary teachings of Marx, Engels, Lenin, and Comrade Mao Zedong. We grew closer than blood family. I had been spilled water to my own family, poured into the unwelcome home of my husband's family. Now I had found the Red Army and come home, like a river to the sea.

"I had been a Red Army soldier for five years when the orders for the Long March came. We started from Jiangxi Province in late October 1934, as an army of ninety thousand soldiers. We marched by night through hills on narrow paths holding bamboo torches. At times our soldiers' train stretched more than fifty miles.

"We fought the first battles of the Long March in these mountain ranges. But our worst enemies were the mountain trails, muddy paths running along cliffs and steep ravines. Hundreds of our comrades fell to their deaths in those mountains.

"Red Army women marched, fought, and died, equal to men, under every trying condition. When our babies were born, we gave them to the peasants in the villages along the way. Premier Zhou's wife lost her baby on the Long March. Chairman Mao and his exwife gave up a son to the peasants, and never saw him again.

"The first half year we marched under fire. The Kuomintang pursued us, trying to wipe us out at strategic points and prevent our river crossings. They bombed us from their planes, and fired on us from the air with machine guns. We could not hide or retreat. It was march or die.

"Do you understand? With death surrounding us and death where we stood, we had nothing to lose. Prepared to endure, suffer, or die, but never to give up; this made us Red Army soldiers. The Kuomintang with their superior numbers and weapons did not have this. Ours was a bond of loyal comrades with nothing to lose and everything to gain. Seeing so many comrades die so bravely made one's own death seem unimportant. Our motherland and her masses alone mattered. We came to feel in each death the pain of a nation giving birth to the future. We were a part of history.

"We left our dead and carried our wounded to nearby villages, where the peasants took them in, adopting them like orphans. Many new peasants joined us, replacing our wounded comrades.

"Our first great battle, fought at the Jiang Xin River crossing into Guizhou Province, cost nearly half our army. The river was wide, swift, and deep. The Kuomintang army waited on the other side. We built section bridges of bamboo, connecting them together under fire. By the time we crossed the river two days later, we had lost over thirty thousand soldiers. Most of you have never seen a dead body. I have seen them by the hundreds, wearing the faces of my comrades. I lost many friends at Jiang Xin River, which for me will always be a river of blood.

"Fifty thousand Red Army soldiers died in those first three months. Then we reached Guizhou Province. Guizhou's main crop was opium, as ordered by the Kuomintang, who collected and sold it. Starvation and addiction were epidemic. In every village we passed, addicts sat or lay on the ground in their opium stupor, pipes in their hands, their clothes soiled. Some were naked and didn't care. Many were children your age. They stared at us with the empty look of cattle as we passed. They hardly knew we were there.

"With opium as the main crop, people used it for money and to deaden hunger, and took it more often than rice. We called Guizhou 'the bottom of hell.' Half the children born there did not live a year. Most adults, except for rich landlords and the Kuomintang, died before the age of thirty. More daughters were sold and drowned in Guizhou than in any other province. Can you see now what Chairman Mao's Liberation means?

"It was on our Long March that Chairman Mao's genius emerged as a historical force. Surrounded by enemies, unable to retreat or hide, only his brilliant, unorthodox strategies saved us. The Kuomintang never knew what we would do next. Unpredictable, zigzagging, doubling back, moving forward again, we seemed ready to attack as we prepared to retreat and appeared to retreat before we attacked. We feinted one way, then attacked or fled another.

"When survival required us to go to one place, we went by illogical routes. We were the pea hidden under one of three cups. Whichever cup Chiang Kai-Shek turned over, we were always under another. Sometimes he turned over all three to find we had disappeared, often over some river he was sure we would never dare to cross. Chairman Mao, the wily Monkey King, often had Chiang Kai-Shek, the fat lion, chasing his own tail. Chairman Mao was the Red Army's backbone and spirit.

"In the dead of winter, we came to Laoshan Mountain. Its steep, narrow footpaths, covered with snow and ice, wound along cliffs and ravines. On this high mountain we learned altitude was our mortal enemy. Many soldiers who lay down to rest near the top could not get up again because of oxygen depletion. We had to leave them. After that, we could not even rest standing up. The longer we stayed in those heights, the more depleted we became. On Laoshan Mountain, to rest was to die.

"By the time we reached Liu Ding Bridge, we had marched for over half a year. We had begun with ninety thousand soldiers and recruited tens of thousands more along the way. Now we were less than fifteen thousand.

"We all know the great battle of the Liu Ding Bridge crossing, that monument to our Red Army's courage. The Kuomintang soaked the bridge boards with kerosene and set them on fire when we arrived. Unable to walk the burning planks, our brave soldiers instead climbed across the chain links stretching over the river, one by one, like monkeys under fire. And they fired back at the Kuomintang soldiers, with the flames roaring up, through the thick, black smoke. As the wounded fell into the river and were swept away, their brave comrades quickly replaced them.

"Unnerved by our courage, the Kuomintang finally scattered in fear. Their paid soldiers fought only for money. They had no great cause to die for and could not understand why we so willingly sacrificed our lives. Our fearlessness terrified them.

"The battle to cross Liu Ding Bridge was the last military battle of the Long March. The Kuomintang's final attempt to destroy us had failed. But two terrible enemies lay ahead. The first was the Jiajin mountain range, over fourteen thousand feet high, called Snow Mountain. By the time we reached Jiajin's feet, we were walking ghosts—more bone than flesh, more discipline than muscle, more will than hope. After Laoshan, we thought we knew the worst of what a mountain could do. But Jiajin proved us wrong.

"Crueler than Laoshan, Jiajin was a soldier's nightmare, covered with snow and ice, higher than the clouds. Her cold winds burned like fire, her snowflakes pierced like needles. Parts of her were so steep we had to crawl up on our hands and knees. Many of us were now barefoot. Our shoes had worn out.

"The descent was worse than the climb—shorter, but steeper. We could not stand up in places and had to slide down on our packs over ice and snow. Many comrades slid to their deaths over cliffs and down chasms. It was like climbing up the blade of a scimitar and down the blade of a knife.

"But Jiajin's height was worse than her slopes. Her thin air fought the lungs. The effort to breathe took the strength one needed for marching. Hundreds died on that frozen mountain of sorrow. And the only words spoken on Jiajin were those of our dying comrades as we passed them by, 'Carry forward the revolution to the end.'

"We finally reached the grasslands on the Tibetan border. They stretched unbroken to the sky, flat, green, and wide as the sea, uninhabited by living things. From the edge they looked peaceful. But we were crossing the border of hell. For days, we marched in knee-high muck that could suddenly become a bog, dragging down soldiers and horses, swallowing them in seconds. We could not save them.

"We marched more than a week in that mud-and-grass sea, dying in quicksand bogs and from illness, starvation, and water poisoning. Each night many who lay down to sleep were dead by morning. We took from them what the living needed, and marched on.

"With no signs of life anywhere, it was like marching on the moon. We did not know how far it was to the other side. For days, in all directions, we saw only a flat marsh meeting an empty sky. We would rather have faced ten armies than that strange desolation.

"When our food supply ran out, we ate grass, leather belts, straps, and harnesses, boiling them in marsh water. And wild marsh wheat that ripped through our bellies and tore open our bowels.

"Five hundred soldiers died in that marsh before we reached the other side. In September, we arrived at the city of Hadapu and the Long March was over. We had marched ten months without rest, across China, over six thousand miles through thirteen provinces. Barely six thousand of us remained, one Red Soldier for each mile of our journey. Starved and exhausted, we looked like walking skeletons. Our will and flesh had pressed beyond human limits to survive.

"In Hadapu, we celebrated and its people took care of us. They fed us like emperors: pork, fish, duck, chicken, eggs, vegetables, and pastries. Whatever we wanted, they gave us. A few soldiers died from eating too much after months of starvation.

"But we survivors were like forged steel. Few on this earth ever matched what we did under Chairman Mao. Yan'an was now a short step away, a stroll across a meadow after our Long March. But Liberation seemed generations from our grasp, a Long March into the future. We didn't expect to see it in our lifetime. Yet here you are in my old age, the third Liberation generation, living in a glorious Red Middle Kingdom that was only a dream forty years ago."

Revolutionary Mother Han Wei looked down at us with two diamond-clear eyes, her lean face lined with hardship, age, and wisdom. I felt awe in the presence of her beautiful spirit.

"But our struggle will not end," she continued, "until all peoples have been liberated. Today, half the world lives under imperialism's tyranny. Whole nations are exploited and oppressed. I have struggled nearly fifty years and I will go on struggling until my last breath, until the whole world is liberated.

"But the torch must be passed. If it goes out, all we have gained will be lost. It is up to you, to your generation. Over a hundred thousand Red Army soldiers died on the Long March. Tens of millions died in the decades before Liberation from famine, sickness, oppression. Their blood colors the soil where we now stand. Do not let their blood be wasted. Do not make their deaths meaningless.

"Many of history's greatest heroes died on the Long March. Their names will never be known. Now I have told you their story. Never forget! Fight with me, with Chairman Mao, with the Party, to liberate mankind from slavery. Never give up! Be Chairman Mao's Little Red Soldiers! Struggle with him till your last breath! And carry forward the revolution to the end!"

Revolutionary Mother Han Wei's final words, spoken with great emotion, brought us all applauding to our feet. Beyond any doubt, she was a great hero who had passed through the fires of hell and survived as a living spark to bring light to others. The truth of Chairman Mao and the Chinese Communist Party, that the individual must selflessly sacrifice for the good of the whole, had come alive for me in her presence. I saw it in her. It was real! And it could be lived!

That evening I wrote Revolutionary Mother Han Wei's Long March story in my journal, ending it with my own fervent declaration:

"I really want to take this bright example of not-afraid-of-bitterness, not-afraid-of-death revolutionary spirit and be a Red Follower. I will never forget the bitterness our old generation had to eat. I will never forget how they sacrificed for our Liberation. I will follow Chairman Mao and do revolutionary things all the rest of my life!"

Filled with renewed energy and purpose, I felt my devotion to Chairman Mao and the Party reborn. I vowed to cultivate the virtues required to be Red Guard. I would take the criticisms of my peers to heart, reform myself, and purify my soul. What were my petty trials compared to those of Revolutionary Mother Han Wei and her Long March comrades?

In the following weeks and months, I became a model student. Each morning I went to class early. I swept the floor, wiped the tables, and carried in coal from the bin. At the end of the day, I wiped the chalkboard and emptied the garbage.

My offers to help my classmates with their studies, after initial refusals, were gradually accepted. I even became more helpful to Mama at home. These outward changes in my behavior signified a corresponding inner change in me that was profound. I had learned the great secret of selfless service. And I was happy.

Several months later, my second Red Guard application was unanimously approved. After a long, painful struggle, I had been accepted by my classmates. And I owed it all to Revolutionary Mother Han Wei. And to our Great Helmsman, Chairman Mao.

Orchids in the Empty Valley

I feared for Mama. Her female medical problem had worsened since her return from Hubei three years ago. Her herbal doctor, specializing in women's problems, had diagnosed a uterine tumor and prescribed an herbal mixture. Each week, I cooked Mama's herbs in a black clay pot, boiling them until they permeated the house with a pungent bitter smell. When the pot cooled, I poured the dark, thick liquid into jars from which Mama drank twice a day, hoping it would melt her tumor away as her doctor had said.

But she was now menstruating two to three weeks in a month and chronically ill and weak from loss of blood. Her flesh puffed and swelled. When I touched her flesh, it sank in a white dent and very slowly welled up again. Finally, the doctor told Mama his herbs could not save her. Had she been treated in her camp it might have been different. Now she must go to the hospital. But it would take six months of "back door" work and bribes to arrange Mama's hospital stay.

An emaciated stranger stood in the dim hall outside our door, his sunbaked skin coarse as weather-beaten granite, his shaved head flecked with white and dark stubble. A worn proletarian uniform, covered with patches and a hundred stitch-line scars, hung loosely on his wheatstalk frame. His hands were covered with strips of white medical tape. He looked like a fugitive, except for two gentle, kind eyes looking out at me from a core of wrinkles. He seemed surprised when he saw me.

"Is your mama home?" he asked softly, with a gentleman's voice.

Just then Mama came to the door and saw him. She paled, her eyes wide, then burst into tears. The stranger looked awkwardly at Mama, not sure what to do. Then he came forward and hugged her affectionately, patting her back while she wept.

"It's all right, Little Sister," he said. "I am here."

"Brother Sea, eighteen years I've missed you," Mama said, and her voice trembled.

Mama's big brother Sea, her favorite person in the world, had spent the last eighteen years in a lime quarry labor camp for criticizing his party supervisor during Chairman Mao's Hundred Flowers Campaign. That was in 1958, when Chairman Mao had invited everyone to criticize the party. But too many people had responded, and Uncle Sea and nearly a million other intellectuals had been sent to countryside labor camps for the crime of attacking the Party. Now he was out on a brief family leave. In two weeks he would return to his camp to finish out his twenty-year sentence.

Uncle Sea came over to me and held my face in his stonelike callused hands. Strips of white tape on his scarred fingers covered fresh wounds, split open with frostbite and poisoned with lime. He looked at me closely, amazed, near tears. I had never seen a man show such warm tenderness.

"Little Sister's little girl," he said softly. "You look just like she did."

I suddenly loved him. Mama brought Uncle Sea inside and made rice porridge for breakfast. Uncle Sea hunched over, oblivious to us, his big bowl held to his face in one hand as his chopsticks swept porridge into his mouth like a threshing machine in high gear. His vigorous eating style and loud, slurping noises didn't match his gentle manner. Mama and I watched him, startled and amused.

When he finished, his eyes eagerly sought the porridge pot. Mama refilled his bowl and made more. To our amazement, Uncle Sea devoured bowl after bowl with undiminished vigor. He ate as if to store away all he could, preparing for a famine to come.

"Have some more, Brother Sea," Mama said after his fifth bowl.

"No, no . . . never mind," he mumbled. "I am full."

Unconvinced, Mama poured the last of the porridge into his bowl.

"Eat," she ordered gently.

Uncle hesitated, as if torn between honor and a primal need.

"No, give it to the child," he said, eyeing me guiltily.

"I'm not hungry, Uncle," I piped cheerfully.

"We're finished," Mama reassured him. "It will go to waste."

Convinced, he finished the dregs and began licking his bowl with mathematical precision. Left to right, bottom to top, he scoured inch by inch with an expert tongue. His face buried in his bowl, he'd forgotten the world. Mama and I looked at each other and burst out laughing. Uncle Sea awoke like a startled child, reluctantly lowering his bowl, its inside polished clean.

"Ha, we don't have to wash this one!" Mama teased him. "I'll just put it back on the shelf till your next meal."

"No wasting," Uncle explained, embarrassed. "You only get one bowl at camp."

"Good habit, good habit," Mama reassured him. "Every grain is a drop of farmers' sweat." But her face looked immensely sad.

That night, Mama brought out an old picture to show Uncle of their mama and themselves when they were young. I squeezed in eagerly between them to look at my eternally twenty-six-year-old grandma. A long silk dress draped her skeletal frame. Her hair, tied back, showed an emaciated face with high cheekbones. Her luminous, sunken eyes stared through the camera into the next world.

This is the last picture taken of Mama and her brother with their mother before she died.

Beside her, holding her hand, stood a skinny little girl staring out with frightened eyes—Mama at three years old, looking much like me at that age. Uncle Sea stood on the other side, glaring into the camera, a defiant little boy protecting his mama and little sister.

This was the last picture taken of my grandma. The family fled in a mass exodus from the Japanese invasion, and she died of tuberculosis on the road. My grandpa kept Uncle Sea and sent Mama to live with his sister in Chong Qing, a Kuomintang stronghold. He didn't know his sister was an underground Communist Party member. She and her comrades treated Mama like their own daughter. They brought Mama to secret meetings and raised her as a true believer. In the worst of the White Terror, as thousands of underground Communists were slaughtered by the Kuomintang and left in the streets, Mama hid in the basement, reading Marx and Lenin under an oil lamp with a flame the size of a soybean that set her heart on fire. To join the Party, Mama drew the line between herself and her father, rejecting her exploiting-class roots. On a winter day in 1953, at the age of eighteen, Mama was accepted into the Communist Party and born into a new life. She declared this her real birthday—that her family had forgotten, that only her mama had known.

Mama didn't show Uncle Sea our hidden family album. He would hurt to see it. Pictures of our family's many Black Gangmembers, including Uncle Sea and my grandpa, had black X's drawn over their faces and labels written underneath: "Anti-Revolutionary," "Big Traitor," "Rightist," and "May 16 Bad Element." Mama had done this so she could keep the pictures and not throw them away, so the Party would see she had drawn the line from the bad elements in her family. Mama warned me privately not to mention Uncle Sea's political condition to him. His years in labor reform camp had stained him deeply, coloring his bones black.

"I haven't seen Mama's picture in so long." Uncle sighed. "I almost forgot how she looked."

"I still have dreams about her," Mama said.

"How does she look?" Uncle asked. "What does she do?"

"She looks like this picture," Mama said. "Sometimes I can't see her face. We walk to the river near our old Jiangsu home to wash clothes. She cooks food for me and watches me eat. She never speaks. But I know she loves me."

Uncle was so moved.

"Where was I, Mama?" I asked. "Did Grandma see me?"

"You weren't born somehow," she said. "In my dreams with my mama I'm always a little girl."

I felt disappointed and a little jealous, imagining Mama's life without me in it. I wanted to enter her dreams and meet my grandma. I asked Mama to dream me in her next dream, or at least tell Grandma about me. But she forgot every time. Mama awaited Grandma in her dreams as I had awaited Mama's return from Hubei. Her mama lived only a dream away, in a place and time where she was always a child and I was always not yet born. And all my reminding could not change this.

For years Mama had told me stories of her childhood with Brother Sea, her most beloved family member.

"After our mama died, Brother Sea took care of me. Our house in Iron Bridge Village was built by a river. The grass and flowers grew so tall in our yard that for Brother Sea and me, three and five years old, it was a forest. That was before the Japanese invaded Jiangsu and we fled to Sichuan Province. I was smaller than the neighborhood kids who came to play. And Brother Sea told them all, 'My little sister is a delicate, tiny doll. She is easily hurt. You must be gentle with her.'

"He always protected me," Mama said.

One night Mama and Uncle Sea sat in the room with me, talking together while I practiced my violin. Mama had recently made me take up the violin when the Party said we could play western instruments again. But we could only play revolutionary music. I played "I Love Beijing Tiananmen," bored and halfhearted, more interested in their conversation. Uncle Sea stared at my violin almost the way he eyed the wok at mealtime.

"What a child." He sighed enviously to Mama. "My two sons are wasted, growing up in the countryside like peasants. They haven't even learned the minimum curriculum. They are so . . ." He searched

Mama, age
two, with
her brother,
Uncle Sea,
age four.

for the right word, then said with pained regret, ". . . uncouth." It
seemed having rough, uneducated children was a worse punishment
than prison labor camp for Uncle Sea. "They hardly know me," he
said sadly. "And they both hate me for ruining their lives. Since they
were young, all the neighborhood kids cursed them because of me,
beat them up and called them Black Rodent bastards. Now they are
older and no one will give them a job. I'm a black mark on their personal records, a big black wok on their backs."

"Ai, Little Jaia is pretty much a waste, too," Mama said, trying to make Uncle feel better about his sons. "Violin learning is only practical. They say if you play a musical instrument now, you may avoid being sent to the countryside in Chairman Mao's Go to the Mountain, Go to the Village Campaign. Many kids have started to play because of this." Mama shook her head, lowered her voice, and said, "Of course, who knows—dog today, cat tomorrow. But better to increase your skill. If a blind cat can catch a dead mouse, maybe Little Jaia can be a real musician somehow."

I played energetically at this, to show Uncle my motivation.

> "I love Beijing Tiananmen,
> Above Tiananmen, a Red Sun is rising . . ."

I dragged and pushed the bow, scraping it across the strings, struggling to follow the tune. But my anthem sounded like two sick cats arguing. Mama cringed.

"Enough for tonight, Jaia! The neighbors will rebel!"

I stopped mid-note, blushing, and sat down next to them.

"Would you like to hear Uncle play?" Mama asked me suddenly.

Uncle Sea play a violin? I'd have to show him how to hold it. I didn't want his big, rough, granite hands to scratch or break my school's precious instrument.

"No, no," Uncle stammered, turning red. "Let the child play."

But when he looked at my violin, his eyes lit up like two embers stirred in a gust of wind.

"Don't be humble, Brother Sea," Mama chided him. "Come on, like old times. Let's have fun. Do it for me," she pleaded.

He looked cautiously at Mama, then wistfully at my violin.

"Well, all right," he said. "But we must seal the doors."

They jumped up like two naughty children about to play with fire. Mysteriously, Uncle checked the window, drew the curtains shut.

Mama closed the door and stuffed rags underneath the crack. Why did it seem as if a crime was about to be committed?

Then Uncle came and took my violin in his scarred hands. His taped fingers caressed it, turning it gingerly with a grace that revealed intimate familiarity and affection. But his hands were no longer clumsy. Eyes narrowed, he lifted the violin to his chin. His back curved in a graceful arch as he raised the bow, his whole being concentrated in an instant, like a flint poised to strike steel. His silent, masterful gestures startled me.

A few rough notes sounded first and quickly smoothed out. And then an enchanted stream of music melted from the taut strings, sweet and fragile as the petals on a jade magnolia. Each note he played grew more sure, vivid, and full of feeling. I had never heard such music before. This was no military marching brass-band anthem, but a lullaby of spirits. Uncle Sea, his dreamy, sorrowful eyes half closed, was far away, drunk with bliss in a celestial realm.

> *"Nobody lives in the empty valley,*
> *where the wild orchids grow.*
> *Spring breezes come,*
> *year after year.*
> *She smiles, lonely . . ."*

Mama's voice came out of nowhere, singing so beautifully, her sad words floating up to entwine with Uncle's haunting melody. My heart felt clean as a blue sky, light as clouds, yet full of a sweet sorrow. A song they sang as children together, remembered on this night, became magic. The feeling in the room changed the season from winter to spring, and the moment to a time long passed. Orchids bloomed in an empty valley under a blue sky. Mama stood there, her sickness forgotten, singing to her brother's violin.

Somehow this song tricked time and made them children again.

They crossed the empty valley, entered the ivy-covered gate of their childhood, slipped past the stone fountain their father built that last spring before the Japanese invasion. They walked hand in hand with their mama along the grassy riverbank, gathering wild goose eggs under the pale Jiangsu moon. They stood at the water's edge watching the Spring Festival lanterns float downriver, casting dancing shadows as silver trout leaped from the water to shimmer in the lantern light.

They crossed the arched wooden Taihu bridge and entered the swaying boathouse, where they found their forgotten dreams still safely docked. And like two little thieves, they untied their dreams and sailed them out upon the water, gently rocking, down the river of their lost childhood.

I adored Uncle Sea. I was just a kid, bumbling and happy to have an uncle who bought me candies, told me stories, and patiently answered my silly questions. He even held my hand when we crossed the street, though I had been crossing streets alone since I was seven. Uncle Sea's noble soul outshone his humble exterior. I couldn't imagine he had ever opposed Chairman Mao and the Party. I wished he could be my father. His visit brought a warmth and new life into our cold home. He even talked to Ba, trying to turn his heart back to Mama again, but nothing came of it.

Uncle Sea's time with us came quickly to an end. The night he left, he gave me a goodbye gift—a golden-hued rosin for my violin bow. I held it in my palm like a rare jewel, deeply inhaling its subtle pine aroma.

"Practice well, Little Jaia," he said.

Mama and I took him to the train station that evening. Standing on the platform under the silver bulb, Mama was silent. Her eyes were red from crying. Uncle watched her helplessly, worried about the illness she tried to hide from him. But anyone looking at her could see how sick she was.

"Don't lift heavy things by yourself, Little Sister," Uncle said gently. "Watch your health and go to the hospital as soon as you can. And don't be sad. Soon Little Jaia will grow up and take care of you. I'll be out in two years." Now he turned to me. "Listen to your mama more, Little Jaia," he said. "Help her every way you can. She needs you. Don't let her down."

The warning whistle sounded. The train rumbled and hissed. Uncle Sea grabbed the rail and leaped onto the step as it lurched and pulled away. Mama and I waved at him until he disappeared. Snowflakes fell from the gray sky onto the empty platform. Mama was crying. In that moment I saw her as a lost little girl, looking for someone to care for her in a harsh world. Ba had abandoned her. Uncle Sea, a political criminal in a labor camp, could not protect her now as he had when she was three and he was five.

"Mama, I'll take care of you," I promised her, taking her arm.

I was certain I could. Seeing into her sadness made me determined. She hugged me, her tears rolling down her cheeks.

"My good daughter! You are only a tiny doll."

I felt so much love and sadness for Mama in that moment. I knew I must grow up quickly.

Several months after Uncle left, Mama had her hospital examination. An X ray showed a large uterine tumor, and a hysterectomy was ordered immediately. But there was another line ahead of her for a hospital bed. Six more weeks would pass before she went in for surgery.

Immediately after her X-ray report, Mama went into a flurry of preparation and new activity. She went through all her belongings and sold many of them to the pawnshop. She spent more time with me—teaching me how to use the bank, and balance an expense book, how to sew and adapt my clothes according to the changing seasons. She wrote down the names and addresses of all her relatives. She even came to school and met privately with my teachers.

As her operation drew nearer, Mama grew more urgent, worried, distracted, and more affectionate with me. I realized she was preparing for her death, and preparing me for independence and life without her. I felt deeply sad and anxious, but put on a brave face, as she did with me. The more I pondered the idea of Mama dying, the more frightened I became, for I saw it would mean our eternal separation. Life would go on for ten thousand years, yet we would never see each other again. How could two people who loved each other as much as Mama and I be parted forever? I refused to believe it. Everything in me fought against this, as if my stubborn will could conquer her death and the terrible negation it implied.

Finally Mama went into the hospital. I visited her every afternoon and did my homework by her bed. Her crowded, gloomy ward was in perpetual chaos. Patients moaned, argued, complained; visitors chatted, wept, and emptied their family members' bedpans; nurses and orderlies went leisurely in and out with medicines and meals, oxygen tanks, and intravenous bottles.

Everyone in Mama's ward had cancer. By coincidence, the woman in the next bed was Old Hua from her Hubei camp who also had a uterine tumor. Old Hua had been in Hubei for seven years now with the rest of Mama's former Ministry of Culture comrades. She had collapsed, bleeding, in a rice paddy, and her son had brought her back to Beijing for emergency surgery.

I remembered all Mama's camp mates being very thin. But Old Hua was skeletal. It made me nervous to look at her. I didn't know about cancer. I thought she just needed to eat more. Yet skinny and weak as Old Hua was, she was always cheerful and kind. She felt lucky to be relaxing in a hospital bed in Beijing while her camp comrades did bitter work in the fields all day.

The evening before her operation, Old Hua told Mama stories about mutual friends in the camp that made us laugh out loud. The next day I came in to find a new woman in Old Hua's bed.

"Where's Old Hua?" I asked Mama. "Did she go home already?"

Mama was quiet. Then, in a small voice, she said, "Jaia, Old Hua's gone. They opened her up and found cancer everywhere. So they sewed her back up and she died. Poor Old Hua." Mama sighed. "Got a big cut for nothing."

We were both silent. I couldn't believe it. Old Hua was dead, in a day. Her life was gone forever.

"How was school?" Mama smiled weakly, changing the subject.

I looked at her. She had lost much weight the last few months. The bony contours of her skull jutted through her sickly dark skin. Her too-large eyes glittered, sunk too deeply in her head. Her hair, once thick and full, was now stringy and thin. Her fragile arms rested on the white sheet like brittle twigs. I realized then that Mama might die.

Ba's only visit the day before Mama's operation didn't help. He arrived fifteen minutes before visiting hours ended, bringing his latest mistress with him—an actress from his studio more beautiful and more famous than Auntie Shang. I knew this woman from her latest movie, and from my parents' recent bitter fights about her. Ba wanted to divorce Mama to marry her. But Mama wouldn't let him go. Now here she stood at Ba's side, glamorous even in short hair and a PLA uniform.

"Here we are, Old Lin," Ba boomed in his stage voice. "We brought you these."

He dumped a net of raw tomatoes on Mama's nightstand. Usually one brought chicken or seafood to a family member preparing for surgery. They needed protein, which the cheap hospital meals of rice and pickled vegetables didn't provide.

"Thank you for bothering," said Mama quietly.

"Oh, this is Comrade Lulu! You know her!" said Ba proudly. "The star of *Battlefield Flowers*!"

A hushed awe fell over the room at this announcement. Everyone knew Lulu from her recent movie and was astonished and flattered that she should come to their ward. Mama bit her colorless lip, looking at Ba, in whose face betrayal knew no shame.

"Comrade Lulu is very concerned about your health," Ba said.

"How are you, Comrade Lin?" Lulu said, looking down at Mama.

She smiled as if extending a blessing, self-consciously fanning herself with an embroidered handkerchief like Ba's concubine. In that moment, I hated her, for flaunting her health and beauty before Mama, and Ba, for his dog-eaten heart. A bold nurse edged in with her clipboard and asked Lulu for her autograph. News of Lulu's presence spread through the ward like a virus. Soon the doorway and the hall outside boiled with nurses, doctors, orderlies, even patients and families from the other wards. Kitchen staff and janitors also came. It seemed a gaggle of corpses might come rushing up out of the basement morgue just to gawk at Lulu, and maybe ask for her autograph, too.

"We came to wish you luck on your operation," said Lulu, with bad acting and a phoney smile.

"Thank you, Comrade Lulu," Mama said weakly, but with dignity.

An awkward silence followed, punctuated by the excited whispers of Lulu's ardent fans. Ba had his camera out.

"Go sit beside your mama." He waved me to the bed.

I sat on the bed beside her and she held my shoulders, smiling bravely into the camera, her eyelids heavy, her world collapsing on this beautiful summer day. She clenched my shoulders, her hands shaking. I didn't move. I wished I could give her strength, that my arms, like pillars, could hold up her world. How long must I wait before iron turned to steel? Ba aimed his camera and snapped two quick shots. Perhaps these would be our last pictures together. The hospital bell rang. Visiting hours were over.

Ba and Lulu went out through a swarm of her fans all pressing to get near her. Only the doctors and nurses with their pencils and clipboards were lucky enough to get her autograph. I could hardly eat that night, thinking of Mama lying in her hospital bed with a net of raw tomatoes on her nightstand. The next day after school I flew to the hospital with Old Hua's shadow behind me. I found Mama lying in her own bed. She was alive!

"Mama!" I ran to her side.

"Jaia." She smiled weakly. "The tumor was benign."

"I knew it, Mama! I knew it!"

I sat on the bed and we held each other. I started crying. "Don't cry, my precious baby, it's over," she said. "It's over." But there were tears in her eyes. She squeezed me harder. "Be brave."

Even from her hospital bed, Mama was teaching me to be strong. Later she told me about her operation.

"Your mama's very lucky, you know. My operation was a comedy. They took four of us in the operating room and gave us all local anesthesia. After they opened us up, the electricity suddenly shut off and all the lights went out. My mind was so clear. The room was like a boiled pot, with nurses running and bumping into each other, looking for flashlights and candles. My doctor cursed the power station leader and shouted, 'Fuck his mama! Fuck his grandma! Fuck his ancestors! The next time his wife comes in, let's grab her and sew up her tubes so he can't have any sons!'

"Everybody agreed with him."

The people near Mama laughed at her story.

"Then someone else said, 'Let's sew up his tube, too!'

"And everybody started shouting, 'Yes! Sew them both up!' 'Tie them in knots!' 'Sew them together!'

"They finished our operations with flashlights and candles. But everyone was okay. See? I'm fine now," Mama said. I must have looked worried. "My daughter, remember this: Whoever survives the biggest disaster gets the greatest happiness later on. I'll be better than ever. We'll go to Bei Hei Park together and climb the White Pagoda. From now on we'll have great happiness."

For several nights I stayed at Mama's side. Because of the large number of patients and shortage of nurses, family members had to tend postoperation relatives at night. I felt my deep love for Mama, grateful that she had been saved from death. Alert and aware, I watched her, jumping up to help her turn over or use her night pot, bringing her water, fanning her, and wiping her sweat-soaked face.

Patients moaned in pain, and nurses came and went in the dark ward. Several times that week, men in white came, silent as ghosts in the night, to carry out on a stretcher people who had died. New patients were brought to their beds within hours. And cries of newborn infants rose up from the nursery beneath our ward.

As I stared out the window into those strange blue nights, I felt surrounded by a mysterious power. It touched me and gave me strength and peace. It made the puzzle of my life seem as clear and simple as the stars floating in its grasp. I saw I could choose it with every breath, every act. Because of it, I knew I could survive any pain, betrayal, or loss, and endure whatever life brought me. And I knew that I would live and grow stronger.

When Heaven Fell
and the Earth Shook

Not long after Mama's operation, Comrade Lulu "blew the stage" with Ba, ending their relationship. The woman Ba wanted left him because the woman he had married would not die or let him go. Ba took Mama's survival in stride. He said her cut-out uterus had left a big, dark cave in her belly that would fill up with cold air and turn her into a strange, ugly personality. Her temper would rival a spoiled monkey's. She'd be as unpredictable as the Party's next campaign. She might, he warned, even grow a beard.

I felt sad to hear Ba say these things. Why couldn't he love Mama just a little? Why did her love for him gain nothing but pain? How had his heart, so shallow, snared Mama's, so deep?

That year my long-lost Red Guard brother, Big Honesty, returned from his Shanxi mountain village after seven years "repairing the globe" as a wheat farmer. He stood at our door, slapping the countryside dust from his jacket, his duffel bag at his feet and his wooden carrying pole leaning against the wall. He looked at me in surprise through his thick glasses, then shyly smiled.

"Little fat Jaia is a big girl now," he said softly.

I barely remembered him, having seen him perhaps a dozen

Jaia, age three, with Big Honesty in Bei Hai Park.

times in my life, and that before I was five. He looked like a farmer, with his dusty clothes, toothy smile, broad nose, and sunbaked skin. His red armband was gone. But he wore the same Red Guard jacket he had worn seven years ago on the day he left Beijing. In the picture taken by Ba at the station on that long-ago morning, Big Honesty stands foreground on a crowded platform, the train behind him, a small, pale sixteen-year-old boy with an uncertain smile, wearing a new jacket and trousers several sizes too large.

Now he stood before me, a twenty-three-year-old farmer with the same smile, a tall, brown-skinned man whose jacket and trousers, patched and faded from years of wear, were too short at the ankles and sleeves. Who would guess his commune had awarded him Party membership for showing special leadership ability, that he had served on its Party Committee, and now they had sent him to a Beijing university on a special mission—to learn microwave communication and return to help modernize his commune? Mama and Ba came to the door, and together we stared at Big Honesty as if he were a stranger.

"Ba, Mama." He bowed politely, forcing a smile.

"Big Honesty! Welcome home!" Ba bellowed.

"How good to see you!" Mama tried to smile.

She didn't seem very happy to see him. She was still weak and recovering from her operation. I didn't know yet she was not Big Honesty's real mama—that he was my half brother. He looked awkward, peering nervously through his glasses. He rubbed his thick, callused hands, and it sounded like two bricks scraping together. He removed his muddy, handmade peasant shoes and came in. We were all so shy. Mama went to the kitchen to make tea. Ba and Big Honesty, uneasy together, sat down to talk. I sat next to Big Honesty, watching him closely, listening to his every word. Brother Big Honesty, Chairman Mao's loyal Red Guard, sent away to the countryside at sixteen, had returned at last to a home where he had never belonged.

I was proud of my big Red Guard brother and asked him many questions about commune life. Big Honesty said his commune was his true family and the people there were his real parents, grandparents, brothers, and sisters. He said if I wanted I could go live with him in his commune when I grew up. He was especially proud of his shoulder-carrying pole. In its center, he had carved Chairman Mao's slogans "Plant your roots in the countryside" and "Serve the people." These, he told me, were his life commitments.

That New Year Big Honesty and I took a train to Northeast China to visit our aunt and uncle, Ba's sister and her husband. Northeast people are famous for their warm hospitality and their unbeatable back-door corruptions. Aunt and Uncle, both doctors, had a thriving back-door practice. For salary, they treated sick people. For profit, they sold sick-leave diagnoses for people to avoid work while drawing full salary. "One-week fever" sick leave cost a fat chicken. A half-year "liver ailment" sick leave cost a large pig. More lengthy and ambitious sick leaves could cost a winter's supply of heating coal or a hundred bottles of Ching Dao beer.

In this poor province where sugar, soy sauce, tofu, and at times even rice and salt were strictly rationed, their dinner table was a banquet every day and their cellar was a warehouse to feed half a village. But they were famous for their generosity, and family, friends, coworkers, and neighbors all knew they could stop by any time for a meal. And they often did. There was always a laughing gathering at their table. That New Year I ate wild chicken, turkey, donkey meat, frozen persimmons, baby pig, quail eggs, and even milk, which was strictly rationed to infants and hospital patients as medicine.

On New Year's Day, their friends and patients streamed into their home with gifts of cigarettes, liquor, and fine foods. A few poor farmers even brought humble gifts of potatoes and sticky-rice balls. That week I threw firecrackers, had snow fights, and learned to ice skate with my cousins. Uncle and Aunt took me, Big Honesty, and my cousins to visit many distant relatives whom I had never heard of.

"This is Grandma Du's brother's nephew." "This is Cousin Lu's mother's sister." "This is Uncle Li's wife's aunt."

But they had all heard of me and Big Honesty and were eager to meet the "treasure children from Chairman Mao's Beijing with a high cadre dad," as Aunt kept introducing us. To them, being from Beijing was almost like being from heaven. And a Beijing high cadre, which Ba was not, was almost an immortal.

Near the end of our visit, Uncle took us by train to Ja Pi Go village to bring big gifts to his hospital leader. Big Honesty got off the train in a village before Ja Pi Go, saying he had to visit other relatives and would meet us that night at home. Ja Pi Go is the birthplace of legendary People's Hero Yang Zirong, whose brilliant deceit of the Kuomintang White Bandits on Tiger Mountain brought down the last enemy fort in Northeast China. This incident, dramatized in the Revolutionary Example Movie *Taking Tiger Mountain by Strategy,* had made Ja Pi Go one of our most famous revolutionary landmarks.

Thrilled to visit Ja Pi Go, I expected to find crowds of pilgrims there. But our train was nearly empty, as was Ja Pi Go station when we arrived in heavy snow. I was shocked to see more than a dozen beggars lined along the fence outside the station, holding out begging bowls. Some were old and fragile, and a few were children my age or younger. Their gaunt, exposed bodies shook in their tattered clothes, pierced by the icy wind.

"Big Uncle! Big Aunt!" they cried out as we passed by, even the very old ones, to show their inferior position. "Have mercy! Please! Begging for mercy!"

They pleaded with everyone, but no one gave them anything. One boy my age silently clutched his bowl, watching me. Two frozen trails of snot marked his upper lip. His bare hand had split open from the cold in a frozen, blood-lined crack. He stared fiercely at my thick mittens, the whites of his eyes showing. I guiltily clutched the gift for Uncle's hospital leader.

"No money! No money!" Uncle shouted, waving them off like flies on his rice bowl.

We spent a warm afternoon in the home of Uncle's leader, a plump old cadre with a smiling pumpkin face who laughed a lot, told funny stories, and fed us tea and sweet buns. Afterward we visited Yang Zirong's famous tomb. His heroic bronze statue stood larger than life on a cement obelisk eight feet tall: his head, crowned with snow, thrust into the gray sky. Tiger Mountain loomed distant behind him, wrapped in a snow shawl.

I was awed by the sight and proud to be in the village where Hero Yang Zirong lived and died serving the people. But I was baffled by Ja Pi Go's gloomy desolation. In the movie *Taking Tiger Mountain,* Ja Pi Go was a lively, colorful town shining under a golden sun, full of fat animals, abundant crops, and liberated, happy peasants. Here, but for a few high cadre homes, I saw a poor, ramshackle village of mud-brick huts. And the people haunting the rutted dirt streets looked as starved and desperate as the beggars I had seen at the station.

We returned to the train at dusk. A few grim beggars stood like statues along the fence, their outstretched bowls filling up with snow. Guiltily, I hid my mittens in my pockets. But the boy with the frozen hand was gone.

That night Big Honesty came home late. The next day we boarded the train to Beijing. I could tell he had been crying. He was silent on our three-day train ride home, sunk in deep depression. Finally I asked him what was wrong. He confessed he had another family near Ja Pi Go, the family of his real mama, Ba's first wife, who died when he was only five. Now he had found them at last. They were poor peasants living on the edge of starvation, begging for food in the streets. And he was no more able to help them than he had been able to help his dying mama when he was five years old.

After that, when I saw *Taking Tiger Mountain* or heard its theme song on the radio, I remembered the real Ja Pi Go, which had become for me a village of contradictions. I saw Yang Zirong's heroic statue with Tiger Mountain behind him; Uncle's leader, a jolly cadre, so pleased by Uncle's gifts; desolate streets of squalid mud-brick huts and a few fine cadre homes; the boy with the frozen hand, devouring my mittens with his white, hungry eyes; and the beggars holding out their bowls. And I heard their voices pleading in the cold wind, "Please! Mercy . . . begging for mercy. . . ."

In early January 1976, Zhou Enlai, our beloved premier and Long March hero, died of cancer. For over four decades, Premier Zhou had radiated a human warmth rare among our leaders. He, after

Chairman Mao, most held the people's hearts. But the love he inspired was not wedded to fear and awe.

Chairman Mao, a paradoxical immortal, dangerous as fire, we worshiped from afar. Like Sun Wu Kong, the mad Monkey King he so admired, he unleashed perilous gifts from his remote heights and watched the chaos unfold below. But Premier Zhou appeared like a serene sage radiating gentleness and wisdom, influencing history by a silent spiritual persuasion.

Always, the ashes of important leaders were kept by the Party. So Premier Zhou's last request that his ashes be scattered over the mountains and rivers of our motherland seemed both a gesture of love and unity with the people and a rejection of the Party that had spurned him before his death to side with his bitter enemy, Chairman Mao's wife, Jiang Qing. Ba said Premier Zhou also refused the Party his ashes for fear Jiang Qing would work her evil magic on them, to persecute him in the land of the dead.

The Party repaid him by leaving his body lying in a shabby hospital room, refusing him the ceremonial honor of lying in state in the Great Hall of the People. This indignity belied his lofty status and certified his fall from political grace. The people were shocked.

On a bitter, cold January day, a lone hearse drove Premier Zhou's body from the hospital, down Chang An Avenue, past the Gate of Heavenly Peace, to Eight Treasure Mountain Crematory. Unexpectedly, more than a million people stood for hours in the snow along the ten-li route, holding wreaths and wearing white flowers and black armbands of mourning. Many wept openly as his hearse passed by.

Spontaneous mass gatherings occurred all over China, surprising the Party and showing Premier Zhou's deep roots in the people's hearts. But it was more than a simple grief displayed. I felt a hidden purpose emerging with these wreaths and black armbands, in these mournful faces weeping as the hearse passed them by. And with this love that flowed in sorrow, a silent rancor also spread. The hearts of the masses had broken open with grief. And an uncontainable force, complex and disturbing to its tangled roots, had sprouted through the cracks.

Beijing's spring arrived. Sultry winds crept over the South Pacific and swept in off the arid Gobi plains, melting the frozen winter. Overnight the clay earth awoke, parks and squares turned green as withered trees and dead grasses sprang to life. In a single day, bare willow branches turned to silky green ribbons. Plum blossoms, swollen on their branches like ripe fruit, burst open and flowered in fiery pinks and brilliant whites. Their delicate, insistent aroma permeated the city.

A frozen stillness thawed in nature, in the people, in my own heart. A restless surging energy awoke in us, coursing through every leaf, stem, and vein. And gentle rains ushered in the season of the Clear Light. Traditionally, April 5 was Clear Light Day, when the people ceremonially honored their ancestors with incense and offerings, sweeping their tombs and raking their graves. But the Party had banned this backward, superstitious custom after Liberation.

Now in late March, for the first time in twenty-seven years, the Clear Light ceremony was reinstituted by the people who began to gather in Tiananmen Square before the Gate of Heavenly Peace. To honor Premier Zhou, they put on black armbands and brought wreaths, flowers, and poems, piling them up by the thousands around the base of the Monument to the People's Heroes.

The days of Clear Light came and went, and the gatherings increased. Though the Party kept silent, all Beijing knew of it by the end of the first day through the "little alley news," usually the most reliable source. The city buzzed with excited rumors. People said Tiananmen Square was half full, that poems and posters to Premier Zhou covered the square, that his flowers and wreaths were piled in a mountain around the Monument to the People's Heroes, and that each night thousands slept under the stars, protecting his shrine. I knew many of my neighbors had gone to the square. Ba had also gone to look, and some of Mama's coworkers too. Later we would hear of similar gatherings in many cities across our nation.

Finally the Party harshly condemned these "antirevolutionary rebels" in strident tones tinged with fear. They were enemies of our socialist order, opposing Chairman Mao, the Party, and the dictatorship of the proletariat. They stirred the muddy waters of Chaos in order to turn back the people's revolution and destroy our Precious Red Mountain. They were evil and insane, rioting out of control, overturning and burning cars and buses, killing innocent people.

We were fascinated, hypnotized by an eerie power emanating from this forbidden, mythic gathering that now threatened the greatest force we had ever known, the Communist Party. Everywhere, people whispered excitedly of this event in awe, with a secret pleasure. And though they were outwardly loyal to the Party, I detected in many an underlying sympathy with these rebels in the square.

The morning after the Party's first report, Principal Guan warned us over the intercom:

"Children, a dangerous antirevolutionary rebellion is in progress in Tiananmen Square. A small group of hooligans, spies, and anarchists wish to destroy our Party and throw our nation back into chaos. Stay away from the square! If there is a riot you will be stepped on, crushed, beaten, or even killed by these reactionary bad elements. Keep out of danger! Be loyal to Chairman Mao and obey the Party!"

Daily after that, from newspapers, radio, and TV, we learned more about these demon rebels. No film or pictures were ever shown. The more I heard, the more fascinated and curious I became. Who were these rebels? What did they look like? How could a mere handful threaten our nation? I had to go and see for myself the event which had cast its spell over us all. Chairman Mao had said, "If you want to know the taste of a pear you must taste it for yourself."

I decided to go and taste it myself. I rode there on the bus after school one day, just to look out the window. I anxiously stared ahead as we turned onto Chang An Avenue near the square. To my surprise, instead of chaos, rioting, burning, and killing in the streets, I saw a celebration of ordinary people like my parents and neighbors, a huge festival almost filling the square.

Without fear, I followed the others off the bus, irresistibly drawn into the crowd to join the human river flowing toward the Monument to the People's Heroes. Flowers, ribbons, poems, and posters covered the bushes and trees surrounding the square, turning them snowy white. Sculpted metal wreaths were chained, locked, or wired to the light fixtures and flagpoles. Then I saw the monument, with pine and flower wreaths piled ten feet high around its base, covering its platform, flowing down the steps to spread out more than a hundred feet into the square.

Everywhere people made passionate speeches, read poems, and sang together, flushed with a joyous fever. They wore white flowers on their jackets for Premier Zhou. Some tied little bottles to the bushes for "Little Bottle" Deng Xiaoping, Premier Zhou's loyal comrade, whom the Party had cast out after Premier Zhou's death. The joy was infectious. An old grandma stopped me with her hand on my shoulder.

"You're a good girl to come and honor our Premier Zhou," she said affectionately. "He was the people's true servant."

This felt so warm and real, as if a shared secret connected all our hearts. I had to take something home with me from this day, to remember this noble feeling, this rare, heartfelt unity. Crowds surrounded the speakers and copied down the best poems as they were read aloud. I wrote many of them down in my notebook.

I was astonished. Till now Chairman Mao had been the sole poet of our Middle Kingdom. I never imagined anyone else could even write a poem. But here were brilliant, beautiful, heroic poems written by thousands of inspired poets. Where had they hid this genius till now? How long had this poetry been stifled within their hearts?

A young man with an accordion stood on a stool and began singing the French "Internationale." We often sang it at public events and rallies. Now its words held new meaning. Instantly hundreds joined in, then thousands.

> *"Arise! Arise! You prisoners of starvation.*
> *Arise you wretched of the earth.*
> *For justice thunders condemnation,*
> *a better worlds in birth.*
> *We want no condescending saviours,*
> *to rule us from a judgment hall.*
> *We workers ask not for their favors;*
> *Let us consult for all.*
> *We make the thief disgorge his booty.*
> *We free the spirit from its cell.*
> *We must ourselves decide our duty.*
> *We must decide and do it well.*
> *This is the final battle.*
> *Let each stand in his place.*
> *The internationale*
> *shall be the human race!"*

It spread like wildfire over a dry prairie till we were tens of thousands singing together, hearts enchanted, voices rising above the square, over the Gate of Heavenly Peace. We could have walked arm in arm to the execution ground and faced the bullets singing.

Part of me knew these acts of love were a slap in the Party's face. But now, feeling this freedom and lightness in my heart, I realized, so long we had smothered inside a drum, awaiting this sacred call. Now we stood in Tiananmen Square, the womb of all our revolutions, with a fire lit in our blood. We had found our voices at last. And nothing could stop our singing. Let our thunder shatter the iron walls! Let our lightning split open the copper sky! Arise prisoners! Free the spirit from its cell! This was a liberation!

I took the bus home and said nothing to Mama about where I had been. The next morning, Principal Guan ended his warning with new information.

"Our space satellites are photographing Tiananmen Square. Our secret police have taken everyone's picture. If any of you have gone to the square you must make a confession of your mistake. If you have collected any antirevolutionary materials thinking your actions harmless, you will be found out. Our powerful satellite camera can read even the tiniest scribbles in your notebook.

"If you know of anyone who has gone to the square, give their names to your teacher. You will be helping these confused comrades. You know our Party's policy, 'Leniency to those who confess, severity to those who hide.' Be Chairman Mao's loyal students."

The Party's noon broadcast confirmed the details of Principal Guan's warning and advised all good comrades to report to the Neighborhood Committee or the Security Bureau anyone who had gone to the square. They would be found in any case, the announcer said, when their pictures were developed.

"When the mud sinks to the bottom of the river, the river becomes clear. When the silver specks on the negatives crystallize each face, we'll know where to go and who to catch."

Sick with fear, I hardly slept that night. I imagined secret police following me, taking my picture as I walked through the square copying down poems. Even now, reels of satellite and police film were being developed and examined. Soon every person who had been to the square would be identified. Uncle Wei would come to my home and take me away. Yesterday I was a loyal Red Guard and Chairman Mao's best kid. Today I was an enemy of the Party. I hadn't meant to do wrong. Now I saw myself handcuffed in back of Uncle Wei's prison truck, a heavy board wired around my neck with bold, black characters reading: JAIA, TWELVE YEARS OLD: ANTI-REVOLUTIONARY HOOLIGAN AND ENEMY OF THE PEOPLE.

With a criminal record I could never join the Party or go to college. And I would be a new black mark on Mama's personal record. I hoped they would send me to Little Plum's camp. How would Mama survive it?

The thoughts raced through my mind as I tried to work out a plan. The Party said, "Leniency to those who confess." The worst thing was to wait to be arrested. Tomorrow I'd take one poem to school. If anyone asked, I'd say I had destroyed the others after returning from the square. I felt guilty and sick. I was a criminal opposing the Party. Yet I had to save myself for Mama's sake.

Next morning, I brought the shortest poem to school. It was on the united strength of the people and didn't sound antirevolutionary. After school I waited for the others to leave and nervously approached Teacher Hua. We had been on good terms since I had reformed my character and been accepted into the Red Guard. Now, meeting her tiger gaze I feared the loss of everything I had worked so hard to gain.

"Teacher Hua, I confess to withholding a crucial detail. Yesterday after school I went to Tiananmen Square. I was only curious. I copied a poem."

I held it out to her. She examined my face intently, then took the poem and read it. She finished it and looked up at me.

"Jaia, you know this was a big mistake, don't you?"

She seemed surprisingly restrained. I had expected firecrackers, harsh words, a trip to Principal Guan's office, and maybe even to the Security Bureau. I nodded, holding back my tears.

"All right, Jaia," she said simply. "You may go."

She returned to her notebook. Stunned, I left the room and started across the schoolyard toward home. I hadn't imagined it would end so easily. Thinking it over years later, I wondered, Had Teacher Hua been to the square too?

The people continued to gather in the square. The Clear Light Rebellion showed no signs of fading. The Party's warnings grew more shrill, and people whispered excitedly about the event. We all felt a spectacular crisis looming that could not be averted. We had poked the beehive and there was nowhere to run. Now everyone was going to be stung. Early in the evening on April 4, a special radio announcement by Beijing Mayor Wu De was broadcast throughout the city over the public loudspeakers.

"Comrades! In the past few days while we were studying our great leader Chairman Mao's important instructions, counterattacking the right deviationist attempt to reverse correct verdicts, and grasping revolution and promoting production, a handful of bad elements, out of ulterior motives, deliberately used the Clear Light Festival to create a political incident, directing their spearhead at Chairman Mao and the Party Central Committee in a vain attempt to change the general orientation of the struggle to criticize the unrepentant capitalist-roader Deng Xiaoping's revisionist line and beat back the right deviationist attempt!

"We must see clearly the reactionary nature of this political incident, expose the schemes and intrigues of these bad elements, heighten our revolutionary vigilance, and avoid being taken in! Revolutionary masses and cadres of the municipality must take class struggle as the key link, act immediately, and by concrete action defend Chairman Mao, defend the Party Central Committee, Chairman Mao's proletarian revolutionary line, and the great capital of our socialist motherland, deal resolute blows at counterrevolutionary sabotage, and further strengthen and consolidate the dictatorship of the proletariat and develop the excellent situation! Let us rally around the Party Central Committee headed by Chairman Mao and win still greater victories!

"Today there are bad elements carrying out disruption and disturbances and engaging in counterrevolutionary sabotage at Tiananmen Square! Revolutionary masses must leave the square at once and not be duped by them!"

Two days later, Mayor Wu De announced the arrest of the small band of hooligans responsible for the rebellion. No innocent people were harmed, he said. The square was suddenly empty, clean, sprayed down with water. No trace of a wreath, flower, or scrap of paper remained. The Party ordered everyone to stay out of Tiananmen Square until further notice. For months afterward, it was occupied and patrolled by armed soldiers and police.

But rumors flooding the little alley news told of a massive, bloody riot the day after Mayor Wu De's first speech, in which thousands of police were beaten back from the square by the rebels. No one knew how the square became empty and clean overnight. Weeks later, my brother, Big Honesty came to visit. He told me he and his Party comrades had been assigned to help police clear out the square at night after the rebels had gone to sleep.

"We beat them up and dragged them into the trucks," he said. "They're in Beijing Prison where they belong! Those troublemakers were putting rat shit in the porridge pot for everyone!"

He seemed angry with the rebels and proud to have performed his patriotic duty. I looked at my sweet, gentle brother and kept quiet. I felt sad and confused. I knew he had only followed the Party's instructions. Big Honesty's faith in the Party was absolute.

A national campaign followed, criticizing the rebellion and its leader, now identified as Deng Xiaoping. At Party and school meetings everyone criticized and wrote anti-Deng-rebellion posters that were put up all over Beijing. One by one, everyone had to publicly "declare their attitude" and align themselves with recent Central Committee documents condemning the rebellion.

On Little Red Soldiers Patrol nights, we searched the neighborhood for antirevolutionary anarchists who had escaped the people's justice. We would know them, Uncle Wei said, by their grim, thoughtful, gloomy faces, teeth gnashing over their failed attempt to destroy our Precious Red Mountain. And we must find them! For even now, in the dark, ghostly corners of their hearts, and in the scribbled pages of their "changing the sky journals," they hatched spidery plots and gruesome intrigues against us.

The Party said that all loyal comrades, in their hearts, hated the rebels. But I searched my heart and found no hatred of them there—only admiration and love, which I hid like dirty crimes. So I stepped like a double-faced hypocrite in two boats at the same time, attacking the rebels with my mouth but loving them in my heart. And I carried a mind full of guilty thoughts.

For months I felt bewildered, struck by an unresolvable paradox. Memories of the events in the square remained powerfully with me. In time a dim awareness grew to a crystal understanding. Our gathering in the square and the joy we had shared were not led or controlled by the Party. The extraordinary power there, the openness, warmth, and tangible sense of brotherhood, were outside the Party's grasp. This was what the Party hated! This was what it feared! This was the crime! Anything the Party could not control was antirevolutionary and evil—even the love and sorrow in the human heart, even the people themselves.

I had discovered the dark, profound secret of the Clear Light Rebellion. And everyone who had been to the square, we who had sung in that forbidden unity, understood. But the joy and freedom we had shared, the liberation of our defiant hopes, would remain in our hearts.

I woke on a hot, humid July night, bathed in sweat, my chest tight. Mama slept beside me as she did now whenever Ba was home. I gazed at the poplar-leaf shadows cast onto my ceiling, by the street-lamp five stories below. The clock said two-fifteen. I went onto the balcony and watched the empty city. Not a soul stirred in the eerie silence of Facing the Sun Avenue.

I went back and lay beside Mama, fanning us both, drowsy with the heat. I must have fallen asleep. The next thing I knew, Mama and I popped up in bed. Thunder rumbled in my head. The walls vibrated like paper sheets in the deafening roar. Our room tossed like a bamboo basket in a hurricane. A million sheets of glass shattered and fell like sleet in the four corners of the world. Mama shouted, but I couldn't hear her words. Was this atomic war? Had the end come? Was I dreaming? I looked in her terrified eyes.

"Earthquake!" she was screaming.

We crawled off the rocking bed and were shaken to the floor. We got halfway up to be knocked down again. Somehow we found our legs and staggered into the hall. Ba stood in his shorts, pulling furiously at the front doorknob. The door wouldn't open. Walls, floor, and ceiling wobbled and swayed. A giant's rumbling, human screams, shattering glass, and an eerie, grinding roar mingled together. Bone-penetrating, marrow-shaking, the earth cried out. Then the door popped open and Ba flew backward past us into the kitchen. He emerged again looking at us with glazed eyes.

"Earthquake!" he shouted, as if it were news. "Run!"

And he ran out the door to merge with our neighbors. They rushed and stumbled through the hall, screaming frantically down the narrow stairwell, carrying children, clutching TVs, radios, and clothes; some in their underwear, some covered with towels and blankets, some stark naked, their butts and breasts shining white in the dark hallway.

It seemed the building would collapse at any second. How strange to hear glass shatter for so long without stopping. The floors glittered and sparkled with diamond shards. Mama only had one slipper on. Seeing my bare feet, she kicked it over to me.

"Put it on!" she shouted, as if it could save me.

"You keep it!" I yelled, and kicked it back.

She kicked it back at me and I kicked it back to her. She kicked it back again, now furious.

"You put that slipper on now!" she screamed over the din.

There we stood in the great Beijing earthquake, playing Ping-Pong with her bedroom slipper. Then the rocking slowed down and stopped. Everything went quiet and still. The earthquake had lasted ninety seconds. It had felt like an hour. Our kitchen cabinets hung open. Their contents lay spilled and broken on the floor. Thousands of windows in Beijing lay in fragments on the ground. Mama and I found our slippers and hurried downstairs holding hands in the dark hall, crunching glass shards at every step. The street was crowded. Everyone was outside. Somehow our streetlight had stayed on. People talked excitedly.

"What a lousy year!"

"Someone up there must be mad at us!"

"I wonder what's coming next?"

Socialism yards had suffered the worst damage. Many of their flimsy, poorly constructed dwellings, made of thin plaster, had fallen in the first tremors. But few people were badly hurt when they fell. The three apartment buildings on our block still stood. But hundreds of buildings throughout the city had collapsed.

I wandered the streets with my friends till dawn, when I saw Ba come out of our building, pushing his bicycle, carrying his black padlocked bag and an armful of clothes. I watched him disappear into the crowd. Later we heard he had gone to Mongolia to do film research. We didn't see him for nearly a year.

For the next five weeks, Mama and I lived in fear with our neighbors, under the makeshift plastic-sheet tents that now filled Beijing's streets. Many buildings had survived the quake only to fall in aftershocks. A tremor could bring disaster. The official tremor detector was an empty soy-sauce bottle balanced upside down on its mouth. When it fell, the watchperson beat a tin pot with a cooking spoon or clapped two pot lids together shouting "Earthquake!" as loud as he could. And we all ran out from under our plastic sheets, screaming and bumping into each other in the dark, often in the driving summer-night rains.

The first week after the big quake, aftershocks came nightly. But other things could topple an upside-down soy-sauce bottle—a rat scavenging for food or a child peeing. False alarms came often. And constant predictions circulated as to the date of the next big quake. Everyone said it was coming tomorrow, next week, next month. And it would be bigger than the first.

In the meantime, earthquake damage and aftershock danger halted work and school. Most people lived in the streets. My class-mates and I roamed the city by day, exploring the destruction. People crawled like ants through the ruined buildings, scavenging for materials to repair their own damaged dwellings. Socialism yards became huge construction sites. Hammers banged and echoed throughout the city from sunrise to sunset.

Many people sat talking all day, playing cards or checkers and drinking tea, listening to the radio for earthquake news. Our favorite card game was "telling a big lie," where you bluffed with the cards in your hand to beat your neighbor, daring him to challenge you. If he shouted, "Show me your cards, you big liar!" and you had the real cards, he lost. If he caught you lying, you lost. Usually, the biggest liar won.

For two weeks the Party never mentioned the earthquake. They reported only mundane news and played sound tracks from the Eight Revolutionary Example Plays: *The Red Detachment Women, The White-Haired Girl, Red Lantern, Taking Tiger Mountain . . .* over and over and over.

Meanwhile we hummed along, living in the streets. We sweated all day in the humid Beijing heat and cursed the torrential rains that fell nightly, and often in late afternoon. When storm clouds gathered, we hastily ducked under our plastic sheets. It was hard to sleep at night. The rain thundered down in bullets and lightning cracked and flashed through the sheets. Water blew into our tents, soaked us in our beds, and flowed in rivers beneath our feet. There was so much water in the streets at night that we peed in our own tents and the rain washed it away. Mama and I secretly joked as we did, reciting a line from Chairman Mao's poem: "Rippling, rippling, flowing river!"

Hot and sweaty all day and cold and damp all night, people grew irritable, grumbled, and cursed more than ever. I heard the word "fucking" two hundred times a day. It was "The fucking rain!" "The fucking food shortage!" "The fucking aftershocks!" "The fucking PLA who never fucking come!" And "Fuck this fucking year!"

But people's sense of humor sharpened as we waited for news and instruction from the Party, for some simple acknowledgment of our plight.

"Didn't someone tell the Party we had an earthquake?"

"They couldn't feel the shaking in their goose-feather beds!"

"I sent them a letter last month."

"It probably got lost in the mail!"

And we waited for the PLA to come help us, to bring us food or at least some real tents to keep the rain off our backs.

"Where are the fucking people's servants when you need them?"

"Lying in their fucking bunks reading Uncle Lei Feng's Diary!"

Also, three slang expressions formerly used by hooligans suddenly became popular. Everything was now "shaking," "smothering," and "out of control." Somehow these words uniquely communicated our frustration, and people said them often with great humor and enthusiasm. The "three hooligan slangs," as they came to be called, salted and peppered our conversations. It became a popular humorous curse to say them all together.

"Fucking! Shaking! Smothering out of control!"

We just loved the sound of it.

Meanwhile, the Party still didn't mention the earthquake, only reporting irrelevant news, and strangely, even some news that didn't happen. It claimed a Beijing pipe factory working at full speed had doubled production. Yet we saw this factory from our street camp. Some of my neighbors even worked there. It was closed because of earthquake damage. No smoke came from its chimney. There were many reports of such nonevents in Beijing, as if to hide our condition from the rest of the nation and deny the earthquake had ever happened. We felt abandoned by the Party. And people were angry. But they joked more than they grumbled.

"Look at me! I'm sawing pipe into lengths!" said a card playing neighbor-woman worker from the closed factory.

"Yes, and I'm shoveling coal in the furnace!" her opponent commented wryly. "See the invisible smoke coming out of the chimney? That's mine!"

Comical imaginary production races were held between workers from different factories over card and checker games.

"Hey! Better get to work! Our factory has just doubled production!"

"Again? We'll catch up! Now show me your cards, you big liar!"

The days passed with endless card and checker games, cigarettes, cups of tea, and lively conversations. People laughed hard to keep their spirits up. I saw true heroism in my people, suffering the ordeal in laughter, turning hell into a marathon ghetto party. I thought Beijing people were the bravest, funniest, greatest people in the world. But while many turned to humor and sarcasm, some grew openly rebellious.

"Who cares? We love chaos! Smothering! Shaking! Who needs to go to work? Let the Party get mad! We'll just live in the street and play cards and pick up our salary once a month! Out of control! Let's piss off the Party!"

I was shocked by things I heard spoken against the Party. Yet it seemed to have vanished before our eyes, fallen through a crack in the earth. All that remained of the Party was a disembodied voice droning on the radio, indifferent to our lives. In its perceived absence a bold new freedom arose. As the saying went, "When the tiger is gone, the monkey is king."

The mice that whispered in the tiger's ears, the Neighborhood Committee's Little Feet Patrol, hovered nearby watching, listening, disapproving. But people no longer feared them. What power did a gang of nosy old snitches have after an earthquake? What could they take from us now that we lived barefoot in the streets, sweating in the heat and soaking in the rain in our dirty shorts and undershirts!

The Four Olds—Old Eyes, Old Feet, Old Tongue, and Old Ears—had lost their power. They made weak attempts to enforce our respect for the Party, roaming about, listening and watching with sour looks, criticizing those who spoke too freely. But people ignored them and even blew them off like flies with irritated looks and contemptuous sarcasm.

"What are you going to do, Old Eyes, confiscate my underwear?"

Finally, weeks after the event, the Party reported that there had been an earthquake. People were not impressed.

"No kidding? An earthquake! Did you feel something?"

"They must have gotten my letter!"

But it withheld news of the destruction of the city of Tangshan, and of the death toll, which had doubled to nearly a million people because rescue efforts were hampered by interfactional squabbling in the Party Central Committee. The delayed report made people even more cynical. Further reports only increased their skepticism.

"Chairman Mao and our Party's Central Committee have sent warmth and comfort to the people of the damaged earthquake areas!" went a typical broadcast. "The grateful people have united bravely to fight this disaster with joyful, revolutionary enthusiasm!"

"Oooeee! I feel warm and comfortable! How about you?" one said, rubbing a sweaty hand delicately over his bare heart.

"I'm too busy fighting this smothering disaster with joyful enthusiasm," another deadpanned, her eyes glued to the cards.

"I must have been asleep when they delivered my shaking comfort. I'm still wet and hungry from two weeks ago!"

Several weeks after the earthquake, the Party proudly announced the news that "we" had rejected all international emergency aid. This, the Party said, showed our strength and independence. "We" did not need anyone's help. Outrage erupted everywhere.

"Fucking! Shaking! Smothering out-of-control bastards! They're not living outside in this wet hell with us!"

"I'll take anybody's help! Give me an imperialist tent! A Soviet raincoat! How is the Central Committee helping me?"

The grumbling reached a fever pitch with this incident. Soon afterward the Neighborhood Committee, backed by Uncle Wei and a high Party cadre, called an emergency neighborhood meeting and announced a ban, for "everyone's spiritual health," on the "three hooligan slangs" because of their "anti-Party nature." "Shaking," "smothering," and "out of control" became forbidden expressions. What was wrong with these words? I wondered. And why wasn't "fucking" banned? As a result, its use went up two hundred percent.

When September's cold rains came, people began moving back into their homes, prepared or not. Better to risk another earthquake indoors than catch pneumonia safely outside, or freeze to death in the street when winter came. Those of us who lived on the upper floor of my building dared not return home. Most of my neighbors moved their plastic tents into the basement. But space was limited, and the fierce real estate grab for it left Mama and me in the street with three other families. In early September we moved into the Beijing Library basement. I was thrilled. Beijing Library was my favorite place, with its sea of books, stately buildings, and large, well-tended grounds. Now it would be my home through the coming winter.

* * *

On the golden autumn afternoon of September 11, 1976, I passed through the crimson library gate into the courtyard as the dirge broke over the public loudspeakers. Its haunting brass tones howled with gloom. It had played to announce Premier Zhou's death in January and our great Long March General Mei Zhu De's death in May. But never this loud. Men and women wailed in an office high above me, harrowing my blood. I knew the end of the world had come. The pillar holding up our Middle Kingdom had fallen. Chairman Mao was dead!

I ran upstairs to Mama's office. She and her comrades huddled around the radio, heads bowed. Mama stared at the floor, pale and in shock. An old woman near her wept inconsolably as the distraught Party announcer confirmed the impossible news: Chairman Mao was dead. I stood numb in the doorway. Chairman Mao was immortal! He would live ten thousand years! Death could not touch him! Now one tragic moment etched in brass had ended our history and plunged our nation into grief. Eulogies began pouring forth.

"Our Great Star has fallen."

"The Light of China has gone out."

"The Red Sun of our hearts has set."

"We are a kingdom of orphans without a father, a flock of sheep who have lost their shepherd."

"We are a ship without our helmsman on a stormy sea."

The dirge played for two weeks with relentless power, covering the days in a dark cloud and making the nights endless. Chairman Mao's paradoxical death bewildered me. Every human being, even infants, wore a black armband. In school I wept with my classmates and teachers. In the face of our unequaled loss, a fearful need to demonstrate the correct response haunted me.

At night, Mama and I sat frozen before the library TV, watching China's gathered masses sobbing, fainting, and tearing their hair.

Mad with grief, they cried for our Great Helmsman to return. And I watched it all, frightened and confused, wondering what it meant. I wanted to curl up in Mama's arms and never go outside again.

Who could replace Chairman Mao? How would his godlike death affect us? Would there be storms in heaven? Would the stars fall? Would famines, disasters, and mad chaos return? Would rivers flood, crops fail, the price of tofu rise? Would the Russian Bear invade us in our moment of weakness? Would imperialist America destroy us with atomic bombs? Who would protect us with Chairman Mao gone? And what purpose did we have to live for without him?

Two weeks later, I was sent to a Tiananmen Square mass memorial for Chairman Mao as a student representative for my school. Over a million mourners in black and white lined up in orderly rows, filling the square and the avenues leading up to it. Long speeches were made by our Party leaders. People fainted from grief and from standing for hours in the glaring sun. Some wept and wailed and pulled their hair tragically. Others clawed the air, beat their chests, and stamped the earth, crying out.

"Chairman Mao! Don't leave us!"

"Come back, Chairman! We need you!"

"Chairman Mao, you cannot die!"

"Ten thousand years alive, Chairman Mao! Ten thousand years!"

What a bewildering, terrifying month it had been. I bent my head low, feeling sick in my stomach. But somehow my fear for our future dissolved like a mist under this bright Beijing sun that came out after all, as I stood in this square in the heart of our ancient motherland with over a million of my people. Perhaps we were strong enough to live on and build a future together without Chairman Mao. Perhaps we could take care of ourselves.

At one point, a palpable wave of force swept over the crowd like wind over a wheat field, and suddenly people around me were convulsed with weeping. I was numb, and puzzled by my lack of emotion at this profound event. And when this wave passed by, leaving me untouched, I became gripped with fear of being seen unmoved, not sorrowful, not weeping as I knew I should have been.

Desperately, I clenched my eyes, hoping to squeeze out a few tears. But it was like squeezing halves of a dried-out lemon. People all around me shook with an epic grief. They quivered and quaked. Their arms and legs flung about like string puppets. They sobbed effortlessly and shed streams of tears. I actually saw wet patches on the ground at their feet where their tears had fallen. I admired and envied their grief. I wished it were mine.

In panic, I bowed my head and made weeping noises, gathering as much saliva as I could in my dry mouth. I glanced around like a criminal to make sure I was not being watched. Nervously, I spat onto the pavement, quickly rubbing it in with my foot to make a wet spot. I spat and rubbed several times till it became a patch like those near my comrades. Then I kept my head bowed and did not look up until the memorial ended.

The period of mourning passed. The Party urged us to transcend our sadness and grief and turn them into strength and renewed commitment to the Party and the revolution.

"Carry Chairman Mao's red flag forward to the end and fulfill his last will to the people!" became the slogan of the period.

Many intensified their devotion to Chairman Mao, lighting incense, praying, bowing, and offering cooked rice to his picture. Death had magnified, not diminished, his powers. Now a Celestial Immortal, a Buddha, to attract his regard through these rituals brought luck, healed sickness, and enabled a man and his family to prosper. Many had believed these things while Chairman Mao lived. But many more believed them now that he was dead.

Yet there was shock when the Party announced Chairman Mao's body would be preserved and set in a crystal coffin in a mausoleum to be built in Tiananmen Square. After Liberation, Chairman Mao and the Party had called preservation and burial customs barbaric and feudal and made cremation compulsory by law.

We were told his mausoleum, to be built before the Gate of Heavenly Peace in the center of the square, would be the world's largest—even bigger than the Red Square mausoleum where Lenin lay. The idea of preserving Chairman Mao gave me chills. I hoped I would never have to see him in person. But ten months later I was sent, along with tens of thousands of student representatives from every province in China, to see Chairman Mao's body. We stood in line for hours one hot summer day, approaching the newly completed white marble mausoleum. Finally, my group reached the pointed iron gate, guarded with electronic sensors. Slowly we climbed the marble steps between two rows of soldiers. We passed from the sun's glare into the dim, cool interior of the first room and stepped onto a thick, spongy red carpet. A gigantic marble Chairman Mao statue faced us across the room, serenely seated on a marble couch atop an eight-foot-high marble base. A spectacular mural behind him showed a landscape with mountains, a river, and clouds.

"First bow!" came a sharp command. Then I saw the PLA officer who stood to one side below the statue. He looked like a toy soldier. We bowed solemnly to Chairman Mao. "Second bow! Third bow!" the officer commanded.

We bowed three times and were sent through one of the doorways at each end of the huge antechamber. One by one, we entered the dim, silent hall. Immediately, I felt the uncanny presence of our dead Chairman. Then I saw his crystal sarcophagus, the source of light, resting luminous on the central platform. And the coolness of the hall, like the coolness of death itself, seemed to emanate from its icelike crystal panes.

Four blank-faced soldiers stood guarding the sarcophagus, one at each corner, their shouldered rifles fixed with gleaming bayonets. I had never seen a corpse or a coffin before. My whole body shivered and shook. And I feared throwing up on the precious red carpet.

One at a time, we approached the coffin to look through the clear crystal at our beloved Chairman Mao. As I drew near, the girls and boys ahead of me began moving faster and faster. I couldn't keep up with them. I was under a spell. With each quivering step my legs sank, the plush carpet sucked at my feet like soft mud.

Then I saw it . . . Him . . . Chairman Mao's chubby, preserved, dead, glowing, crystal-encased body. To my huge relief, his eyes were closed. His face was as red and shiny as a waxed apple. His chest was puffy and round inside his gray uniform, like a stuffed panda under our Party's red flag adorned with a crossed golden ax and sickle. Here was Chairman Mao at last. He looked shorter and smaller than I expected. It shocked me. He had always looked huge in his pictures. Articles I had read called Chairman Mao a giant at 1.90 meters tall. But here he looked a meter and a half.

All my life I had wanted to see Chairman Mao. Now the sight of his stiff, waxy-red form reclining in crystal splendor awakened terror. I ran with my schoolmates out of the hall, hearing a soft, rapid "cush cush" of footsteps coming after me. I ran through a third chamber out the door, out of the haunted mausoleum into bright sunlight. The pale faces of my classmates told me they were as frightened as I was. We walked silently to the bus. I was too nervous to ask my comrades the most disturbing question on my mind. But I couldn't stop wondering, "Did Chairman Mao shrink?"

The mystery of it haunted me. Except for the shrinkage and the slightly unreal color of his skin, he looked healthy, peaceful, profound. On the ride home, I timidly asked an older boy sitting across from me what he had seen. I hoped he would either confirm or deny the change in Chairman Mao's size and set my mind at rest. He hemmed and hawed anxiously. His eyes roamed here and there, up and down, looking for a place to look. Finally he stammered in a nervous squawk, "Uh, boy . . . the carpet's really thick . . . I was so moved, huh?"

Then he turned around and wouldn't look at me all the way home. I decided he must have closed his eyes when he looked at Chairman Mao. I wished I had closed mine, too.

On October 22, with Chairman Mao six weeks dead, the Party announced the arrest of a Gang of Four: Mao's widow, Jiang Qing, Party Vice Chairman Wang Hongwen, and Party Central Committee leaders Zhang Chunqiao and Yao Wenyan, who held four of the top six Party Central Committee posts. We heard first of Jiang Qing's dramatic arrest: how the PLA soldiers burst into her room at night, automatic rifles aimed; how they did not lower their guns even when she collapsed on the floor crying, "The Chairman's body is not yet cold and you have the gall to stage a coup!"

Jiang Qing, Chairman Mao's Best Student and our Revolutionary Standard-Bearer, became the White-Boned Demon, hated by all, pitied by none. And her Gang of Four achieved infamy overnight. Tales of their criminal excesses flooding gossip vines and all media, gave them mythic status. The Party said their crimes numbered in the millions. The little alley news gave the wicked details: Jiang Qing had a stable of male prostitutes serving her perverted whims day and night; to retain her youth, she had drawn blood from the veins of young soldiers and injected it into her own; she had fed exclusively on delicacies like panda paws, live monkey brains, and rare green-haired turtles, and had sat to shit on a swan-feather toilet seat. Were these things true? How could Chairman Mao and the Party not have known? Why had they let her do these things?

Since Premier Zhou's death, the people had hated Jiang Qing, cursing her in their hearts while biting their tongues. Now the image of Jiang Qing as a cultural vampire was etched deeply in our minds. People spoke freely, calling her a "blood-sucking goblin," "poisonous bitch," and "vampire skull under a pretty scarf." She had sat at Chairman Mao's feet, like Lucifer at the right hand of God. And she had stolen heaven and plunged our motherland into darkness.

The day the Gang of Four's arrest was announced, ecstatic crowds poured into Tiananmen Square. The fall of these powerful criminals proved justice real. It felt like a new liberation. A national celebration followed. For a week from dawn to midnight, jubilant masses packed the streets, parks, and Tiananmen Square, singing, cheering, marching, drinking, writing poems and posters, beating gongs and drums, and dancing the Yanga, red sashes waving like flying dragons. Beer and wine sold out all over China. Firecrackers exploded like a roaring tide, and rainbow fireworks lit up our cities at night. Noisier than New Year's and more passionate than National Day, it seemed the Clear Light Rebellion had spread to the whole nation. And the Party had finally joined in.

The celebration culminated in a mass Tiananmen Square rally. Before a crowd of nearly two million people, with all of China listening on the radio and watching on TV, Beijing Mayor Wu De made an epochal announcement: "Chairman Mao's Great Proletarian Cultural Revolution has been victoriously completed!"

The crowd in the square cheered for five minutes. I heard the roar in my home a mile away. An indescribable surge of relief and euphoria flooded through me. The great cleansing was over! My family would no longer live in fear of exile, under the black shadow of their political labels! Uncle Sea would be released from his camp! Now I could write freely in my journal and we would live happy, untroubled lives!

When the pandemonium subsided in the square, Mayor Wu De continued:

"Our victory over the Gang of Four clique is the great victory of the Great Proletarian Cultural Revolution! We must usher in a new wave of learning Marxism, Leninism, and Maoism! Thoroughly reveal and criticize the antirevolutionary Gang of Four clique! Continue criticizing Deng Xiaoping and his reversing-the-verdict wind! Enhance and continuously develop the victorious result of the Great Proletarian Cultural Revolution! Use class struggle as a key link, to 'do revolutionary things, improve productivity, improve war preparation,' and continuously develop the excellent situation! Long live the great, glorious, ever-righteous Communist Party! Long live invincible Marxism, Leninism, and Maoism!"

No one was sure what this meant, or where we now stood, or where we were headed. The ambiguity left a lingering confusion that would build and gather over our nation like a pall. Yet the Cultural Revolution was over! We had awakened from our long nightmare. And our spirit now stirred to life in the smoldering ruins of an era, and rose from the ashes.

Exoneration!

Weeks passed, the mood of celebration waned, and euphoria gave way to confusion and anxiety in millions of scarred veterans of chaos—and in the uncertain masses. And the litany of crimes charged to the Gang of Four increased. They had done it all, the Party said. Now they were under arrest and everything would be right again. Yet no one asked the obvious question: "How could the Gang of Four have done everything?"

We instinctively believed the Party's claim. Perhaps the Gang of Four *had* caused all our problems. Yet with our world turned upside down and black changed to white again, a dilemma arose with compelling urgency. As always, we relied on Central Party documents for our opinions and beliefs. And we had to know, on what common truths did our lives now stand?

Was former Chairman of the Nation Liu Shaoqi, killed by the Red Guard, still a Big Anti-Revolutionary Traitor? Or was he now a Gang of Four victim? Was the Clear Light Rebellion still the counterrevolution of a few bad elements and hooligans? Or were those arrested in the crackdown also Gang of Four victims? What of Big Criminal Deng Xiaoping, now in confinement and expelled from the Party? He had opposed the Gang of Four in the past. Didn't this make him a hero?

Our most urgent issue was a hundred million "problem people," "political criminals and ghosts" with black labels in their personal records. These family members, neighbors, former coworkers, and friends formed a vast subculture of untouchables and exiles in our midst. Cultural Revolution victims: persecuted, imprisoned, tortured, crippled, killed, driven insane; their reputations and careers ruined, their homes and lives destroyed. Our fates intersected in so many ways; we were trapped together in a vast shivering web.

What of these black-labeled and dishonored problem people whom we had shunned for years, fearing political contamination? Could they and their families now come out of exile? Could they be exonerated? Could they be restored to our communities and live among us as our neighbors and friends once more? These terrible questions burned in our minds and hearts, becoming an unavoidable force moving upstream through every channel to the highest levels of the Party. A cultural conversation began that could not be silenced. The People wanted justice. Their suffering souls cried out for it. And the Party had to respond.

In my own family were nearly thirty Black Gangmember relatives who had spent years in prisons, cowsheds, and countryside labor camps. A handful had died, two violently, leaving large families behind to carry the black wok on their backs. My family history was common to intellectuals in our era.

The Party's Gang of Four answer was a broom to gather up our haunted past and a carpet to sweep it under. But it did not reveal the new truths of this post–Cultural Revolution era. And now we feared to speak, for today's wrong words could tomorrow mean prison, exile, or worse. We needed issues clarified and questions answered. Our history and our future were at stake.

The exonerations began a year later with Liu Shaoqi and then Deng Xiaoping. Then the Clear Light Rebellion was renamed the

Tiananmen Movement, and the rebels arrested in the square were released as national heroes. Many spoke on radio and TV and became superstars.

Over the next few years, Mama and Ba attended frequent exoneration ceremonies to honor former friends, neighbors, coworkers, and relatives who had died stained in the Years of Chaos. They returned grim-faced, wearing their black armbands, emanating a strange acrid odor that for me became the smell of death.

With these exonerations a remarkable period began. Millions were allowed to petition for the removal of unjust labels from their personal records, and for token payment for their losses, called a comforting fee. Special offices were set up to process these petitions. Other offices were created to investigate all crimes committed in the Cultural Revolution. Most reported crimes were automatically charged to the Gang of Four. Minimal comforting fees were awarded to all these "Gang of Four victims," and their cases were officially closed.

But for the desperate or persistent few who felt they had not received justice, or who wished to push further in testing the Party's goodwill, a special office opened up in Beijing. It came to be called, unofficially, the Office of Last Hope.

Mama and I went back to our former Ministry of Culture living compound to see our old friends Grandpa Li and Grandma Yang. They had just returned to Beijing after seven years in Mama's old camp. Seven years of hard labor and privation had aged them, bent their bodies, and whittled them thin. They hugged us warmly when we came in and seemed very happy to see us, even though we had rejected them in the camp and avoided them the whole time we were there. They had been Black Gangmembers then. Mama had been a Gray Ghost fearing contamination. And I had been Chairman Mao's best kid, following his instructions. But today we didn't mention those painful years.

Grandma Yang, now seventy, watched me as tenderly as she had ten years ago. She still wore her short gray hair pinned behind her ears revolutionary-style, as she had at seventeen when she had followed Chairman Mao to Yan'an after the Long March, earning the honorary title of Chairman Mao's Red Doll. She and Grandpa Li were busy petitioning the Party for an exoneration and the removal of the black labels that now stained their personal records.

Since I was two they had been my surrogate grandparents. And this old room had been a second home of my childhood. Often I had sat at this table on Grandma Yang's lap while she stroked my hair, fed me sweets, and told me fairy tales. And Grandpa Li had watched me, his humorous eyes magnified to the size of ripe plums by his thick lenses. Writer, archaeologist, art historian, and former head of the Department of Historical Treasures, he might have been a Mandarin scholar in an earlier era, or a Buddhist priest.

Their old room, once cheerful, cozy, and bright, now seemed small and somehow sad, full of dust and a moldy smell. The walls were stained, dirty, greasy, splattered with soy sauce and a riot of black firecracker scars. The paint peeled. Spiderwebs threaded the ceiling like map lines, gathering in every corner. Glass shards protruded like malformed teeth from the doorframes of a once-elegant bookshelf. The books were now a pile of torn pages swept into a corner, guarded by a lonely broom.

Grandma Yang spoke of Auntie Willow, who had returned with them on the train from Hubei. Auntie Willow had been ill this last year in the camp. Wang Ma, my old nanny, had gone to live with a new family. Bing Mei still worked in her butcher shop and never touched her piano anymore. Captain Chen, their neighbor and head of their district's Security Bureau, was in prison for raping one of his daughter's classmates. He had made a big mistake. The girl's parents were cadres with powerful connections. Cold anger burned in my belly at this news of Captain Chen. I had never told Mama about him.

Grandpa Li told Mama about Old Dai, who had lived in the room upstairs for fifteen years. One night a week ago, he had gone mad and hacked his wife and two daughters to death with a meat cleaver. No one had dared to go in until the screaming stopped. By then Old Dai had slit his own throat. The compound was still in shock.

We talked for a while, and Grandma Yang and Grandpa Li invited us to stay for dinner, like old times. But Mama said we must go. Walking down these dim halls in my old building, I felt the haunted presence of tormented souls. A silent hiss slithered in our echoing steps. An unspeakable secret whispering mingled with children's laughter and the screams of the dead.

We walked in the silent dusk through the Ministry of Culture compound. It had the barren look of an abandoned town. Eerie lights glittered like ghost fire behind the windows of each room. The snowy honeysuckle and pink fairy-furs, the green lawns and purple vine arbors, had long ago been uprooted and cleared away. My childhood playground had become a graveyard. But the ten-story chimney still puffed dragon smoke and fire into the peculiar twilight. The ghosts from our past still wandered within this mist of ash and cinder, beneath this gray sky.

On the bus home, I thought of Captain Chen sitting in a tiny cell, and of the snake spirit demon he had kept locked in his basement. Perhaps he had raped her, too. I felt sorry for Round Round, whom I had not seen in years.

And I saw Bing Mei in her butcher shop, her bloodstained apron clinging to her knees, flaying carp, splitting pig joints with an ax, sawing cow bones with a serrated blade, attacking pieces of meat with her cleaver. Her coarse red hands swam like eels through mountains of flesh, forests of bone, rivers of blood. Severed tongues, intestines, livers, and burgundy hearts lay scattered at her feet on the blood-slick floor. She split a pig's head open with her ax, hacked off its ears with her cleaver, and scooped out its transparent, jellylike brain, a delicacy to be divided among her clamoring patrons.

As a child, Bing Mei's nimble fingers had danced across black and white keys as hundreds listened, enthralled. Now Mozart and Beethoven echoed in the sealed chamber of her heart. And she slapped the carnage of her life on a scale, wrapped it in old newspaper, and calculated her perplexing fate on a bloody abacus.

"Jaia, go tell your grandpa dinner is ready."

Mama whispered to me in the kitchen of our new apartment. Ba had returned from Mongolia after nearly a year's absence. Within two months, he had finagled this new three-room apartment, and Mama and I had rejoined him from our library basement.

I cautiously poked my head in Mama's room. My black-wok grandpa sat there, as he had all week, in a black-tea fever, working on his last-hope cases, hunched over and scribbling in his notebook like a large, bald fetus doing homework. His table was strewn with Chairman Mao's four-volume *Collected Works,* copies of various Central Committee documents, and the Chinese Constitution.

The exoneration tour had come to our home—Grandpa, his third wife, three of his seven sisters, and his fourth son. Grandpa's two-year struggle with the Party had won them all partial exonerations. They had pooled their small comforting fees to travel the country visiting family, proclaiming their newly won reversed verdicts. Mama had not seen her father for fifteen years.

"Dinner is ready, Grandpa," I called softly.

"Ignore me!" he barked, not looking up. "Eat without me!"

I fled to my room where my study table was set for dinner. Seven of us waited for Grandpa: his three stoic sisters; his third wife, Moon Jewel, her face pinched in frustration; Mama, looking nervous; Ba, yawning with boredom; and smirking Ting, Grandpa's fourth son, cool as usual.

I liked Ting's monkey humor, sharpness, and proletarian charm, his indifference to the family quarrels and tensions. Three years in a Shanghai prison for gambling and black-market dealing had taught him patience and perspective and heightened his sense of humor. (Two of his brothers were still there.) Ting took me as his little sister and was full of hooligan street wisdom that always began with "Look!"

"Look! If someone pulls a gun on you, just do whatever they say! Never resist a superior force!" Or "Look! It doesn't matter what you do! You can dig shit or paint a picture! Who cares? As long as they give you the money!"

He winked at me across the table, nibbling slyly at a plate of fried peanuts. Grandpa knew we wouldn't eat without him. Two of his sisters were older than he. But Grandpa, an only son with his father gone, was the authority and oldest living "root" of his family.

"Stubborn old man! Let's eat without him!" fumed Grandma. "A bull's temper in a granite head! A fortune of suffering I got marrying my Dead Old Man."

Since Chairman Mao called intellectuals "dead people," Grandma used the label as Grandpa's pet name. Now in her sixties, Grandma Moon Jewel was still pretty, with finer skin than Mama's. Moon Jewel, the sharp-tongued daughter of an exploiting-class landlord, had married Grandpa on the eve of the Cultural Revolution. They fell together from the weight of their wrong political backgrounds. Muttering, she marched to his room, delivered a feisty tongue-lashing, and returned with Grandpa scowling in tow.

"Look at my wife, who can share all the sweetness but none of the bitterness," Grandpa grumbled.

"My Dead Old Man! When did we ever have any sweetness?"

We sat quietly. Mama brought in a plate of roast duck and a bowl of stir-fried vegetables. A bottle of Grandpa's favorite green-plum wine sat open in front of him.

"I'm just having wine for dinner," he said.

We knew the ritual. Grandpa filled his cup and emptied it in a long swallow. His eyebrows relaxed and he began looking peaceful. He grabbed his chopsticks with his four-fingered hand, snatched a fried peanut from the plate, and maneuvered it deftly into his mouth. His first bite was our permission. Now we could eat.

I marveled at Grandpa's four-fingered chopstick skills. His right thumb was sawed off nine years ago in the Shanghai mill where he was sent to have his thoughts reformed. I never tired of secretly observing his small, mangled stump. It looked just like a mushroom.

"You should eat more and drink less," Grandma advised him.

Grandpa replied proudly, "A man with ocean capacity never gets wine-drunk! He only gets inspiration! All the great poets drank. Remember T'ang-dynasty Wine Celestial Li Bai!" Grandpa raised his glass. " 'Never leave your golden chalice empty under the moon,' " he quoted Li Bai passionately. "Never!"

He emptied his in gulps and refilled it with a steady hand.

"When did you ever wait for the moon to come up?" muttered Grandma. "And what have you written since we were married? Self-criticism reports the first ten years and exoneration appeals the last two. The only thing improving is your calligraphy!"

Grandpa had been a talented poet and calligrapher, Mama said. But his poetry was flawed by classical, bourgeois man-woman themes and a sentimental love of nature. His refusal to write politically relevant poetry after Liberation had ruined his literary career. But he kept writing secretly, even courting Grandma, his "Moon Jewel Beauty," in lyrics years ago in Shanghai. Then the Cultural Revolution began and he was put in a cowshed.

"Father, try the roast duck," Mama said, trying to postpone the quarrel Grandma provoked.

"Is that so?" Grandpa muttered back at Grandma. "We'll see tomorrow!"

His veiled reference to tomorrow's visit to the Office of Last Hope brought troubled looks to his sisters' faces.

"Isn't your belly full of bitterness yet?" Eldest Sister sighed.

Grandma frowned at her. She wanted Grandpa to fight the Party

Grandpa
and his
newly wed
third wife,
Moon Jewel
Beauty, in
Shanghai.

hard and win whatever he could. But Eldest Sister had suffered more and only wanted peace. She had witnessed her Kuomintang husband's execution with their three children after Liberation. Then they had paid the Party's one-yuan bullet fee and dragged his body to the crematory, living as outcasts in their village till the Cultural Revolution came when they were put in cowsheds and labor camps for their Kuomintang connection.

"Eldest Sister is right," Second Sister spoke up. "Hear her. Be happy for what you've been given, and for what you have left."

Second Sister's husband was hanged in a Sichuan cowshed in the first year of the Cultural Revolution—a murder called suicide. She and their eight children had come and cut his body down from the tree. Most of them were later put in the same cowshed. Her eighteen-year-old son, tortured there by the Red Guard, had both his legs broken when he was run down by a car while trying to escape. His brother fled to a tiny island off the southern coast, where he lived seven years as a fugitive. Mama said he had come home changed.

Third Sister glared fiercely at Grandpa. This talk, with its forbidden subtext, disturbed her. She considered Grandpa the agent of discontent in the family, and waged an ongoing campaign to convert him back to faith in the Party by proving the Party right—which only made him angrier and more determined than ever to do battle.

"This is why you didn't get full exoneration!" she erupted. "You won't be reformed until you trust in the Party's righteousness! This is your test!" She lectured not only Grandpa, but all of us. "Fight the Gang of Four, not the Party, which has suffered more than any individual!" She dramatically waved her arm, almost knocking over the soy-sauce bottle. "The Party led China into the light! It is self-cleansing and pure! Even its mistakes are honorable and lead to greater justice later on!"

Grandpa called Third Sister "Screw Spirit Grandma," a "Maoism-Marxism parrot" who lived "to justify the Party's errors." Before Liberation, she had been an underground Communist agent in Kuomintang-held Chong Qing, where many thousands of underground Party members had died. But in the Cultural Revolution, after all her heroic service, she was called a Kuomintang spy and sent to a labor camp for nine years.

"She's right, father," Mama timidly agreed. "Besides, it's too risky. Best not stir up a wave. Who knows what the next campaign will bring? What you do now may be used against you then."

"Who knows," echoed Second Sister.

All heads but Third Sister's nodded sagely. Mama had voiced the secret fear. Ba, busy sweeping the tenderest pieces of duck into his bowl, murmured in assent. Plopping a big juicy piece into his mouth, he began chewing and talking, waving his chopsticks.

"Mmmmph! To win here you must be a big criminal or a big hero. Then you get everything. Look at our high cadres. Warlords! They take the meat while the rest of us fight like starved dogs for one skinny bone! Look at Chairman Liu Shaoqi. So many years we spat on him for the Party, and then he's the first one exonerated! Look at the Gang of Four. Even locked up, they live better than us. Jiang Qing's prison cell is nicer than my apartment! She has padded walls and we don't even have a carpet! And she drinks milk and eats an egg every day! It makes me burn! We're small potatoes, worth less than a fart! All our words only make the room stink!"

Ba snatched another piece of duck and stuffed it angrily into his mouth. Grandpa's eyes lit up and burned. He was angrier at the Party than anyone I had ever seen. His scowl held down a volcano. It drove him as it ate him up from inside. I shivered at the crazy, criminal words he spoke against the Party in his thunder voice.

"China has thousand-year rot!" "The Party has betrayed the people!" "I will never eat bitter and call it sweet for the Party!" And "I'll make the Party pay more than sesame-seed comforting fees and stinking half-exonerations!"

Grandpa's wine-soaked belly stored decades of bitterness. He couldn't forgive or forget his family's suffering. And he bore a terrible guilt, convinced he had brought his children to ruin. Grandpa turned his sad eyes on Mama, who had to publicly "drawn the line" with him to join the Party at seventeen. Wearily, he emptied his wineglass in a long, reckless swallow.

"You all take your sunny thoroughfare," he said. "I'll cross my single-log bridge. Tomorrow I go to the Office of Last Hope."

This was his final word. Ba snatched one last slice of duck from the plate and sneaked into the kitchen. Mama grabbed several dishes and followed him. Now Grandma Moon Jewel spoke up, like gleeful firecrackers going off after a cannon.

"Good! You fight hard, my Dead Old Man! I want at least a few good years with you! Otherwise, what a waste!" But from her tone of voice and her look at Grandpa, I saw he was her secret hero.

Next morning Mama, Grandma Moon Jewel, and Grandpa's three sisters went to the Summer Palace. And Mama had me escort Grandpa to the Office of Last Hope at Zhong Nan Hai Gate. Behind this massive gate and immense stone walls lay the Forbidden City. Here ancient petitioners had kowtowed till their foreheads' blood stained the pavilion stones, hoping the emperor would hear their pleas and render justice. When the Cultural Revolution ended, the tradition of seeking justice at Zhong Nan Hai Gate began again.

Grandpa and I arrived to find hundreds of people standing and squatting in a line before the gate. These were Last Hope People, their cases closed by local Party officials. The little alley news hummed with their tales of persecution and torture: tales of family members murdered or missing; of wives and daughters raped by cadres still in power; of corrupt Party officials who protected themselves by suppressing evidence and threatening, harming, even killing those who persisted in seeking justice.

As my eyes stole through the crowd, my senses recoiled at their desolation; their torn, filthy clothes, starved, haunted faces, and terrible wounds; their limbs maimed or missing; their bodies and faces disfigured and scarred. Some behaved strangely, maddened by suffering, shouting, twitching, weeping, babbling, hysterical, or silent.

And the sharp, sickening odors of urine, excrement, and undefinable illness permeated the air.

Grandpa winced, silently surveying the crowd, and his wrinkled old face went tighter than a walnut. We went to the end of the line. A skinny clerk came by handing out numbers to newcomers. Our number was nearly three hundred.

"Don't lose your ticket," the clerk instructed. "We renumber every four hours. If you go to the bathroom, have someone save your place. If we renumber while you're gone, you'll have to start at the back of the line."

Grandpa clutched his ticket in his four fingers. I stood behind him like a nervous shadow. Gloomy and preoccupied, he stared at the two PLA soldiers with rifles guarding the massive red gate. Ahead of us in line, an old blind farmer with dark, leathery skin stood beside a tiny girl in a dirty little jumper. His eye sockets were holes carved deep in his head. A string tied to his wrist was fastened around her waist so he wouldn't lose her. He held a battered tin cup painted with fading red characters reading LONG LIVE PEOPLE'S COMMUNE. A drooling man stood by his old father, clutching an ash box to his chest. A woman with half her face burned crouched, nursing a baby, in the square beyond the gate. Passersby stared at her. A silver-haired grandma leaning on a stick limped up to a guard, knelt down, and kowtowed at his feet. Her forehead met the pavement and she held a petition outstretched in one hand. But he ignored her with military firmness.

I saw people from many provinces, heard strange accents and dialects, recognized the features of various regions and tribes. There were thick-bodied Mongolians with sheer foreheads and fierce warrior faces wearing sheepskin coats and clumsy leather boots; small-boned, narrow-eyed Cantonese with two-dimensional faces, their baggy trousers rolled to their knees fisherman's style; dark, leathery-skinned Tibetans whose piercing onyx eyes I could hardly look away from, their coarse hair like black wire under colorful Sherpa caps; lizard-eyed Korean-border Chinese with sleek, flat noses and proud, noble faces; and a strange, round-eyed, bearded white Chinese from Ulu Moochi on the Russian border, wearing ragged tribal clothes and moccasins. His curly blond hair stuck out in tangles around a face as long as a wolf's. A noisy crowd surrounded him, gaping in amazement.

Hours dragged by. Suddenly, the heavy red gates lurched and floated open and a shining black Red Flag limousine rolled out, silent as a cloud and longer than a dragon. White curtains covered its tinted passenger windows. Instantly everyone awoke. The two soldiers snapped salutes and froze in the hot sun. The kowtowing old woman, still on her knees, stared up at the creeping limousine in whose plush, air-conditioned chamber a high cadre people's servant rested. Was it Deng Xiaoping? Would he stop to hear our petitions, and give justice to his people?

A horn like a ship's whistle exploded the silence. The engine growled in warning. People scattered like frightened chickens. The burned woman looked up dazed and lowered her nursing infant, exposing her naked breast. Before she could move, the limousine roared and lunged past, missing her by a foot. Black fumes spread out in a cloud and enveloped her.

We stared as the limousine sped away down Chang An Avenue to vanish in a ripple of heat and black smoke. Then the gate began to close. Instinctively, people moved toward it. But a soldier sprang forward, his hand upraised as if to push them back.

"Halt!" he barked. "It's not open yet!"

The spell broke. People began talking excitedly. I looked up at Grandpa, who stared after the vanished limousine. I saw hate burning in his eyes. In a moment, he turned and handed his number to an old man behind us. For the first time he looked down at me.

"Let's go," he said quietly.

The last week of his visit, Grandpa didn't touch his case file. He

From the "Exoneration Tour": in the back row, Ba, Grandpa, Ting; in the front, Third Sister, Eldest Sister, Second Sister, Moon Jewel Beauty, Jaia, and Mama.

had Mama return his reference materials to the library. Each morning he went to a nearby park to do tai chi. He became a tourist, almost a grandpa. And we became almost a family, visiting the Temple of Heaven, the Forbidden City, Bei Hai Park, the Underground Palace, and the Great Wall.

For days after our visit to the Last Hope line, no one dared ask Grandpa about his quest. They knew something had happened. Mama asked me privately, but I didn't know. We had talked to no one. At our family meals, Grandpa had a faraway look and hardly spoke. One evening, Grandma bluntly broached the subject of his campaign.

"Hey, old man!" she said. "What's happening with our cases?"

Grandpa regarded her, silent and aloof. Then he said simply, "There is no justice left in China."

The Office of Last Hope stayed open for a year. Then one day I passed by and the line was gone. I wondered if the people had all been helped. Years later, I learned the office had been closed without explanation. Resolving these cases required digging up secrets the Party felt were better left buried. So it closed the Office of Last

Hope and sent the people away. Many of them wandered for years as living ghosts on the streets of Beijing.

At the time of Grandpa's visit, his bitterness toward the Party offended me. I sympathized more with Third Sister's Party-line orthodoxy. But Grandpa was a lonely Don Quixote fighting windmills for justice; a hero-fool choosing honor over obedience at a terrible price; a bold wanderer rejecting the safe, sunny thoroughfare to cross his own fated single-log bridge.

"Better an empty life than a hero's death," cautioned a proverb of our time.

But to this slave philosophy of fear and resignation, Grandpa had replied boldly in the spirit of an ancient poet he loved, "I would rather be broken jade than flawless clay."

Light and Shadow

I was changing. My body grew shaped in waves. I had strange feelings and thoughts. I lived in urgency. I dreamed about boys, watched them secretly in class, noticed their eyes, their movements, their changing voices, and the way they laughed. I felt awkward, nervous, self-conscious. I longed to be invisible, to watch the world and not be seen, to live on a distant star. I wondered who I was, who I would become. Mama noticed my changing and grew restless and anxious about me—and critical.

"Jaia is just too tall," she said to her coworkers when I visited her one afternoon. "A big leaf on a thick branch."

I felt ugly. I wanted to be a gold leaf on a jade branch, as an old expression described the ideal woman. The Party said the best women were Iron Girls, the unstoppable village worker girls with iron arms and legs, who leveled mountains, dug reservoirs, built roads and dams; who walked like the wind for Chairman Mao, carrying hundred-jin sacks of rice and corn on their iron backs, and baskets of rocks and buckets of water slung on poles over their iron shoulders.

But I didn't want to be an Iron Girl. Mama caught me looking in her mirror once too often. She called it a useless act of vanity, shallow, stupid, and a waste of time. I secretly examined myself in the rusty bathroom mirror hanging over our basin and grew deeply disappointed. My face looked ordinary and plain. I had none of Mama's beauty or charm. I had Ba's strong legs and too many muscles on my arms and chest from swimming. No matter what the Party said, everyone secretly admired a gold leaf on a jade branch and thought Iron Girls were ugly. And I was an Iron Girl.

I was growing wild, out of control, rising like a monsoon river. Though one or two years younger than my classmates, I was the tallest student. Years ago, Little Plum had warned that if I did not stop growing I would be taller than Chairman Mao. Then no man would marry me. She had told me if I stayed under an open umbrella indoors I would stop growing. I hadn't believed her then. Now I was worried.

For two months, when Mama was not home, I fixed my umbrella open over my table while I studied. I tied it to my headboard at night, leaning open over my pillow while I slept. One night, Mama caught me asleep under it and made me stop. She called it superstitious anti-science and against Chairman Mao's teaching. Besides, it didn't work.

In my fourteenth year I entered a state of grace. It had no dramatic beginning; it drew me in unawares. Peace descended on me like snow, and I surrendered to it almost without volition. Gradually, I lost all concern for self, family, school; I ceased wondering whether life would work out or not. I knew it would. The mysterious world revealed itself floating in a vast sea of exquisite harmony. An infinite wheel turned the sun, earth, moon, and stars, spun the seasons in their cycles, and made dynasties rise and fall. A mysterious force turned deserts green, melted glaciers, drew the tides. It opened blossoms and drove tender shoots through the frozen earth. Even the boiling, churning, wonton course of history followed a golden path to a great, heroic destiny. Life was magical, miraculous, and good.

In this state, I conceived a fantasy of a beautiful Chinese goddess, a fairy-tale being. She seemed to be a part of my new condition, perhaps even its cause or source. I thought of her daily as if she were an intimate friend. I communed with her, absorbed her perfect presence. She was peaceful, loving, angelic, and glorious; I believed she had come from heaven.

Her slender body, serene face, and long shining hair appeared often to my inward vision. Her smile and sparkling eyes were like a baby's. Pure and direct, they looked inside me and revealed me to myself. By her light, I often felt ashamed for my wrong doing and thinking in daily life. She was a shining mirror, reflecting my imperfections to me in order to correct and restore my spirit. She was a reminder of a wholeness I had forgotten. She made me see a purpose to my life of flesh and led me to a fearless, bright, and peaceful center of my being.

Over time my imagination explored her qualities, her history, her miraculous nature. My visionary musings seemed spontaneous acts of creation and discovery. She had witnessed endless births, deaths, resurrections; the millennial rise and fall of passions; the whirlpool of love and hate. All-seeing and all-knowing, she watched over the sparrow's eggs, the mountain creatures, and the children of men. To her, the planets and stars were dust motes scattered in the fields of space. She was a source of miracles, an enchanted healer, a magical dancer. Her wisdom was beyond genius, science, or art. And she loved everyone. For in her eyes all were destined for the peace, joy, and glory of her own radiant nature.

Through her eyes, I glimpsed a vision that lit up my soul. For months I walked through life down a broad, paved golden avenue, watched over, taken care of, guided. I breathed new life from an indescribable realm, and heaven's light shone down into my being.

I felt things in a new way: the metallic radiance of poplar trees; people's splashing laughter; the rich, poignant smell of fried greens;

the liquid orange sun setting in our rectangle window; streetlamps pouring down cascades of silver light that swooned in pools in the streets; the electrified air rising from the earth in huge scintillating waves to fill the sky.

But inarticulate and intoxicated, without a need or ability to speak of my experience, I could not share my vision with anyone. Mama and Ba, our neighbors and friends, the people in the streets, didn't notice. I saw them asleep, dreaming frantic, hopeful illusions which they mistook for real, standing before a curtain that would one day rise. And I knew they were only a dream away.

As before, I lived swallowed up by the masses around me. But I was at peace, while they struggled bravely in pain, bent with invisible burdens, hoping, fearing, wondering. Sometimes, in the crowded streets, an inner quietness crept into my heart. And I felt an extraordinary mystery. We were children lost in play, alive, bewildered, not knowing our source, our purpose, or our destiny.

It seemed we had entered these bodies to witness, experience, and feel life at its source. And one day we would realize this peace together and surrender our hatred and revenge, resolve our contradictions, drop our burdens, put down our hoes, guns, dustpans, and butcher knives, and become one family.

We lived in a mystery we could not grasp or explain. Yet its presence could not be denied. It was more subtle than a mist, more exquisite than a rainbow, more ordinary than dust, more mysterious than silence. And it contained the whole of life within itself. It emanated from the sea of faces surrounding me, and I loved them all. Then everything in me grew calm. For I knew we were all its children, born from and playing within its luminous form.

I spent many afternoons reading in Beijing Library. Only high cadres and workers with company research passes could enter a library, and few came. So Mama and her coworkers took long naps, gossiped, and knitted for hours. Knitting absorbed their passions and made them happy. They sat in one of the great world libraries surrounded by classics of all cultures and eras, and the only books and magazines I ever saw them read were on knitting.

Pouring themselves into this safe art made them accomplished craftsmen. They knitted shields against chaos—orderly rows of stitches in measured symmetry, unlike their lives, which chaos had unraveled. They hand-copied exotic patterns from foreign magazines onto engineering draft paper and made elaborate, military-coded charts with darkened squares, crosses, and complex shadings to represent raised weft and lowered warp threads, three-dimensional popcorn knots, and needle points for paisley and fancy Venetian lace.

Mama's United Nations Information Department grew renowned for its knitting expertise. Women and even some men pilgrimaged from other departments for instructions and updates on the latest international fashion trends, respectfully calling Mama and her coworkers Lao Shur, "Teacher," and even Shi Fu, "Master."

I sat nearby with my nose in my books, discovering a world of banned literature. I also read foreign literature; biographies, fairy tales, novels. I read *The Scarlet Letter* and saw a familiar struggle victim in Hester Prynne. I wept over the Little Match Girl dying in the street, and the Little Mermaid trading her freedom for unobtainable love and happiness, dissolving heartbroken in the waves and turning to foam. I thrilled as Madame Curie discovered the first glow of radium in the dark; at Beethoven composing musical masterpieces in his deafness; at Helen Keller, locked in a world of silent darkness, achieving liberation through an inner light.

I read Chinese history: how Ch'in-dynasty emperor Shih Huang-ti buried all the scholars in his kingdom alive and burned all the books; how Han-dynasty writer-historian Ssu-ma Ch'ien was castrated by his emperor for writing true history, then went on to complete his legendary twelve-volume epic; how Qin-dynasty minister

Shang Yiang was torn apart by five warhorses for implementing just reforms; how our emperors indulged in pools of wine and forests of meat while the people lived and died in wretched poverty.

I read of our modern heroes like sixteen-year-old Liu Hulan, the rebel patriot captured by the Japanese invaders, who walked through her village facing her enemies, head raised, eyes clear, her fearless young spirit unbowed. She would be slaughtered under the knife, her short, brave walk to death and her hero's spilled blood serving the liberation of her motherland.

I studied the works of master calligraphers and diligently began to practice this ancient art. I discovered our classical poetry; words used in ways I had never seen, an alien language of sublime sensuality, new to me, yet thousands of years old. Its haunting depths of beauty and sorrow opened my heart. I felt ecstatic and guilty. I knew it was forbidden to read these works. But I couldn't stop. Over time I memorized three hundred Song and Tang Dynasty poems. I was surprised to learn from Mama that children in every generation before mine had memorized these poems. Only my Red Generation had never heard of them.

I sat beside Mama and her library coworkers, former scholars, writers, and artists, some fluent in several languages. They had attained great knowledge and skill in their fields, and spent years in cowsheds, prisons, and labor camps because of it. They were steeped in the richness of our heritage. I now looked to them as precious teachers, and listened to their discussions.

"Old Zhou, how many stitches do you use to make that fishbone stitch look so good around the neck? How many for the weft and warp threads?"

"Little Jing, where did you get that triple-ply nylon yarn? I've searched all over Beijing, but I can't find it anywhere!"

"Old Yao, your seamless sweater looks like it was made in heaven!"

"Don't waste all your time reading, Little Jaia," they advised me. "What can you do with so much book knowledge? Learn to knit!"

So I did. Gloves. Slippers. A scarf. But I kept on reading.

One afternoon a man came into the library to see Mama. He told her Ba was having a dirty ghost-mixing affair with his wife, an actress in Ba's studio. He asked Mama to help him stop Ba from making his wife a stinking shoe behind his back.

"It isn't true," Mama said. "I don't know what you're talking about."

She knew it was true, but couldn't admit it to a stranger. Who knew who he really was or what he really wanted? The man was desperate, to ask for her help. What could she do?

"Must I kill him?" the man said, raising his voice.

Mama's coworkers looked in their direction.

"You must leave," Mama told him. "What you do is your business."

He looked at her a moment, then left. Mama told her coworkers and they urged her to divorce Ba. Not long after, Mama told Ba she wanted to leave him and submitted a petition for divorce to her work unit. I was ecstatic. But Ba was shocked. Now that Mama wanted what he had thought he wanted, he didn't want it anymore.

Mama's coworkers immediately began matchmaking for her, plotting her revenge against Ba. They fiercely competed in placing their candidates before her, arguing back and forth over their merits.

"Old Jin is best. Mr. Hua walks like a crooked melon!"

"Old Jin looks like a cracked date! Chan is best!"

"Chan! Are you kidding? He smells like a sour pear! Old Tao is best for sure!"

"No, no, no! His ears are the size of palm fans!"

"That's good! Big ears are lucky! Buddha had big ears!"

"Wasn't Buddha antirevolutionary the past ten years?"

"Wasn't everybody?"

"Well, when we were in the cowshed I didn't see Buddha protecting you with his big elephant ears!"

"Yes, but Chairman Mao said, 'Seek the truth from facts.' Big ears have many advantages."

"Name one!"

"They are windy on a hot summer day. Every time Old Tao turns his head, you get a free breeze!"

Old Tao, a widower poet from the periodicals-indexing office, became candidate number one for Mama's next husband. Old Tao could smuggle them copies of the new seasonal patterns, colors, and fashion forecasts from the foreign magazines in his office. A Liberation veteran and exiled intellectual, Old Tao wrote passionate patriotic poems about Chairman Mao, the Party, and the revolution and sent them to magazines for publication. I first met him in the library cafeteria, where he tried to win Mama's heart by pleasing me with his magic tricks.

"Watch this, Little Jaia," he said. "It's called Tropical Fish."

I imagined him pulling exotic colorful fish wriggling from his hat and sleeves or plucking them from my ears. Instead, he poured steaming hot water into his tea jar and set a piece of paper on top, followed by strips of newspaper. The strips began to writhe, twist, and curl, looking vaguely like fish in a hot wok. Who did he think he was fooling? But his eyes watched my face so eagerly that I had to act surprised. He roared a laugh of pleasure, and I immediately loved him. His sweet, wrinkled, childlike face radiated kindness and fatherly love.

"Do you want me to show you how I did it?" he asked mysteriously. "You can show your little friends!"

I pretended to learn his secret trick. He began coming over to Mama's department daily to talk with her and show me new tricks. He took me for walks in the library compound, to the parks and the zoo. He treated me as his daughter and urged me to become writer too, and serve the Party with my pen.

Before long I was begging Mama to marry him. I dreamed of our new life together. He would move into our apartment and we'd be a family. We'd have a new crystal water pitcher in a frosted cherry-blossom pattern with matching glasses, an embroidered tablecloth, and pearl-white lace curtains opening on the crisp blue sky. And a big, red, wedding paper-cut pasted on the front door would say "Double Happiness." Ba would be in prison. I found myself joyfully planning their wedding as if it were my own.

Mama liked Uncle Tao and encouraged his attentions, yet kept an ambiguous distance. And Uncle Tao waited patiently for his love to be returned. But I saw her heart moving slowly toward his. And I was happy.

In school, I made my closest friends since Little Plum. Our gang of five girls and four boys defied the taboo against girls and boys talking or being friends. We ignored the gossip and loved each other like brothers and sisters. For three years, we gathered in one another's homes, drinking tea, eating dried sunflower seeds, and passionately planning the future of China as if we had been appointed leaders of our generation.

We'd end rationing of peanut butter and walnuts; solve traffic problems by inventing flying bicycles; permit people to exchange letters with foreigners and visit their countries; let all children live with their parents; shut down all labor camps; stop class wars; and broaden people's vision by promoting science, art, and literature. We'd turn Party leaders into elected officials who could be voted in or out of office. And everyone would be able to say what he really thought. Our country would be better for our generation. And maybe the world. Our group's slogan was "The Cantonese dare to eat everything. We Beijingese dare to say everything!"

Of course, many things we dared not say, many criticisms and observations we dared not make, and many questions we dared not ask. But Mama and Ba listened to our conversations, disapproving.

"Don't fool with fire!" Ba fumed at us. "A bunch of milk-stinking kids talking politics! How many people got bulleted for commenting on things they shouldn't have mentioned? If I turned you in now, you wouldn't see sunlight for ten years!"

I saw Uncle Tao often and spent much time in his Jasmine Alley socialism yard. He was a father, mentor, and friend who taught me, disciplined me, cooked meals for me. We read together and discussed poetry, novels, plots, and characters. He even gave me half of his desk to use, to practice my writing and calligraphy, and we dipped our brushes in the same inkwell. Uncle Tao encouraged me to become a writer, thinking I would follow in his footsteps.

His patriotic poetry, published in newspapers and magazines, finally got him invited into the Writers' Association. Now he was an official poet. And every time he had a new poem published in a magazine, he spent part of his royalties on a big fish for our celebratory meal. We cooked it with colorful vegetables, and I imagined I was Uncle Tao's long-lost daughter come home. After dinner I went outside to catch water in the kettle to wash dishes and make tea. The neighbors sniffed the fishy air like hungry cats and talked to me good-humoredly about Uncle Tao's literary luck.

"That Old Tao, each character he writes earns a jin of fish!"

"Too bad I was a book-burning activist in the Cultural Revolution. Otherwise he might give me the leftover tail."

"It's strange," an old man once told me, seeming puzzled, "how words suddenly became precious again."

"Yo!" his neighbor joked with him. "The policy changed way back—two weeks ago! Don't you listen to the radio?"

"I'll start writing poems if the price of food keeps going up!"

"Ya! The only thing that doesn't go up now is Deng Xiaoping's height and our salaries!"

"Ai ya . . ." Everyone sighed in consensus.

Though I loved Uncle Tao and his reputation thrived, I felt something missing in his poems of noble idealism and romantic devotion to the Party. He hated the new poems of the younger generation. They evoked love without the Party as its object, and introduced darker personal themes. Uncle Tao called these writers egoistic fishbowl poets, moaning without real pain while admiring their sad reflections in the mirror. He warned me to be extremely careful of what I read. An innocent mind could easily be poisoned. I did not tell him I was already reading these new writings.

One night Ba stumbled into the house so badly injured he could barely walk. When I saw his puffed face, an unrecognizable mass of cuts, bruises, and abrasions, and his blood-spattered pants and shirt, I broke into sobs. Ba mumbled about being hit by a bus, then staggered and fell moaning into his bed.

Mama removed his pants, jacket, and shirt. His legs were also bruised and cut. I brought a rag and a basin of hot water, and she began washing his wounds. Seeing Ba like this shocked and terrified me. I took his clothes, damp and heavy with blood, into the kitchen and plunged them into a pail of water. When I squeezed, a cloud spread out of the blue cloth to fill the pail, turning the water red. I pulled my hands out in shock. Then my tears were falling into this bucket of Ba's blood, and I was ready to forgive him everything if only he would live. It seemed that only disaster could bring us together. I wrung his blood out, again and again, emptying the bucket and refilling it till the water grew faint pink and finally stayed clear.

Ba refused to go to the hospital. So Mama stayed home and nursed him, sitting by his bed day and night. Her devotion to Ba was still there after all their bitterness in love and all his betrayals. She looked so tenderly at him, so hopeful as he lay there oblivious in his delirium. When Ba came back to this world, he and Mama seemed turned to each other in a new way.

One afternoon Ba groaned and sighed gravely, his face crimson, his hair askew. Tears of sincerity swirled in his limpid eyes. He looked up at Mama and me like an injured child lying at the bottom of a well. Finally, he turned to Mama and expressed profound remorse for his unforgivable mistakes.

"My dear, I've hurt you terribly. I failed you! Abused you! I betrayed our love! I hate myself! Let me be born as a pig in my next life to pay for my crimes!

"I love you," he continued. "You are no cheap woman. Anyone can add an extra flower on a brocade, but how many will fetch the coal in winter? You are the dearest to my heart. How much merit my ancestors must have accumulated for me to have found you. You have swan-white virtue! And I am a man with a lizard heart."

He wiped a stream of real tears from his cheeks, blinking his lizard eyes. I had seen Ba's studio's movies, with their contrived dialogue and stilted acting. This was better. Mama was sobbing with him now, reaching for a handkerchief. But I could not let myself believe him.

Ba was swept away on a wave of remorse, self-pity, and sorrowful eloquence. He had become the wounded Red Army hero in the revolutionary drama *Yi Mong Mountain,* whose noble suffering moved the heart of the beautiful peasant widow.

"I want to give up evil and return to good, correct the tilted and straighten the slanted. I want make a new path and start fresh with you and our daughter. No more wicked thoughts, evil influences, and heretical ideas. I'll remold my subjective world while changing the objective world. I beg for your forgiveness. Help me cleanse my filthy soul, change my spiritual complexion, and renew my flesh and bone. Don't throw me away. Lift me up! Give me a chance to perform good deeds! Let me atone for my guilt! I beg you!"

This was truly Ba's most amazing performance. He quavered and whimpered, his voice rose and fell in all the right places, and his tears did not stop as he delivered thought-reform lines used in a thousand political meetings. With a keen agony, it seemed he would scoop out his heart from his chest and offer it to Mama as barter for atonement. But he didn't. Several times, he glanced across the room at me. I dared not go near him. My face flushed at Mama's gullibility. She believed Ba. He was saying everything she had wanted to hear for years. And he seemed convinced by his own performance.

He had memorized too many scripts and survived too many struggle meetings and campaigns, negotiating the changing waves and perilous shoals. And his long immersion in the pickle vat of third-class movie production values had marinated him to his bones. Mama sobbed and sighed. Ba swore and promised to be true, ". . . till the ocean dries up and the mountains wear down."

Mama knew herself too little. Ba knew Mama too well.

"Ai . . . " she said shyly, tenderly, at last. "Let the past be over."

I left the room. Mama finished Ba's script. She is healed. The family is reunited. The moon waxes full. Everyone lives happily ever after. To be continued. . . . The screen flashes and the reels wind to a stop.

Mama turned off the light, and their conversation became a susurration in the dark, mixed with odd noises, patches of silence, and Mama's girlish giggling. I couldn't take it anymore and shut my door. Why light a candle for the blind? Mama warmed a frozen snake in her bosom. And I feared a poison bite would follow the thaw.

That week Mama withdrew her divorce petition. Ba finally healed. He even joked about his near-fatal traffic accident.

"You thought I looked bad," he bragged. "You should have seen the bus!"

His sweetness lasted two weeks before he went back to his old habits. Then he packed his bag and left home again. But Mama was still in love with him. To my dismay, she drew back from Uncle Tao just as it seemed their hearts would meet. But he became my best friend. I raged inwardly over her mad choice. Uncle Tao loved her dearly and Ba couldn't love at all. Now I watched her choose for her own strange reasons to remain unloved.

Not long after that, the stranger who had visited Mama at the library called to tell her he and his friends had taught Ba a bitter lesson, to cure him of his bourgeois appetites. "Next time," the man told her, "we'll kill him." So Mama learned the true cause of Ba's terrible injuries. Months later, Mama learned from old Ministry of Culture friends who worked near Ba that he was having a new affair.

Nursing Ba as he lay vulnerable and weak before her and hearing his longed-for confession had raised Mama's hopes. She had saved Ba. Now he had risen from near death, healed by her loving care, and crawled into another woman's bed.

Months passed. My ecstatic vision, so clear, began to fade as the world swirled in chaos, oblivious to this peace. Cancerous doubts invaded my mind. Other people seemed so urgently busy, frantically motivated, passionately absorbed in their anxiety, hopefulness, and desperation. A powerful vision, obscure to me, intoxicated and infused them. A ceaseless hunger drove them. Their purposeful intensity drew me irresistibly to follow them, to join in their adventure.

All their milling in the streets, shouting at merchants, their gossiping, worrying, fighting, seeking, and grasping seemed to give them life. I felt they pursued a rare treasure, knew a great secret that gave their frantic lives meaning. And in their blind, mad rush toward their goal, they trampled, without noticing, the mystery that possessed my heart.

I began to wonder, Was I missing out, chasing a mirage, standing on the wrong side of the curtain believing in illusions? I felt ignorant. I needed to test my own ability off the golden avenue, to join them and find what they sought, to see how I would do and what I was made of. I thought I could return at any moment, that my vision of life's purity would never fade.

Part of me resisted, not wanting to go that way. But step by step I was drawn back to that other world, without the will or clarity to hold my place, to be blinded by the red dust again. One day, I realized I had lost my vision and the grace of the goddess who had been my companion and guide. I was reborn in chaos, disconnected, bewildered by life. The mystery had vanished. The silence had disappeared. In their place I found a fearful buzzing, a shrill emptiness, a restless drive. For this, I had traded my peace.

After Ba's last betrayal, something in Mama changed. She grew more possessive of me. I became her hope, her burden, her bridge to the uncertain future. She feared my unknown destiny and wondered how I would live. She forged me for survival through invulnerability, criticizing my social awkwardness, my average intelligence, my serious look, my reluctance to flatter people when necessary, and my strange, quiet character. She said I was not fit for the big people's world. And she mistrusted my friends.

"You waste yourself on your friends!" she argued with me. "Who are they to you? What have they ever done for you? How can you trust them? You never know which one will be your enemy!"

"But Mama, they're not my enemies!"

"Anyone can be your enemy! In a split second! Even your best friend! I've seen it many times. You were my enemy in the camp when you accused me of not loving Chairman Mao because I dropped his pin in the mud!"

"But Mama, I didn't mean . . . "

"My best camp friend became my enemy, reporting my harmless words to the PLA and making them sound evil! Ba is my enemy every time he ghost-mixes with his cheap women behind my back! Look at Chairman Mao and his Long March comrades. They all turned on each other! He had to kill them one by one! Or they would do the same to him. Everyone has the enemy seed in his heart, waiting a change of weather to sprout. And your arrogant political discussions with your friends! Idiot! Behind every wall is an ear! The neighbors might hear! Who knows, one of you might report the others! And if none of you do, who says I might not?" She gave me a strange, urgent look. "Don't you understand?"

Mama was preparing me for life in the bitter sea.

In my junior year, all China's high school students were divided into levels according to their grades. The top twenty percent in each grade went into Priority Classes. They had the best teachers, more class hours, the most rigorous curriculum, more frequent testing, and stood the best chance of being in that three percent of high school graduates who would be allowed to go to college.

My whole group of friends made it into Priority Class. But a fierce competition began, and we stopped our gatherings. With one eye on each other and one eye on the future, we competed in class by day and studied late at night, fueled by black tea. We damaged our eyes and began wearing glasses. We grew anxious, haggard, and unhealthy. And we feared the future. We were fifty drowning children racing to a lifeboat for three. The prolonged, desperate struggle killed our pleasure in learning, separated us from one another, and broke our friendships. That year we began hearing stories of Priority Student suicides all over China.

Meanwhile, Mama poured herself into her work. When I was sixteen, she was promoted to the Beijing Writers' Association. There she wrote magazine articles and translated English-language works into Chinese. She showed a good face in her office and worked hard to prove herself capable, loyal, and trustworthy. She began leading foreign writers' delegations on diplomatic tours throughout China. Mama achieved position. But she still felt vulnerable.

Comrade Lai, Mama's supervisor, was the daughter of Deng Xiaoping's vice premier. Comrade Lai began actively cultivating Mama's friendship. Mama was charming and diplomatic. People instinctively liked her, trusted her, opened up to her. Mama was thrilled and flattered by Comrade Lai's special interest, even grateful and relieved. A friendship with the vice premier's daughter might offer future political protection, ensure a bright career, and open many back doors.

One afternoon Mama came home from work seeming nervous and preoccupied. Ba came home that night. After dinner I heard them in the kitchen talking in low voices. I listened closely. They were discussing Mama's supervisor, Comrade Lai. What I heard shocked me.

Comrade Lai was an agent of the Ministry of Public Security, our KGB, planted in the Writers' Association to uncover suspected antirevolutionaries and secret individualists. And she was recruiting Mama to work under her. I went into the kitchen.

"What's this about Supervisor Lai?" I asked bluntly.

"Hey, cease fire!" Ba said, extremely annoyed. "Who asked you to mix in your mama's business?"

"She has a right to raise her voice in this family." Mama took my side in diplomatic tones. Then I found out Supervisor Lai had offered her an "invisible position" in the Ministry of Public Security.

"Yo, who would have guessed?" Ba shifted into euphoria, trying to steer the mood to one of ecstatic appreciation. He returned to Mama. "Even with your obedient air of harmless stupidity, these sharp Public Security people saw your talents. You'll be a big gray wolf wearing a little white furry sheep's skin. How perfect! I have to wipe my eyes and take a new look at you. Esteem, esteem!"

"You're encouraging her to be a spy!" I was shocked.

"No! A spy opposes the Party!" Mama protested. "This is for the Party!"

"What's wrong with being a spy?" Ba blinked innocently, turning to Mama. "It's patriotic. It honors your ability. Also, now you get the Party's special protection. We all do. Be grateful!" Ba snapped at me. "Even if the wind blows the grass away tomorrow, we won't be touched. This makes your mama a big tree with deep roots. We can stand in her shade. Plus, it's a second job with no extra hours. She gets overtime pay and some of that greasy Party soup they save for the Inner Chamber. After all she's given them, they owe her a little something back. This is justice!"

"Why does the Party still need underground work?" I asked Mama. "And pretending to be someone's friend to get trust, then sending a behind-the-back report—it's not right. Besides, it might be dangerous. What if somebody gets in trouble by mistake, or comes back years later to even the debt?"

We had all heard stories of victims paying back their persecutors with revenge murders years later.

"Ho! She has sets-full of theories! When did you become so smart and cynical? How dumb!" Ba was really mad. "You can't even tell big from small. You Red Guard are truly shallow. No wonder they call you the Lost Generation. You should watch your mouth! You're speaking against the Party even now!"

"Would you do it?" I pinned Ba with a fiery look.

I knew it was a stupid question the moment I asked. Ba blinked and smoothly turned to Mama, smiling cheerfully.

"Of course I would! I envy your mama. She has real proletarian consciousness. Being underground for the Party is heroic! Go see the movie *Shajiabang*. Your mama's just like the heroine. And *Taking Tiger Mountain* had hero Yang Zirong. In fact, every movie has an underground hero. Without underground heroes the Party wouldn't exist! We'd all be Kuomintang Party members today!"

I left the room. Who could argue with Ba's slippery tongue? Later that night, Mama came in to talk to me. She sat at my table looking anxious and fragile. In that moment, I hated Supervisor Lai with her easy insider life and her privileged birth, giving Mama a test like this. Mama looked at me as if I were twisting her arm.

"How can I say no?" she finally said. "Her father is a vice premier. What will it look like to the Party if I refuse? They'll think I'm hiding something! You don't understand. I won't do any harm. They only want to hear about bad people, troublemakers. Your Ba's right. It's patriotic. And it could give us all the Party's shade from now on. Plus practical benefits. This helps you."

Mama was doing this for me, too. It was her way—empty herself to fill me up, sacrifice her present to my future. She probably spent her winters shivering and wondering how to keep me warm. I remembered when I was little how she had sheltered my childhood, how she fed me revolutionary fairy tales and Chairman Mao's teachings, passionately believing our Party was the best thing ever to happen on this earth. She had told me our motherland's bright future would defeat the darkness of the world through communism's inevitable victory. Then we would have the best of everything, she had said. Now her faith and idealism had died, and a fearful obedience had replaced them.

The idea of my lonely, tired Mama being a Security Bureau snitch made me angry and sad. I struggled with myself about it. I judged her, pitied her. I blamed Supervisor Lai, Ba, the Party. I told myself she would be patriotic, working for national security and world peace, protecting our motherland from enemies within.

I finally discussed my feelings about Mama's spare-time spy job with Uncle Tao, to see what he would say. He was surprised at me.

"How can you call it spying?" he asked indignantly. "This is honorable revolutionary work! It's necessary as long as imperialism and antirevolution strive to overthrow our Precious Red Mountain! Class struggle is a never-ending, complex war! Enemies live in our midst! Your mama is being loyal. Loading this heavy responsibility on her shoulders proves the Party's trust in her. I would volunteer if I hadn't been a Black Gangmember. I still have too much egoistic consciousness. Your mama is selfless. This kind of work is the most patriotic! Remember, the Party only aims at bad people and could not be any busier protecting the good ones."

"What about all the mistakes that were made before?" I asked.

"That was the Gang of Four's doing!" Uncle Tao exclaimed hotly. "Don't you listen to the radio? How can you be so narrow-minded as to bring up these cases? And the exonerations followed right away. That was the Party's doing, making up for the Gang of Four's ten million crimes. This proves the Party only works on the positive and not the negative side. You're not confused, like some ignorant people, are you?" He looked at me with concern, and I shook my head, feeling like an antirevolutionary. "You are young. You should believe in our Party. Eliminate all individualism and egoistic instinct from your nature. Purge your heart bright red! Be the Party's humble servant, like the cow that eats grass and squeezes out milk; like the worm that eats leaves and spins out silk; like the coal that burns to ash and radiates heat. Communism is the hope of mankind! Don't hesitate. You'll be led down a forked road and corrupted by the sophistry of our class enemies. I have great hopes for you, Little Jaia! Make your commitment now!"

Uncle Tao spoke passionately, his lyrical eyes shining like Wine Celestial poet Li Bai in a drunken trance, chanting spontaneous, white-hot verses from his inmost fiery core. I felt I was being sworn into the Party under a luminous crossed-axe-and-sickle flag and Chairman Mao's picture, before the Gate of Heavenly Peace.

As I looked at Uncle Tao, my heart filled with admiration. He was no hypocrite, but a true Communist. He wasn't like those Party members who said and did anything to get the greasy soup. Everything he said, he believed and would live and die for. Even though I didn't agree with him, I felt like a shallow, cowardly fraud, living a hidden life, plotting strategy to protect my egoistic self. I admired

Uncle Tao for his unshakable certainty. His ears didn't even look too big now. How I loved him.

Meanwhile, for weeks Mama lived anxiously under the magnifying glass, her lips cracking with the spice of fear as she awaited Supervisor Lai's first underground assignment. The unbearable tension finally resolved itself unexpectedly. Mama had a heart attack. She took several weeks' sick leave from work, and finally informed Supervisor Lai she must regretfully decline her honorable promotion because of her unworthy constitution. Her EKG showed renegade lines, running like cracks through her heart. I was frightened by her condition, but grateful that it had ended her new career before it began.

Ba grumbled about Mama's lost promotion. A big back door of opportunity had slammed shut, leaving us out of the Party's shade. If the wind came up tomorrow and blew the grass away, we would probably go with it.

One day, hoping to inspire me and correct my path, Uncle Tao took me to see Chairman Mao's private home in the old Imperial Palace in Zhong Nan Hai Compound. We passed an ancient pavilion with a nine-dragon water channel carved at the base. We walked through the Imperial Garden between rows of arching willows by a shimmering lake and arrived at his quarters. The guide took us into Chairman Mao's private chambers. To my surprise, his bed was piled and the room was filled with ancient scrolls and manuscripts.

"See Chairman Mao's diligence for the masses' sake?" The guide proudly indicated Chairman Mao's treasured collection of ancient literature, poetry, and calligraphy. "He lived with these books. He stayed up for days and nights reading, writing down his brilliant thoughts and charting the course of history."

Uncle Tao's eyes grew watery at this proof of Chairman Mao's love for the masses. But I was shocked. For years I had read these banned works in the library, guilty as a thief in a treasure cave. Each character I had read felt like a jewel stolen, a crime for which Mama and I might be caught and punished. Now I knew these forbidden works were my cultural heritage. They had been stolen from the people. Chairman Mao had hoarded them like an old landlord in his greedy warehouse, keeping us in the dark. He had devoured the precious banquet of our heritage while we worshipped his Little Red Book. I felt betrayed, yet I knew now I was not a thief.

Uncle Tao still loved Mama, but his love could not reach her. I watched him grow slowly resigned to her friendship, and saw my chance for a new family vanishing before my eyes.

"Mama, don't you love Uncle Tao?" I asked her once. She looked at me as if my question were the stupidest thing she'd ever heard.

"Love is a sickness," she said. "It burns you up and leaves you cold and scarred. It's a game. Whoever gets most from the other wins. That's all. Love is a stalking tiger, an assassin in the shadows. I won't be a victim again! Neither should you! Be the tiger crouching to pounce. Be the one hiding in the shadows. Forget love. Armor your heart. How else can you survive?

"Who can you trust? Everyone wants what you have. Let them in close and they find your weakness, make strategies to defeat you, and take what is in your hands. Women hook and seduce your man with their nasty tricks. They destroy your family and ruin your life. And men fall for your rivals, one after the other, younger than you, to make you old before your time. In every relationship, one person suffers the knife above the heart. Love anyone and he will betray you. Never fall in love. Close your heart and grab all you can. Save it up for your old lonely nights."

I knew Mama's teachings came not from her heart, but from her pain and her fear for my future. She tried to weave me unpierceable armor against life, the way she knitted me sweaters and scarves against the cold.

I didn't want her armor. But slowly I drifted into a familiar darkness. It was everywhere in these disillusioned years; in the gloomy air and the predatory streets; in people's wary, mistrustful eyes; in the Party, ruling by deception and treachery, betraying the sacred trust of the masses it had once liberated.

We were a haunted people, numb, trapped in lies, made cynical by hypocrisy masquerading as the sacred. What was real? What was true? A few clever people climbed a ladder out of the flood to exploit the rest of us. Our Great Helmsman incited us to betray and murder one another to prove our loyalty to him. Now he lay, an immortal corpse in a crystal coffin, posing for posterity while we waited in lines stretching across Tiananmen Square to kowtow like fools.

What could we believe in now? Self-cleansing purity? Screw Spirit morality? Serving the masses, Comrade? Lies! Illusions! Only what we could grab with our hands was real. Only facts, weighed and measured, wouldn't betray us. The only virtue was survival. We urged each other to falseness, warning, "Only speak thirty percent of the truth!"

"The guns always shoot the leading bird!"

"Better a mediocre life than a heroic death!"

Thanks to you, Chairman Mao, to your three million Cultural Revolution deaths, your hundred million exonerated victims, and all the horrors of your decade-long geriatric madness. We close your Little Red Book of fairy tales, where the sublime and the absurd joined hands with a nightmare in a convulsive dance. Where we drank your myth and went mad together, and tore our world apart for your Great Illusion.

Keep your struggle meetings and labor camps, your utopian chaos, and your revolutionary apocalypse. We survived your mad assault on history and don't want any part of you now. We don't want to hear one more story that ends singing your praises. And we don't want to spend our future crouching in your shadow, swimming in your abyss, worshiping your sanitized myth.

What did you teach us through all your chaos, your purges, and your class-hatred wars? To outsmart, flatter, and be slippery, and act dumb to survive. To gird ourselves in steel and wear ambiguous masks. To smell danger, to fear one another and pinch our throats against the truth. That friendship is a practical equation, a shield of flesh in a world of potential enemies, a back door to a better deal. That we are only a wink, a blink, an insignificant flash in the millennial darkness. That the only immortals are Taishan Mountain, the Yangtze River, and You.

I wondered what could happen to me. And I hid behind my mask, shouting slogans, writing tired political posters, radio and newspaper words, echoes of Chairman Mao. I marched and danced the Yanga, waving my red sash and grinning my mask in the Victory Parades we had for each new campaign. Dog today, cat tomorrow. The grass points where the wind blows. "Down with Deng Xiaoping!" becomes "Welcome back, Comrade Deng!" "Oppose feudal Lackey Confucius!" becomes "Study Great Master, Sage Confucius!"

Cynicism armored us all. We feared being duped again. For what horrors might we commit in the next collective madness, following the next Great Leader? Like many people, I armored myself by believing those who had suffered most had brought it on themselves with their hot blood, standing too tall and speaking too loud. We blamed the victims. Who asked them to save us? Did they imagine they were historical heroes dipping courageous ladles in the cyclone soup, shaping the globe like giants, distilling earth from sky?

Someone should have told them, "Ya! Don't get so excited. Your blood pressure will pop out the mercury dial. Sit down! Be a bit humble! Of course you got your mouth washed out with lye and your tongue burned to the root, speaking freely like that. Of course you had your eyes poked out with hot irons, looking so arrogantly at the world instead of lowering your gaze and sighing like a shy girl before Chairman Mao's picture!

"Did you hope to be Chairman Mao—to change history? Chairman Mao was only Chairman Mao because fate chose him. He collided by chance with the lightning bolt of history's fiery need. If fate chose you, of course you'd be a brilliant emperor, chairman, whatever. You'd offer graceful toasts at international banquets. The *People's Daily* would tell how you granted audience to important foreign leaders to discuss issues of common concern in a frank, cordial manner. Your simple words would be prized as jewels, recorded in the history books and studied by future generations.

"At history's pivotal moment you'd sit poised in your command tent, regarding destiny with your ten-thousand-li piercing gaze. You'd devise infallible strategies for crucial battles, guide massive armies, beckon thunder and lightning, chop waves of enemy soldiers down like ripe harvest wheat, and lead your people from victory to victory. After your rise to glory, we'd praise you as the emperor seed, recognize the moment you snouted from your mother's womb. We'd make myths of your humble origins and tell one another:

" 'A herd of smoking dragons coiled beneath his kang on the night he was conceived! He levitated before he walked! His cry was like a silver casting hammer striking pure gold, and his first words prophesied his immortal destiny! He didn't even have a bellybutton or an asshole like the rest of us!

" 'We poor, weak mortals sold our souls for a bowl of rice, while he tightened his belt and manufactured the ultimate destiny! On his way to glory he wrestled with the wind and danced with starving tigers! He rode on a hurricane and smothered tornados in the palm of his hand! He swam in the political abyss and walked laughing through the rain of bullets! And then he conquered heaven!'

"These are the myths we would weave in your name—if history chose you. And when our tap water came we'd think of you, the Well

Driller, our faces flushed with everlasting gratitude. And we'd chant your name and drink to your health and glory for ten thousand years.

"But history didn't choose you. So sit down! Go home! Why risk the only life you have making trouble for the rest of us? Isn't it enough simply to exist? Why raise a pulse about your political ideals? You want to change history? To purify the world? The fish would die if the ocean were too clean!

"And you're just a farmer like the rest of us, even if you can recite the ancient classics. An intellectual is just a peasant who got drunk on a dead man's words, forgot his roots, and imagined he could fly. How many generations past was your family picking corn husk and sorghum from their hair, planting rice shoots in the paddies, their baggy trousers rolled up their muddy legs and their wives squatting to give birth in the proletarian fields?

"Take a look in the mirror and remember Darwin: 'The strongest live and the weakest die.' Then multiply one by nine hundred million and even the strong are lucky to survive. Even the 1.8-meter-tall, handsome-faced, perfect-bodied examples of pure proletarian virtue arrive in truckfuls. A blind man can walk down any street and sweep them up with a broom. But you, with your tilted spine, crooked teeth, and pimple-scarred nose, what can you hope for when the straightest backs worry that their shadows are slanted? Even if you were flawless, your skin like silk, your teeth gleaming like pearls, your forehead square as a cliff, and your jaw jutting like a hoe; if you remained supremely obedient, malleable, bent your perfectly erect spine in the presence of your superiors, never made them feel threatened by your humble existence, made them believe your life was bestowed by their noble hands and your sesame-seed ability was inspired by their greatness; if you poured them tea, lit their cigarettes, and flattered them like a eunuch in the emperor's court day and night forever . . . even then, perhaps, you might only survive your haunted life to die of old age the day before your execution.

"So forget about us. Save yourself! Be ambiguous. If you must make a noise, only speak the allotted thirty-percent truth after you've heard it said first by your betters. Better yet, be a brain-dead block-headed simple wooden idiot waiting for the herd to move first. Then when you hear the new truth on the radio or read it in the newspaper, be completely, enthusiastically enlightened! Let your conversion be passionately displayed! Be a dumb crippled bird suddenly shooting into the sky, flying like a swan and singing like a nightingale, giving all credit to the Great You Know Who. What a touching story of transformation you'll be! People will sob, " 'A thousand-year iron tree blooms! A million-year skeleton rises from a tomb and walks praising the Party and Chairman Mao!' "

This was how the world appeared to my cynical mind in my darkest period. This was our cultural philosophy behind our loyalty masks, forged in chaos by the brutal facts of our daily lives, in the absurd nightmare of our tormented history.

Ba, busier than Chairman Mao, worked diligently to salvage his failed revolutionary career. He felt thwarted by wrongful persecutions and the pettiness of inferior people. All his pleasurable triumphs ended in painful consequences. A cruel fate had followed him like a dangling tail, staining his former glory, ruining present opportunities, and cursing his noble destiny.

He should have been running the whole movie studio instead of one movie crew! He was brilliant! He had wisdom! He was witty, charming, handsome! What was the big deal? So he made a few little mistakes! Chairman Mao made big mistakes! Ba wanted an exoneration, too! People fussed over his trifling errors, made mountains of his molehills. Petty jealousy! Small-mindedness! Peasant consciousness! Little people's prejudiced, narrow hearts! Ba raged over corrupt, incompetent idiots slipping through the spider's web to grab the great prizes he deserved, while he got caught like a fly. Ba was mad!

He and I fought often now. He saw me and felt the shame of the unresolvable dilemma his life had become. I saw him only through the lens of Mama's pain and his betrayals, and I challenged him bitterly at every opportunity. At times I became a crazy person, raging at him, criticizing him, wanting to see him suffer for his whole history of wrongs and family crimes. Ba would roar, mad as a hooligan, "Don't get between your mama and me! Don't make this your battle!"

But I wanted a battle with Ba. And I was gathering ammunition. One winter night, I stared through iced panes down to streets emptied by the white chill. Mama was in Shanghai on a diplomatic tour. Ba, as usual, was gone. Goose-feather snow fell from the invisible sky, on a curved wind, into a creatureless void. I heard footsteps in the silence, coming up the stairs to stop at our door. A soft chink of metal like a doorknob twisting. Then a muffled thud of a gloved hand knocking. Who could be out so late on this cold night?

I padded to the door and opened it. A solitary figure stood motionless in the hall, wrapped in a thick black coat, black gloves, head wrapped in a black scarf, and face hidden behind a white cotton surgical mask. It appeared like a shadow projected by the weak light of the bulb dangling from the ceiling. Except for two bright, glittering eyes.

"What . . . who are you?" I stammered under the glare of those alien eyes.

A clear, measured, emotionless voice came out of the white gauze, indistinguishable as man or woman, cold and precise as a radio.

"Jaia, do you want to know a secret? About your father."

"Ai!"

I tasted coldness in my marrow, staring at the wrapped figure with its chiseled voice, its unblinking eyes staring like an assassin above the white cotton mask.

"Do you want to know the truth about your father?"

The voice came again, cool and insistent, its nature hidden in a dry, sexless tone. Looking up at this ghost standing a head above me, I shivered like a dry husk in the wind.

"Who are you?" I shouted to give myself courage, hoping my neighbors might hear me and open their doors.

"An old friend of your father's."

"Leave! Get out!" I screamed, terrified.

I tried to slam the door. But it banged against a granite hand in a glove.

"Do you want his secret to be buried?" the voice hissed at me through the crack in the door. "Won't you wonder?"

"Get out of here! You don't even have the guts to show your face or use your real voice!"

I was almost crying in anger and terror, pushing the door as hard as I could. But a greater force held it open. The masked face leaned tilted into the gap, staring at me.

"I overestimated you. You're a little coward—your father's daughter. Afraid of the truth!"

The ceramic eyes were black holes in white porcelain spider-webbed with red cracks, eerie and tormented. I pushed harder. Suddenly the hand went slack and the door slammed shut. I locked all three bolts and stood shaking like wheat in a sieve. Cold ice spread from my stomach up through my chest. Footsteps started down the hall and faded, descending the stairs.

That black-shrouded ghost with its radio voice and malignant stare haunted me for weeks, filling me with dread and heating up my rage at Ba. Was it man or woman? Ghost or demon? I felt it stalking me like a shadow through Beijing's wide streets and narrow, twisted alleys, circling and crossing my path, burning with an alien urgency, carrying a secret from the pit of Ba's cryptic past.

For years I had felt the tangible presence of a secret that followed Ba everywhere, made him come and go at strange hours, constantly change his schedule, unpredictably appear and disappear, padlock the compartments of his life from the world, and sleep holding the keys. For years I had wondered: Who was Ba? What crimes had he committed? Now I regretted not asking the ghostly visitor when I had the chance.

I observed Ba carefully the next few days. But the closer I examined him, the more elusive he became. He had the same pitiless eyes as the winter ghost, portals into a world of dark forces and strange urges. He was a haunted shadow armored in human flesh, a spy from the abyss driven by mysterious intentions. But I didn't know if my perceptions were real or simply my own imaginings. For sometimes he seemed a transparent idiot, a comical fool. Yet when I looked at him, I also saw myself. In some ways I was more his daughter than Mama's. I saw his shadow in me, and his strength. And since I could not embrace him, I became his worthy opponent. Our relationship was a battlefield.

One night not long after my strange encounter, I pushed Ba too far. I came into his movie-studio room and found him massaging a woman on his bed. Instead of quietly leaving, I started screaming like a madwoman. Rage shot out of Ba's eyes. He rose from the bed in his shorts, shrieking back at me, his face red as a ripe tomato. I thought it would burst. Ba had finally had enough.

"All right!" he exploded, buttoning his shirt. "All right! You want to try me out, you rabbit's whelp? Are you ready for me? What haven't I fought? Tiger, bear, wolf, soldier! Clear blade in, red blade out! Let's go! Let's settle it right now!"

I couldn't believe my ears. He smashed his huge, meaty palm on the table and it cracked like gunfire. He was rolling up his sleeves, stalking me like a street fighter. I looked into his fierce, burning eyes, and my anger fled. Ba was really going to hurt me! In panic, I turned and ran out the door, down the stairs.

"Oh no! Don't chicken out now!" Ba roared. "Don't cheat me out of this!"

He came bounding after me, his powerful fifty-six-year-old body flexible as a young wolf's. I took three steps at a time, screaming for help. But Ba caught me from behind, grabbing my arm and neck in his powerful hands. I struggled as he shook me. Slowly I twisted around in his iron grip. Then, with all my fear and rage, I sank my teeth into Ba's forearm and tasted his blood.

"Yaaaaa!"

Ba howled like a mad, wounded beast. He released me and stood transfixed, staring at me in shock, pain, and disbelief. Blood seeped from the tooth marks dug deep in his arm. Doors opened and people stared out at us. I ran down the stairs and took one last look at Ba. He stood there deflated, in a pitiful slump, shoulders sagging, examining his wound.

For days Ba covered my bite with a medicine cloth. He even told Mama about our fight, minus the woman in his bed. Mama seemed to sympathize with Ba the most when I opposed him. She told me he felt sad that his own daughter had bitten him and drawn blood. I felt sad, too, but mostly angry. I was Ba's judge. Someone had to punish him, to make him pay. But a week later I apologized. Ba didn't look in my eyes. Waving his hand awkwardly as if it were no big deal, he pursed his lips like a boy and shook his head.

"It's nothing," he mumbled.

But I knew Ba still had my tooth marks on his arm.

Family Matters, American Dreams

Brother Big Honesty graduated university with an electronics degree and was hired by Beijing Electronics Department. He was going to marry his fiancée, Mimi, after a four-year engagement. He would not be returning to his commune after all. To celebrate his new job and his upcoming wedding, he invited me to Hundred Goods, Beijing's largest department store.

"Buy anything you want, Little Sister," he told me proudly.

Reluctant to spend his first-earned money with his wedding coming soon, I got a panda-head fountain pen and a bottle of blue ink, totaling sixty cents.

"So! What did your rich brother buy you?" Ba asked when I came home. I showed him my purchase. "Ha!" he burst out. "What a cheapskate!"

"He said to get anything I wanted," I told Ba. "I picked these."

"You little fool! You had him by his scrawny chicken's neck! Ask for something big! Make him pay in installments! Ha! Ha! Ha!"

He and Mama both thought this was hilarious. But I knew Big Honesty and Mimi needed their money for the wedding. Big Honesty and I had grown close since his return from the countryside five years ago. So he came to me one afternoon, his "precious Little Sister," to discuss his "big problem." We sat at my study table.

"Mimi's family wants a big wedding," he announced mournfully. "She is their first marrying daughter, and the prettiest."

"What do they mean by 'big'?" I asked.

"Big," he groaned. "They want a big wedding party in a big restaurant. They've invited all their relatives and friends—at least fifty people. On the wedding day, I have to hire a big car to pick Mimi up at her house and bring her to a big banquet."

"That's big!" I was impressed. "How much will this cost?"

"I'm not finished yet." Big Honesty heaved a big sigh. "The worst part is the 'colorful gifts' the man has to pay the bride and her family. Mimi's parents want a five-hundred-yuan 'labor fee' for raising her. They want me to give Mimi a new Phoenix bicycle, a sewing machine, an imported Japanese watch, a four-season wardrobe, a TV, a screen-test opportunity in Ba's film studio, a new set of furniture, a room with at least forty square meters . . ."

With each item on the list, Big Honesty's head sank further into his shoulders and his chin drooped down onto his chest. My poor brother! I was shocked by this exorbitant shopping list.

"Whose son do they think you are, Deng Xiaoping's?" I asked when he had finished. "Besides, the Party says colorful gifts are a feudal custom and must be rejected."

"My naive Little Sister, forget what the Party says," said Big Honesty wearily. "Who believes it anymore? All parents want everything they can get for their daughters. They think the husband won't honor the marriage if he gets it cheap. Most men go into debt for a wedding. Besides," he said, lowering his voice, "Mimi and her family think Ba is a high-level cadre with big power in the movie industry. So they are asking cheap. They only want black-and-white TV instead of color, a set of furniture instead of a Japanese motorcycle, and five hundred yuan instead of a thousand. They think if they don't act greedy now, Ba will be a bigger back door later."

"What a discount," I grumbled. "But Ba is not a high cadre."

"Please don't tell them that!" Big Honesty was distraught. "I'm lucky to get Mimi at all. If they find out he's only midlevel they'll look for someone higher up than me."

This was the worst wedding scenario I had ever heard of. It seemed Big Honesty would lose face in front of his new wife, her whole family, and everyone they knew.

I tried joking with him. "Maybe we'd better have Mimi marry Ba."

"Silly girl! Shut up!"

"What if you can't get all these things?" I asked, knowing he couldn't.

"Then her father says we have to wait. He won't let Mimi have a cheap wedding. He may even look around for better offers."

"It sounds like they're selling Mimi." I was angry for Big Honesty. "Let's add it all up and see how much she costs per jin."

"Be respectful." Big Honesty looked down helplessly. "Please, Little Sister, help me. I promise I'll help you later. I need you to ask Ba for two thousand yuan." He was desperate. "I need five thousand, but Ba will never do it. My friends and I can make the furniture. I'll get a used bicycle cheap and paint it." He frowned. "I'll work the rest out somehow."

"Can't you ask Ba?" I suggested.

"Not possible! Talking about money makes his liver shake. And you know he doesn't like me."

"He doesn't like me, either!" I protested.

"I know," Big Honesty said. "But between us, he dislikes me the most. It's better if you ask. Please!"

"Okay," I agreed reluctantly. "But don't expect too much."

"Two thousand yuan!" Ba jumped a foot in the air when he heard my plea for Big Honesty. "You rabbit whelp! You white-eyed wolf! Even your elbows bend outward!"

"It's not for me!" I reminded him.

Now he remembered—Big Honesty was the thief!

"That criminal! That greedy bastard! I gave him my extra apartment! I gave him my bicycle and camera! Huh! There was even film in it! What more does he want?"

"Mimi's parents won't let her marry my brother if he can't provide a good wedding. He has to buy the colorful gifts."

"In this Communist era?" Ba exclaimed righteously. "Feudal lackeys! Those greedy people aren't even Party members. They should give Big Honesty their daughter to serve the Party. Isn't that enough payment?" He shook his head like a revolutionary uncle in one of his studio's propaganda movies, as if baffled by their lack of patriotism. "If they would deny the Party for their own greed . . . well, let them." He paused heroically, savoring the moment. Then, unable to restrain himself, he added gleefully, "I guess Big Honesty will be a skinny old bachelor forever! Ha! Ha! Ha!"

"When I married your Ba," Mama fumed, "no one mentioned colorful gifts. And who went to a restaurant? We got married on our lunch break! After work we walked to Dong Si photo studio, rented wedding clothes, and took one wedding picture."

"That's right!" Ba burst in heatedly. "When Big Honesty was a Red Guard in the Cultural Revolution, he tried to take that picture to his teacher so she could burn it. The little bastard called it vain and bourgeois! Now what kind of vain, bourgeois wedding is he planning? I didn't pay your ma's family a yuan! She was free!"

Mama's face froze. Hurt and insulted, she left the room. Ba's skin was thicker than the Great Wall, bragging about a free bride in front of her. In the end, he refused my request.

"A father shouldn't foster gross materialism in his children," he explained nobly. "It erodes their revolutionary spirit."

I wondered what he would try to get from my future husband's family if I got married. He'd probably bankrupt them and mortgage their ancestors. In the end, Big Honesty acquired substitute gifts with friends' help, even making the furniture set himself, and greatly simplifying the other arrangements. Big Honesty and Mimi were married on May Day morning. They went to the Security Bureau office to sign their marriage certificate and returned to their new home, where our party had gathered to celebrate their union. Now they were man and wife.

I became interested in moviemaking by watching Ba at work on the set. I loved being with the cast and crew in his studio. I went there often to watch him, to study his territory. Now I secretly wanted to write and direct my own movies.

Mostly, the studio set was like loose, scattered sand before Ba appeared. The director baby-sat his toddler. The shifty-looking actor who played Class Enemy characters flirted with the script woman. The cameraman played poker with the lighting technician. The fat set designer napped on a narrow bench as though balancing on a horizontal bar. The young actor playing the Vigilant Commune Boy target-practiced with his slingshot and cavorted with the extras on the set. The actress playing a Commune Barefoot Doctor in a village costume with fake patches and grubby dirt makeup put on high heels and tried the rotten exploiting-class hair curler, then admired herself in the mirror with dreamy eyes, striking gross, nonproletarian, tilted-shoulder poses.

The swarm of extras in peasant and soldier costumes roamed the set like excited children. They tramped up and down the fake vinyl hill and plucked plastic leaves from the artificial trees as souvenirs. They rippled the sheet of blue silk water and rocked the paper sailboat, dazzled by the realness of the fake. They climbed ropes and poles to the spotlight catwalk or clambered up the camera dolly crane and sat, legs dangling over precarious ledges, jostling each other, joking, and casually dropping sunflower shells onto the set.

Suddenly Ba appeared in the doorway, tall and stern, chief of this wild tribe, gazing at their desecration of his domain.

"What the fuck's going on here?" he thundered.

People froze, freeze-frame, squeezed apologetic smiles on their faces, and swiftly lined up like guilty kindergartners. Ba glowered at the huddled gathering.

"Do I have to talk about those big, glorious revolutionary theories today? We've all been bombarded enough by the radio. You're not school kids! And I'm not some constipated Party Secretary! I see you really deserve a whipping today." Ba had lowered his voice ominously. "But I'm in a good mood. I just heard our regular Political Bureau censors have fled to their little beach-town resort to hide and play for the whole month. So we have a chance to slip this movie uncut past their milk-stinking junior stand-ins . . . *if* we get it done on schedule, I remind you. So the most important thing for you to remember is, *if* we finish today's shoot on time, you each get a free noodle dinner with lion-head meatballs, plus a snack to take home to your kids."

People's eyes glittered and applause rose, with heartfelt shouts of "Snacks!" and "Meatballs!" Ba waved them to silence.

"You have five minutes to get ready to shoot the 'Barefoot Doctor saves a poisoned pig for Chairman Mao' scene. Makeup lady, get those bourgeois curls out of the Barefoot Doctor's hair! Who are you playing in those high heels?" he asked the Barefoot Doctor. "Madam Chiang Kai-shek?" Ba glanced up at the extras perched on the crane and catwalk. "All you monkeys get down! Let's go!"

The whole set sprang to orderly, purposeful action. The makeup lady flattened the curls of the Barefoot Doctor, who gazed at the horizon, rehearsing her noble, proletarian expression. The dolly-crane climbers and catwalk daredevils slid heroically down poles and ropes like PLA marauders to sweep all their shells off the set. The sneaky Class Enemy skulked beneath the undefeatable red flag, plotting to poison the commune's pig.

The director found his script, everyone took their positions, stage lights blasted on, background music rose, the camera rolled.

The fake trees looked radiant. The blue silk lake rippled and the sail-boat swayed gently in the uneven gusts of the wind machine. Then the Vigilant Commune Boy cried out and the extras rushed onto the set to surround the poisoned pig. Even without eyedrops, they welled up plentiful proletarian tears and revolutionary vigor. The Class Enemy acted guiltily innocent. And the Barefoot Doctor rushed in and saved the pig, who seemed expressive and convincing in his role as a victim of the never-ending class struggle.

I watched Ba in awe as he surveyed the set from his high chair like triumphant Genghis Kahn viewing a sacked kingdom from his palanquin, plotting how to get a *People's Daily* reporter to come in Friday to write a praising article before the film's completion to help him muddle through an easier release, and how to get his studio leader to pay for the free dinner and snacks he had recklessly promised. He pondered how to keep his cast and crew motivated till the last reel was shot without exceeding his budget or losing his authority by being too tough or trying too hard to please. Ba was a lion tamer, a spurred whip in one hand and a fistful of meatballs in the other. Expressionless, he worked to figure out another flawless scheme.

To my surprise, in spite of all our conflict, Ba believed in me. He always urged me to try for what seemed out of reach or beyond my ability: the United Nations Training Program, the Rockefeller Scholarship, the International Olympic Math Contest. No matter if they only wanted a handful of candidates out of a billion Chinese.

"Who can stop you?" Ba would say, utterly serious. "You're my daughter. Success is in your genes!"

I felt his affection in these encouragements, yet I feared not being able to meet his expectations. But when the coy Barefoot Doctor actress suggested to Ba that he take me as his apprentice, he replied firmly, "No! I won't ruin my daughter's future. I don't want her mingling in some sweaty, ass-kissing, grabbing-after-crumbs studio to make fake movies more boring than a sneeze. She's above this kind of bug-carving skill. She has a brain!"

I think he also feared I might go into the movie business and end up working in his studio. But at the end of my senior year I applied to one of Beijing's best film schools, more determined than ever to write and direct my own movies someday. I had read many of the scripts that passed through Ba's hands and had seen directors in action on the set. I knew I could do it too.

For months I studied the filmmaking books in the studio library, preparing for the exam. Four out of seven hundred applicants would be chosen. The examination took three full days. I made it to the final seven, two girls and five boys. They would pick only one girl.

The last test took all day. We seven finalists each performed a monologue, wrote a frame-by-frame screen treatment for a short story, giving the reasons behind all our choices, and answered impromptu questions from the judges' panel in a stand-up interview.

By the day's end, I knew I had made it. Waiting excitedly for the judges' announcement, I wondered about this other girl and how she had come this far. Extremely introverted and fearful, she spoke in a soft, mosquito voice, had been unable to concentrate on her tasks, became confused during her interview, and gave rambling, disjointed answers. The judges had treated her with surprising delicacy.

When they announced their decision, to my astonishment, they had chosen her. I was devastated. My future melted and disappeared in front of me. One of the judges, a kindly woman in her fifties, came and took me aside. I was crying.

"You did extremely well, Jaia," she said. "We would have picked you, but there were special circumstances. Her father was our school chairman before the Cultural Revolution. He was tortured and committed suicide in our cowshed. Her family has suffered terribly. We owe it to them, to her father, to give her this. Can you see it's right? You're two years younger. Come back and try again next year."

I saw the justice of it. But I felt cheated, betrayed, utterly powerless, that no matter what my abilities or qualifications, I could never succeed in this tortuous maze of invisible debts and favors owed, of inside relationships and comforting fees. A strange feeling came to me in that moment, hatred of the Gang of Four. They had been abstract enemies till now. I knew as I left the auditorium that I wouldn't be back.

"Your mama and I are sending you to America."

Ba announced this to me thoughtfully at dinner one night. Puzzled, I looked at him, then turned to Mama.

"Yes, we're sending you to America, Jaia," she echoed firmly, lowering her eyes. "Even if we have to sell everything and borrow against our future salaries. We want you to go."

I thought they both must be crazy. I was halfway through my first semester of college. How could I just leave them, China, everything I knew and loved, and move to the land of the American Ghost? Yet I understood. Our whole country fantasized about getting out. It was all my college friends talked about.

Just the other day my friend Red came to class in a daze to dazzle us with her pearl inlaid jewelry box full of colored gems, an engagement gift from a fifty-six-year-old Hong Kong businessman she'd met in Bei Hai Park the week before. We were awed by her treasure and sudden, heaven-sent destiny. Many girls were now strolling through our parks, palaces, and other tourist sites, made up like Taiwanese go-go dancers, looking for rich foreign men with magic treasure chests to come and change their fates.

Our national vision of the West had changed. The poor, bloodsucking, capitalist masses, starving in the streets and ghettos of the crumbling imperialist empire, were reborn in our imaginations as a kingdom of overfed tycoons, movie stars, and exotic women glittering with jewels like curved cloisonné vases, all living in mansions, signing million-dollar contracts over lunch, sipping champagne, and disco-dancing on moonlit beaches till dawn. And in our minds, America was the pulsing heart of this new utopia.

Capitalism beckoned irresistibly, her sultry smile and gaudy flash far more seductive than Uncle Lei Feng's Screw Spirit. In her fevered embrace, even steel warriors became entrepreneurs the first week and tossed their revolutionary volition aside like old aprons. We had all heard about this new, golden West.

Masses of my countrymen now rushed over the precipice of our failed communist utopia into capitalism's freefall. Everyone with a back door was getting out and going West. First the high cadres and their kids and cronies went. Then artists, athletes, scientists, musicians, actors, actresses, doctors, architects, singers, dancers, writers, engineers. Our Central Opera Orchestra stopped performing because the conductor and a third of the musicians had all gone West.

The national fleeing frenzy had begun in the late seventies with Deng Xiaoping's Open Door Policy. Deng's Open Door let the big fish swim leisurely through, but set a fine-mesh sorting net for the rest of us. Still, people stampeded by tens of thousands, elbowing up to the door, hoping to slip through before Deng narrowed it to a crack on a whim, or slammed it shut altogether.

Gone, the ancient tradition, "Do not travel far while the parents live." Now parents sent their children out in droves, to Singapore, Hong Kong, Russia, Japan, America, Britain, Canada, France, to a better life. They were human escape hooks flung over a high wall on a filial cord, for many children brought their parents over once they stabilized in the West.

I was sure the Western myth was false, that its glitter was tin, and there was no heaven on earth. But Ba had feverish dreams and plans. He would send me sailing to a Western shore to pick up gold nuggets in America's streets.

I watched him across the table. "I'd rather stay here," I said. "I don't like capitalism."

"Yo!" Ba snorted. "Proletarian patriotism is out of fashion. And when did you become such a Marxism grandma?"

"Can you talk decently to your daughter?" Mama looked sad.

"Oki, yoki." Ba imitated the American "okay" to charm Mama, and turned back to me.

"Don't be so puffy. I've observed you for years now. You don't have a future here. You've barely muddled through this far. Your Mama spoiled you. You don't like the taste of blood. You never even saw a dead body, except for Chairman Mao, and he's fifty percent wax! So what if you have a brain? Your skin is too thin and your teeth are too wobbly. They stole your director scholarship and you didn't even squeal! And you think you can climb the white-bone ladder and grab a future here? You don't know what it takes! This is social Darwinism! How tough can you be? How nasty can you get?" He glared a challenge at me till I looked down. "The Party is rotten and China is a wrecked, sinking boat. Don't be naive. Flee the fire for the safe side of the river. Remember that documentary where the big fox kicks the baby fox out in the snow, so the little shit-ball can learn to survive? We're like that big fox now."

Ba, the big wily fox, looked at me, his little shit-ball offspring, and concluded his sophistry.

"Go to America, little fox." He grinned. "Then come back to get us."

Ba and Mama were serious. Ba mustered all his creativity, preparing to slip me through the Party's net. Mama's cousin, my aunt, had been in America three years now, and might be able to help us. I knew her from the two years she spent in Beijing after her release from her labor camp. She had lived in a socialism yard near us, in a one-room dirt-floor hut with her dying mother. But my aunt had found a way to America. Now Mama wrote her a letter bemoaning my bleak future in China, telling her I would be useful to her in

America, not a burden at all. I'd get a job right away, work hard and support myself.

Ba claimed even low-class American jobs paid more than high cadres earned here. He told us stories of poor Chinese who got rich in America, shining shoes in airports, cleaning toilets in hotel rooms, shoveling horse shit in American barns. His favorite story was about a pair of peasant brothers who grew fabulously wealthy as partners in an American funeral business. One brother carried dead bodies around on his back, stuffed them in coffins, and got to keep whatever he found in their pockets. The other brother who buried them got paid a hundred American dollars per grave dug, plus tips!

"Don't be afraid to eat bitterness!" was Ba's slogan.

I knew I didn't want to dig graves or carry dead Americans around on my back. The easiest way for me to get out was by student visa. But my sixty-year-old aunt, who wrote back offering to help, couldn't show sufficient financial support on paper to sponsor me. So Ba devised a caretaker scenario to fool the Security Bureau Passport Office. We'd tell them Auntie was old, lonely, and needed me to come take care of her. But this wasn't complex enough for Ba. His style and habit of improving scripts required more drama.

"We'll say you two were deeply bonded since you were born. She was like your second mama. Now she needs you for her lonely heart. You must exchange richly intimate letters like an affectionate mother and daughter. And you must call her Ma."

Reluctantly, I agreed. I knew I could not dissuade Ba once his mind was set. I felt an obligation as well. My going to America might help our family. Perhaps I could make a new home there for Mama. At least I could have a life of my own without offending them. And maybe they would even miss me. So began our letter-writing campaign. For a whole year I wrote my aunt a letter a week; future documentary evidence to show the Security Bureau at my passport hearing. They were touchingly sad.

"Dear Ma, I miss you profoundly. I cry at least once a week, thinking of you far away and lonely, in the cruel American land, being exploited by blood-sucking capitalists. Come back, dear Ma! Oh, how I miss you day and night! Come back to the arms of our motherland! Come back to me! Although we're not rich, we have enough. And we'll have each other. I'll take good care of you. But if you can't come home soon, take me there quickly! Tearfully yours, Little Jaia."

Ba helped write these letters, defining their tone and style. He insisted on dramatic emotions and political correctness, as they were intended for the eyes of the Security Bureau. But I was ashamed of them. Before the date of my passport hearing, my aunt sent photocopies of all my letters. We brought them, with her replies, to wait in the line outside Chang Ann Avenue's Security Bureau Passport Office. Across the street at Beijing Hotel, the exalted comings and goings of rich foreigners, laden with shopping bags, confirmed our fantasies of Western life.

Mama, Ba, and I finally made it inside for my interview. The officer heard Ba's compelling story outline, then read several of our letters. He was unimpressed, even a little irritated.

"Who do you think you are fooling? These letters are stagy as a revolutionary example drama! Aiyo, you think you're so smart! Who doesn't know you can put even a cow and a horse together and have them exchange some letters? This trick is an old mop by now. Do you know how many thousands of people already tried this? Please, don't stink up my office with this crap. Be a little bit original. I'm not some blind old farting grandpa you can fool with phony chicken scratches on paper! You must do better than this!"

Mama and I were humiliated. Ba blinked, unfazed.

"Which part didn't work?" he asked sincerely, as if discussing flaws in his movie script.

He spent the next five minutes charming the old officer, trying to pick his brain for the next interview. Wheels turned in his head.

He was already devising future scenarios. To him, this was only a creative challenge. We had prepared for a year, waited in line for five hours, and the meeting had taken ten minutes. As our feet hit the pavement outside the Security Bureau office, Ba said, "Oki yoki, next time we'll say she adopted you when you were ten, no, five! She bought all your diapers and clothes, paid for your tuition and food. You lived half the time with her and half the time with us. How can they disprove it? I'll fake an adoption paper and find a notary to sign it. We'll make that old Security Bureau fart like a mute eating bitter herbs!"

Since our government operated manually—no computers, no database, and only random filing—and with thousands of emigration applicants arriving daily and more faces than could ever be remembered, no rejection was final. If one scenario failed, we'd make up a new one and return. We could try until we succeeded or lost hope.

Ba worked several months on the new adoption angle, inspired by hints from our interviewing officer. But this also proved to be a paper tiger poked through by a Security Bureau pencil, and another humiliating incident for Mama and me. The new officer located my aunt's personal record. She was in a Beijing cowshed when I was three and a countryside labor camp till I was twelve. She couldn't even have seen her own daughter, let alone have adopted me. Years of engaging class struggle had made the Security Bureau a tempered iron fist, much smarter than Ba thought.

We had to find connections to some official in the passport office. Then, with the right gifts, any scenario could work. We'd bribe one officer to jump me ahead in line, another to squeeze my passport through, and maybe a foreign embassy worker from my host country. This was how things worked.

Without this, I might never get out. I didn't care. But Ba and Mama wouldn't give up. They went hunting connections everywhere. They explored all their contacts, seeking a back door out.

They gave gifts to every Party official they met. They even managed to bribe an American Embassy official. He came to our home for a feast one night, accepted our gift of a valuable antique painting, promised to help, and then refused to return any of our phone calls afterward.

And every few months we returned to the huge lines outside the Security Bureau Passport Office with Ba's latest scenario. Ba always came with us, certain Mama and I would bungle it without him.

Daily, year-round, rain, snow, or shine, thousands came to this line, fishing for a passport out. Many camped overnight to get an early number. Each morning a predawn mass of silhouettes in dark-hued proletarian uniforms, a muted wall of restless shadows buzzing with anxiety, wild dreams, and desperate strategies, greeted the sun. The ultimate prize sought, a visa to the West, was a life-changing totem more potent than Chairman Mao's unearthly, immortalized corpse. I felt a sadness in these lines, that people felt so trapped here, that our motherland was like a prison from which they sought escape.

People stood together like comrades on a march, talking of anything to do with getting out, with life in the West. Many passed the hours practicing foreign languages, exchanging study tips and discussing various textbooks. No more Chairman Mao's Little Red Book or Uncle Lei Feng's Diary. *900 English Sentences* was a national best-seller. So was *TOFEL, Test of English as a Foreign Language. TOFEL* in Chinese sounds like "tuo fu" which means "pray for a blessing." People practiced everywhere for this blessing, even on the buses and in the food lines.

Many people said Hong Kong was the best place to go because you could enjoy capitalism without learning a foreign language. Canada, Britain, and France were also popular. But America was the most desired place, and its embassy had the longest lines. It was famous for its star and noodles flag and its gold plaque of a vicious-looking eagle clutching a clawful of arrows and a branch ripped off a tree. This pickiest capitalist country picked and chose whomever it wanted, as if selecting potatoes to stuff in a shopping bag. To stand in its line, everyone washed and ironed their clothes, hoping to be the desired potato.

The hot news of the day was often about some big fish who had leaped over the dam. When our top woman tennis player sought political asylum during a tournament in America, people were either thrilled or outraged.

"Some patriotic hero! She cried her eyeballs out on TV when our national five-star flag was raised. Now she sneaks like a hungry dog into the American camp at the first opportunity!"

"What are you doing in this line, Mr. Patriotic?"

"I only want to visit America. I would never stay there!"

"Ya, don't brag about it! Everybody knows the only people who come back from America to live here are losers and idiots."

"Who can blame her? She only made ninety-five yuan a month here. Now in America, even a cheap towel company will pay her millions to blow her nose on their brand!"

"If I get to America I'm staying! Making a fortune there is like making instant noodles here!"

People had many theories about what influenced their chances of visa success at the American Embassy. Prior to Thanksgiving and Christmas was good, but near Fourth of July was best. Presidential election time was iffy; Reagan or not could decide everything. But who knew which way? Flu season was the worst. And even trivial things like a new baby or a birthday could play a major role. Those Americans loved to make a big fuss about the day they were born!

People were outraged by America's application form, which asked if we'd ever been Communists, then asked if we'd ever been Nazis. Were Americans comparing us with our Nazi enemies? Did they think we were the same? This was grossly offensive! To us, Nazis were cold and vicious. But we Communists were warm and passionate. And the Communist question was totally ridiculous.

"Are you now, or have you ever been a member of, or in any way connected or associated with the Communist Party, or ever knowingly aided or supported the Communist Party directly, or indirectly through another organization, group, or person, or ever advocated, taught, believed in, or knowingly supported or furthered the interests of communism?"

Of course we had! All of it! Every one of us! What was wrong with that? But only an idiot would answer "yes" to this question. Even though we allowed imperialists to visit us, we would deny our communism to go to the West. We always had to deny something to get ahead. As the saying went, "Whoever has the milk, call her Mother."

1984

When I was nineteen, in the summer of my second university year, Mama and Uncle Tao were invited to a two-week writers' conference in the beach town of Qing Dao. So they took me with them. Sixty of China's foremost writers also attended the Qing Dao conference. Permitted to write again after their ordeals and exonerations, they were reestablishing their ruined literary careers. I had read many of their pre–Cultural Revolution works and expected to witness passionate literary discussions that would inspire me and illumine the writing craft.

The first conference meeting disillusioned me. For three hours, they rose one by one and read formula works in progress to the inevitable praises of the group. The high point of the meeting came when a famous old PLA poet stood and dramatically recited one of his poems in a thundering voice.

> *"Attack in the morning glory!*
> *Patrol under shining stars!*
> *Sweat in the burning sun!*
> *Welcome thunder and storm!*

Under a PLA soldier's uniform,
steel rib, iron bone!
Inside a PLA soldier's chest,
red heart, bright liver!"

He sat down with huge dignity as everyone cheered, applauded, and shouted praises.

"A great poem!"

"An epic!"

"Too powerful!"

"It made me smell the gunpowder!"

The conference was mostly a gossip fest of educational outings, shopping trips, and fine restaurant meals. The main issues debated were the calorie count of a roast duck and the cholesterol content of tea-boiled quail eggs. And the most dynamic theorizing revolved around who was having an affair with whom in the literary field. And all literary discussions toed the official Party line.

In the main conference event, a famous woman writer read her new novel about a group of reform-camp hooligans and the warmhearted PLA warden who embraces them with proletarian compassion. Each chapter ended with one of his edifying lectures on proletarian virtues, the need for eternal vigilance, the Gang of Four's evil, Chairman Mao's greatness, and the Party's purity. In the final chapter, the once-rebellious hooligans returned home loyal to the Party, grateful to Chairman Mao, and burning with desire to carry his red flag forward to the end.

The conference declared the book an inspired masterpiece, but I churned with disgust at its two-dimensional falseness. If it were true, Little Plum would have returned from her camp by now. This novel focused the burning issue of the conference: "How to influence today's youth through art and literature."

This raised a key question, which a short conference debate quickly resolved: "Do today's youth have a brain or not?"

Opinion on the matter was divided. Two or three people thought we had a brain. The rest insisted we were shallow and spoiled and needed to be guided down the right path. The famous woman novelist summarized the no-brain position.

"Today's youth are spoiled idiots with no real experience of following Chairman Mao's revolution! They don't know how our Precious Red Mountain was acquired! They only think of their own comfort and trivial body sensations!"

These writers defined the creative challenge of literature in the eighties: "We must develop more sophisticated propaganda methods than those used in the past."

The most controversial conference issue was Bei Dao, a young Chinese poet recently nominated for a Nobel Prize. These older establishment writers despised Bei Dao and gnawed at him for one whole afternoon like a pack of starved dogs on a meaty bone.

"How stupid and shallow that Nobel Committee is!" they declared. "Fooled by Bei Dao!"

"What rotten taste!"

"He has lost China's face in front of those foreign devils!"

"Shameless people like Bei Dao shouldn't be called poets," the famous woman novelist commented sourly. "The best you can say is that he puts characters next to each other and calls it poetry."

The discussion ended in unanimous consensus: Bei Dao was a rotten poet and the Nobel Committee was stupid. Everyone felt great pride at not having been nominated themselves.

I loved Bei Dao's subtle poems. Their stream-of-consciousness style and haunting moods explored repressed and forbidden themes, evoked longing, despair, love of sensual beauty, and a passionate urge to freedom. The Party had labeled him a dangerous influence because of his wide appeal among my generation. His poems, translated and read in many languages, were presently banned in China. These conference writers declared it their patriotic duty to undo the damage done by Bei Dao and all literary hooligans like him.

"Listen to his ambiguous poem," one indignant old poet said.

Rising from his chair, he contemptuously read one of Bei Dao's poems from an old poetry journal, his nose wrinkled in disgust.

> *"The orange ripens,*
> *the sun-filled orange ripens.*
> *Let me walk into your heart*
> *heavy laden with love.*
> *The orange ripens,*
> *its skin exudes gossamer mist.*
> *Let me walk into your heart,*
> *sorrow melts into a source of joy."*

The magazine now shook in the old poet's hands. His face quivering with indignation, he managed to continue.

> *"The orange ripens,*
> *each sliver enmeshed in bitter threads.*
> *Let me walk into your heart,*
> *to find my shattered dreams.*
> *The orange ripens,*
> *the sun-filled orange is ripe."*

The old poet threw the magazine on the table. Bei Dao's literary insult brought cries of outrage from the group.

"Ooh, gross! That's pornography!"

"Talk about petty bourgeois! This generation is hopeless!"

"What he wrote is just a basic body urge! Totally trivial!"

"Too many feelings!" Uncle Tao exclaimed hotly, rising from his chair. "It's all love and sex organs! Who needs it? These poets invite the love god Pan to seduce and corrupt our bright youth! We must drive him out!"

I thought the poem was beautiful, and kept my mouth shut.

On the fifth day of the conference, our writers' group walked along the bluff of the military fort overlooking Qing Dao Harbor. We followed our PLA tour guide to a seawall fortified with a row of enormous, polished black cannons. Literary exclamations erupted from the group.

"The shield of our nation!"

"A second Great Wall!"

"A glorious symbol of our Party's invincible strength!"

They scribbled these inspirations in their notebooks, crowding around the gleaming guns, laying their hands on them as if they could absorb the power through their palms.

"Aren't you going to write something in your notebook?" Uncle Tao nudged me.

"And look there!" The PLA commander proudly pointed to the bay, where an enormous submarine floated on the water's surface.

"A gleaming leviathan!"

"An iron dragon!"

"The glory of the masses!"

More inspired scribbling followed. I dreaded the poems they would make of this day. I would probably be reading in next month's *Poetry Journal*:

> *Guarding a PLA submarine's shell,*
> *steel hull! Iron decks!*
> *Inside a PLA submarine's chest,*
> *red engine! Bright fuel pump!*

I could smell the gunpowder. I wandered along the stone wall looking out on the barren sea, contemplating my bleak future as a writer in my country. Hearing footsteps, I turned to see a man in his thirties approaching. He had a calm, handsome face and deep-set eyes. Several times in the conference room I had caught him looking at me. He hadn't spoken a word all week.

"Are you bored?" he asked, coming up to me casually.

"Aren't you?" I tested him.

"No," he said with a slight smile.

Crafty double-face! Another shallow revolutionary poet? Or a Party snitch sent to observe and report on Secret Individualists? Everyone knew the snitches were here. But few knew who they were. I wondered how many opinions were uttered in the conference for the benefit of these invisible Party ears.

"Then why don't you take notes?" I asked curtly, meaning for his art if he was a writer, or for the Security Bureau if he was an informer.

He smiled at my boldness and said slyly, "I'm observing carefully, taking notes and pictures in my mind." Whatever he was, he was sharp. Then he added, "If you want to be a writer, you can't let things bore you. Anything can become part of art or literature. Even this."

He nodded toward his scribbling comrades with a deep tolerance. For me, these were the first real words of the conference. I felt instinctively I could trust him. I glanced at the group, feeling all my bitter disappointment welling up.

"They're so empty," I said. He wasn't shocked.

"Look deeper," he said. "Find the mystery in their emptiness. They're not as stupid as they seem. They wrote the truth once and were persecuted for it. What they lost in the cowsheds and camps couldn't be restored with their exonerations and comforting fees."

His softly spoken words amazed me.

"What do you write?" I asked.

"I used to write poetry," he said.

Looking away, I saw Mama and Uncle Tao watching us at the edge of the group.

"I have to go," I said.

"What's your name?"

"Jaia."

"Jaia," he said. "I am Yangtze. See you around."

After that, in the conference room and restaurants my mind was on Yangtze. I saw him listening, observing everything with quiet intensity. He disappointed me, never speaking out or sharing his work. I wanted to hear his voice, his poetry. I wanted to talk to him again. If anyone could teach me about real writing, it was Yangtze. But now all eyes, especially Mama's, turned on us like searchlights if we came near each other.

One day, a PLA boat took our group a mile offshore to a beautiful cadres-only island, lush with tall grasses and arching palms, and surrounded by beaches of soft golden sand. It was a paradise floating in a topaz sea. Awed by its beauty, we forgot our serious opinions and became children again. Shouting and cheering, we dove off the boat to splash and swim about in the warm blue water.

I walked down the beach collecting pretty stones and shells and sat in the sand to polish them. My most beautiful, a creamy orange shell, had whirling white spirals on its smooth surface. When I looked at it closely, I saw a sailboat in the clouds.

"Have you found any treasure?"

I looked up. Yangtze stood beside me.

"Look at this."

I proudly handed him my beautiful shell. He became completely absorbed in it, turning it over slowly, examining every part of it with great interest.

"What do you see?" I asked him.

"A ship," he said. "Sailing on an ice-cream sea."

"You can have it," I said impulsively, and immediately worried that I was being too forward.

"Thank you, Jaia," he said.

He was utterly sincere. I saw depth and kindness in his eyes. He wrapped my shell carefully in his towel. Then something behind me caught his attention.

"It's my turn to go." He smiled.

I turned and saw Mama approaching. Yangtze walked toward her, nodding pleasantly as he passed. I jumped up and ran into the sea.

Mama was furious after this "second incident." Her comrades had begun gossiping about me and Yangtze, and she had lost face. That night in our room she gave me a stern lecture.

"Don't even look at that old man! A no-virtue, nameless poet, seducing a young girl to satisfy his dirty lust! He'll ruin your life! And you'll give me another heart attack!"

The rest of the conference, Mama and Uncle Tao supervised my every move. I remained at Mama's side, an obedient daughter, avoiding Yangtze. I felt a great sadness and longed for the conference to end.

It rained torrents the day our ship left Qing Dao Harbor for Beijing. Writers from other cities came to see our group off at the dock. These old-timers had enjoyed the conference immensely. They shook hands, patted shoulders, exchanged addresses, and swore to stay in touch.

Mama and Uncle Tao chatted beside me. I scanned the crowd for Yangtze and saw him standing alone at the end of the dock, watching me through the rain. He had no umbrella, and his hair and jacket were drenched. Our eyes met, and I looked down. When I looked up again, Yangtze was striding across the dock. He came right up to us, smiling, and held out his hand to Mama.

"Comrade Lin, good-bye," he said. "Pleased to have met you."

He was so polite she forced a smile and shook his hand. After he shook Uncle Tao's hand, he turned to me.

"Good-bye, Jaia. Keep in touch."

To my astonishment, he openly handed me a folded piece of paper. What could I say with Mama there? Clumsy words stumbled off my tongue and drowned in the ship's blaring horn. Mama grabbed my arm and led me up the ramp onto the deck. I looked back and saw Yangtze standing on the dock, watching me through the veils of rain. As we entered our cabin, Mama suddenly clutched her chest and leaned dramatically against the wall.

"See what you've done!" she hissed. "I'm having a heart attack! Promise me you won't see him! You mustn't even think about boys till you have your Ph.D. Otherwise I won't live long!"

She grimaced in pain. It seemed the cost of my own selfish happiness was Mama's life. I promised, half doubting her, yet full of desperate guilt. Slowly she took her hands from her chest. Her breathing became normal.

When I read Yangtze's address and phone number, I saw he lived in Beijing! I considered calling him, despite my promise to Mama. But the longer I waited, the harder it became. What would I say to him? Why would he want to talk to me? I was a stupid, clumsy girl half his age. He would see my shallowness and realize his mistake. Months passed. I had waited too long. He would be angry by now. So I didn't call. I concentrated on my studies and kept my promise to Mama. But I didn't forget the poet Yangtze.

Chinese New Year came, 1984, covering Beijing in a blanket of snow. Mama had a cold and gave me her invitation to the Chinese Writers' Association New Year's party, to be held in the exclusive high cadre club at Zhong Nan Hai compound, where Deng Xiaoping and the Party Central Committee played. The club's iron gate was guarded by a row of PLA soldiers with automatic rifles. I showed my invitation and entered, passing armed soldiers patrolling the snow-covered grounds in pairs under bare snow-frosted plum and poplar trees.

The club's ground floor had an Olympic-size pool, a bowling alley, two Western-style bars, three restaurants, and a banquet hall with floor-to-ceiling velvet drapes and crystal chandeliers. An orchestra played Western dance music in the ballroom, and two hundred people stood drinking punch, eating snacks, and not dancing. I went to the bowling alley, where I had arranged to meet Uncle Tao. It was more crowded than the ballroom. People piled behind each lane, eager to play this high cadre, Western game.

Uncle Tao and several old men stood in one lane, hefting huge black balls and walking up and down a long wooden floor. A skinny grandpa with glasses and a white chin beard walked all the way to the pins and picked one up. He examined it closely, tested its weight. Suddenly an angry voice shouted over the loudspeaker, "Put that bowling soldier down! Do not walk past the black line! Put that soldier down now and return to your seat!"

The old man looked up, startled and confused. Everyone laughed.

"Yaaa! Put it in your pocket, Old Shur!" shouted Uncle Tao.

"Keep it, Old Shur!" called his partner. "It's made of gold!"

The old man stooped, placed it carefully on the mark, and walked with dignity up the lane to rejoin his comrades, who cheered and slapped him on the back like a conquering hero.

"Uncle Tao!" I called. He looked around and saw me.

"Oooh! Fresh blood! Little Jaia!" His high voice twanged like frayed arhu strings. "Come bowl with us high blood pressures!"

"I've never played," I protested.

Uncle Tao came and dragged me happily onto his lane.

"Neither has anybody else here!" he said.

My white-haired comrades peeled off layers of winter clothes, faces flushed and excited. Uncle Tao went first. A veteran of two wars, he stood holding a ball to his nose peering down the alley at the pins as if facing Kuomintang soldiers across Liu Ding Bridge. Motionless, he meditated on his death blow with deadly purpose.

His comrades squirmed in their seats, anxiously cracking their knuckles and rubbing their hands as if their lives depended on his shot.

"Throw that thing, Old Tao!" one finally shouted. "They're not getting any closer!"

Uncle Tao turned and fiercely shushed him. Then, glaring at the pins, he shuffled up to the black line, swung the ball back, and flung it forward with a fierce grunt. It sailed through the air, hit the floor with a bang, and rolled slowly down the lane, knocking over a side pin. His teammates cheered. His second ball knocked down several more pins, and a chorus of whoops went up from the crowd behind us.

"Make room for Little Jaia, Comrade Lin's daughter!" Uncle Tao shouted. "All you high blood pressures! Make room for our fresh blood!"

He put a heavy ball in my hands, stuffed my fingers into the holes, and steered me to the front line.

"Go, Little Jaia!" my teammates shouted. "Add oil!"

They began chanting, "Little Jaia! Little Jaia! Little Jaia!"

I swung the ball back and just managed to bring it forward before it slipped from my grasp. My teammates cheered wildly as it rolled slowly down the center of the lane.

"Hit them!"

"Hit them all!"

"Knock them dead!"

It rolled to a dead stop halfway down the lane, and a great "Aaii yoohh!" went up from the crowd behind us. I turned bright red.

"She hit glue!" shouted a wit in the crowd, and people laughed.

Uncle Tao went to retrieve my ball, and I threw the next one into the gutter, ending my bowling career. When Uncle Tao turned his back, I slipped into the crowd. To my surprise, I nearly walked into Yangtze, who had been watching my bowling debut. He smiled, and his black eyes sparkled like oiled onyx.

Jaia, twenty years old, just before leaving China for America.

"Where have you been, Fresh Blood?" he asked.

"Yangtze . . ."

"Come back, Little Jaia!" Uncle Tao shouted. "You must do it again!"

Yangtze laughed at my nervous expression.

"Follow me, Little Jaia," he said.

I followed him without hesitation, down the hall to a crowded café. We found a small corner table. The room buzzed with conversations. Music from the ballroom next door vibrated through the walls. Yangtze watched me quietly.

"Are you a strong person, Jaia?" he asked simply.

"I want to be," I told him.

"You know you are," he said. "You just don't believe it yet."

How unconventional he was! These simple words began the most real conversation I had ever had. His calm strength melted my

awkwardness. The shell of concerns normally occupying me quietly dissolved. We talked for hours, and I learned much about
Yangtze. To my joy and surprise, I learned he was one of my heroes, a rebel-poet of the 1976 Tiananmen Square Clear Light Rebellion, arrested in the crackdown, imprisoned, and exonerated
after the Gang of Four's fall. I knew then I could trust him with my
life. We talked of being writers in our country. And when I mentioned my disillusionment at the conference, he looked around the
room, apparently casually, and said, "The Party silenced these writers for decades. Now the Party says, 'Speak!' What can they say
when the Party's ears listen to their every word? You thought I
might be a spy at first. Do you remember?

"Put yourself in their shoes. 'What will happen in the next Cultural Revolution?' is the question you face every time you write. So
you churn out formula revolutionary dramas to please the censors.
Write the truth and your career ends in a labor camp. Write a novel
called *Follow the Red Sun,* or *At Last, the Dark Night Is Over,* and
you get a salary plus royalties, the Party publishes half a million
copies in a literary magazine, and you're a success.

"Your best work was bulleted and got you thrown in the cowshed and exiled to a camp. To survive, you shit formulas. But it's
like pulling the trigger yourself. You believed in the Wonderful Life.
You fought for it for twenty, thirty years. Then your faith met the
Party censor. Bulleted." Yangtze looked grim.

"We have two fates: Fear breaks us, or cynicism corrupts us. We
become eunuchs for the Party either way. We believe the lies we tell
and the masks we wear till they become real. And we die inside. This
is how we survive."

Hours later, we walked the snowy path under frozen trees, past
the armed patrols to the front gate. We stood on the sidewalk before a row of motionless soldiers. Yangtze wrote his address and
phone number, handing them to me for the second time.

"This time use them, Little Jaia," he said with a faint smile.

He passed into the shadows of the tree-lined sidewalk, and I started for home. Two weeks later, I called Yangtze and arranged to visit him and read his poems. He lived in a two-room apartment with his father. A former scholar, poet, and historian, Yangtze's father had survived the labor camp where his wife, Yangtze's mother, had died after a prolonged illness.

Yangtze's room, a monk's cell three meters square, contained a bed, a small desk, and a chair. The seashell I had given him in Qing Dao sat at one end of a bookshelf.

"Have a seat." Yangtze handed me a sheaf of papers. "These are my best poems."

There were perhaps twenty poems, lyrical and inspired, drawn in bold calligraphy. I read them all, enthralled. Yangtze was a gifted, impassioned poet. The last poem I recognized. I had read it a hundred times before and knew it by heart. It was included in many poetry collections from what we now called the Tiananmen Movement. Yangtze was one of the leading poets of the Clear Light Rebellion.

"This is your poem?" I asked, amazed.

He nodded. He knew the one I meant.

"The 'proletarian anthem,' " he quoted ironically. "First it got me in trouble. Then it made me a hero. It's a good poem."

"It's a great poem. And you are a hero. You all were."

"We were naive rebels," Yangtze said. "Then Party-manufactured heroes and political pawns."

I asked Yangtze to tell me about the crackdown and his life in prison. And he told me his story.

"After the Mayor's radio speech ordering us to leave the square, over half a million of us ignored him and stayed till sunset. Several thousand of us had camped out every night around the monument to protect Premier Zhou's shrine. Early next morning, an army of police trucks converged on a hundred thousand people who had already gathered. Thousands of police poured from the trucks wearing helmets and carrying clubs and shields. A voice on the public loudspeakers ordered us to go home. But everyone stayed.

"When the police started toward the monument, we roared and rushed to defend it. The riot lasted twelve hours. Many people were injured. Some died. But we held our ground and the police finally withdrew. Most people went home again at dusk. But our core of several thousand stayed behind. Late that night, police battalions moved in and surrounded us in the darkness.

"Suddenly the floodlights went on and lit up the square. Thousands of men in black carrying clubs and shields surrounded us in 'closing the net' formation. They moved in, swinging their clubs, attacking with no mercy. We couldn't escape. The square turned slick with our blood as they struck us down and dragged us away.

"I was hit in the head and woke in a crowded prison cell. My wounded comrades lay everywhere, moaning on the bloody floor. Some never woke up. Later we were separated for interrogation. I don't know how many days mine lasted. My room had no windows and the light was always on. They beat me and threatened execution if I didn't cooperate fully. Many times they put a gun to my head.

"People who went to the square the next morning found it wet, clean, and full of soldiers and police. They had washed our blood away in the night with hoses and removed our wreaths and posters. Not a sign of our battle remained.

"I was put in a cell with a thief and a hooligan. The Party separates political criminals so they can't support each other. They fear two rebels will start a revolution. My cellmates also loved Premier Zhou and respected me for supporting him.

"Every day they played cards, and I studied. I read the same books you were allowed to read outside: Chairman Mao, Marx, Lenin, Engels, and Chinese history. But I truly studied them in prison. And they showed me what had gone wrong. We're raised on slogans, not Communist philosophy. We're conditioned to believe and obey. The Party herds us through campaigns and turns us against each other to control us and hide its own corruption. We've lost socialism. And we'll never know communism.

"The more I understood, the hotter my blood grew. I wanted freedom to be a true revolutionary. But I knew I might not survive. People are executed all the time. No need for a trial. I could be dragged out any day. And if the Party called me a dog, I'd be remembered furry and four-legged.

"Politics and history are mindless forces, like floods and earthquakes. Pressure builds, the masses erupt, and many people die. All our revolutions and campaigns hold no more logic than this. We are at the mercy of great, blind, irrational forces. We are swept along.

"My comrades and I never dreamed the Party would release us and call us heroes. Then Chairman Mao died and the Gang of Four fell. A year later the Party named our rebellion an 'Anti–Gang of Four Heroic Movement.' Nonsense! Our movement was pro–Premier Zhou and anti–Party corruption!

"But we were exonerated. And we naively saw the Gang of Four's fall as the big change the party claimed it was. We swallowed the Gang of Four lie as most people did. We all wanted to believe the nightmare was over—that we were really free. But the Gang of Four were just the criminals who lost.

"The gang who won, who rule us now, seized power by blaming them. Many bloody-hands used this trick and used foolish people like me to secure their political fortunes. We naively helped them because they called us heroes and made us famous. But the deck had simply changed hands. And we were only shooting stars. So you see, Little Jaia," said Yangtze softly, "I'm not a hero at all. Just a tool that has lost its use. I'm only a survivor."

I was so impressed by Yangtze, and honored that he had opened himself to me. He became more of a hero in my eyes. All that evening at home, I saw him in my mind, a beautiful statue carved in marble, radiating calmness, wisdom, and strength. And his dark eyes watched me from their profound depth.

For two weeks I found myself thinking of Yangtze. One day I received a letter from him, asking me to come see him. I went the next day. I was so happy to see him when he opened the door. But he looked serious. Something was on his mind. We went into his room. He watched me in silence.

"Little Jaia," he finally said, "I knew I could trust you the first time we met in Qing Dao."

His confession moved me. In our era of betrayal and fear, trust was rare and precious as desert rain, its bond deeper than blood.

"I trust you too, Yangtze," I said.

It felt like a confession of love. He watched me steadily.

"I wrote a new poem," he said.

He handed me two sheets of paper. Silently, I began to read.

This is the end of the good-bye road.
Let go of the hand once held.
So many springs have tasted like bitter red wine.
But now the falling castles and barricades
no longer make me grieve.
The phony, solemn voices in their aged throats
no longer make my lips twitch.
Our history's gray echo is drowned
in the spring flood of your youth.
Over stiff bodies and barren skulls,
I saw your rosy smile, your green aliveness.
An orchid blooming on a mountaintop,
you shattered my icy calmness.
Your shining smile, your tender eyes,
called down the hidden stars,

to wheel and circle like white gulls
over the ocean of my soul.
A forgotten voice sealed under the dust of aeons cried,
"This is what I have longed for!"
Now inspirations awaken from their frozen dreams,
and the world shines in a radiant dawn.
Heavenly fireworks explode in the funereal sky,
and perfumed images rain down,
as the coral dances in the sea.
The blissful waves serenade my little mermaid,
sitting shyly on her throne of golden sand,
polishing shells.
And I, who have nothing,
am suddenly richer than the glory of Solomon . . .

I read on.

"Do you like it?" he asked when I had finished.

"It's beautiful!"

"I wrote it for you."

"Me . . ."

"Little Jaia, I feel I've known you for a long time. You opened my heart when you gave me your shell."

His intensity overwhelmed me. He came and knelt before me, holding my face in his hands, staring into my eyes with such tenderness. We kissed and embraced for a long time.

"My Little Jaia," he whispered.

I felt such peace in his arms, a shimmering stillness at an infinite depth. Joy coursed through my blood. It swept through my desolate life. I could have grown old believing love the illusion, the lie it had become for my parents, my culture. But I was dis-illusioned by this. The winds of chaos had blown a thread through a needle's eye. Against all odds, love had broken a spell and turned my heart from stone to flesh again. I had found one with whom I could walk hand in hand and look death in the eye. I meditated on his silent form. And I savored his name: "Yangtze . . . Yangtze . . ."

He was like the river. And he was taking me home to the sea.

That day was unforgettable. I had fallen in love with a great man, a wise mentor. All my life I had sought heroes in humble peasants, or soldiers made of iron and steel. Now I had found a living hero, a flesh-and-blood poet emanating brilliance and tender warmth, whose love had awakened me.

Yangtze and I began spending weekends together. We had picnics in Tiananmen Square; we strolled the Heavenly Temple paths strewn with fallen cherry blossoms; we told our secrets to the circular stone Wall of Echoes and our voices danced around and around, disappearing in whispers, ascending to heaven; we wandered through Bei Hai Park in the shade of the jade magnolias, their large white blossoms fragrant as sweet gardenia.

Spring's tender romance bloomed into summer's splendid passion. And I hid it all from Mama. Telling her would mean having to choose between them. There would be painful scenes.

Yangtze lent me his most precious books, banned in Deng Xiaoping's Anti–Spiritual Pollution Campaign; translations of Sartre and Schopenhauer, both of whom Yangtze felt had seen to the core of life. Under Yangtze's guidance, I began to see the world with new eyes. And with my encouragement, he began writing again for the first time in years.

Each month, Yangtze met secretly with a small circle of former Clear Light rebels and artists. I was invited to their discussions. Such meetings were dangerous. Theoretically, our Constitution allowed people to gather and speak freely. But in reality, meetings not "hosted" by the Party were forbidden. To be caught exercising our rights meant imprisonment. Even disco and video parties were raided and their participants arrested, except for the children of high cadre.

Yangtze's friends belonged to Beijing Spring, an anticorruption, pro-democracy movement that had sprung up like a weed in a sidewalk crack during Deng Xiaoping's brief Open Door Campaign. Deng had quickly crushed the fledgling movement, arresting its leaders and supporters. But many Beijing Spring members had left, taking their movement overseas. Now an international human-rights organization with increasing worldwide support, its waves came back home to disturb the Party and give hope to many people.

But Yangtze had little faith in it. I had been to one of its original rallies and was impressed by the passion of the people I saw there. But when I called Beijing Spring the beginning of a new revolution, Yangtze disagreed.

"It's not a revolution," he said quietly. "It's a tiny movement, a spasm. And it will fail."

"But you saw their rallies!" I said.

"Yes," Yangtze said. "And I read their pamphlets. They're true heroes, risking their lives and futures for their ideals. But they are too few, too naive, and they don't represent the masses." Yangtze looked at me. "Think about it, Jaia. We have eight hundred million poor peasants who can hardly write their own names. What is free speech to them? As long as their bellies are half full they believe what the Party tells them. And the Party knows a nation of half-full bellies is the best defense against a handful of pesky intellectuals clamoring for freedom."

"You're just being cynical," I protested. "Beijing Spring is the beginning of a profound cultural movement!"

Yangtze regarded me soberly.

"There's no revolution without the masses. What do peasant farmers in Sichuan or Qinghai Province care about a radical Beijing-Shanghai intellectual's salon? They'll never hear of it. And if they do it will be an 'antirevolutionary gang of hooligans, spies, and enemies of the people working to destroy our socialist motherland.' Just like the Clear Light Rebellion.

"Our peasants are taught to despise intellectuals. We live in the realm of ideas, on the fruits of their labor, while they battle nature to feed us and survive. We are jokers to them who know nothing of real work. I lived with them for seven years. Do you know what they loved to say? 'Bourgeois intellectuals, cheap like dirt!' " I winced at his words. "Remember, when Beijing Spring wouldn't dry up on its own, the Party crushed it and swept away the dust. And the masses didn't even blink."

Yangtze's words were disturbing. Being with him, I felt torn. I was twenty, confused, struggling, and afraid, full of doubts and hopes. And it seemed Yangtze and I needed from each other things neither one of us had. The closer we grew, the more I saw our lives leading down two diverging paths. And I was saddened.

I had been working for three years to get an American visa, with mixed feelings. America had caused tragic hardships for my country. Yet the Party denied freedom to our people, while America promised freedom to all who came. I had long ago rejected my childhood dream of joining the Party. Now I was prepared to go into exile to find my freedom.

"Don't you see any hope at all?" I asked Yangtze.

"Not in this century, Little Jaia," he said, quietly certain.

"But the Clear Light Rebellion . . . why did you risk your life?"

"I believed then," he said. "Beijing Spring is a lesson for others."

"What do you think we should we do?" I challenged him.

He looked at me tenderly.

"You and I should get married. We could have a child. I'll take care of you. We'll have a happy life."

His words made me sad. They felt like defeat. Aware of my gnawing doubts about our relationship, Yangtze seemed to want to provoke my crisis, to see which way I would go. Several times he had said, "You're not clear about us, Little Jaia. I can wait. If you choose me, I'll be here. If you go to America, I'll understand. My love for you also has a father's blessing and a brother's responsibility."

Later, I saw his long poem to me had anticipated each phase of our relationship, predicting its outcome even before our first kiss.

One night I dreamed Yangtze and I walked on a desolate plain dotted with abandoned huts and surrounded by hills of soft brown earth. Canyon walls towered in the distance on four sides, sealing us in a wide basin. The midnight sky burned with an eerie red glow, casting an orange haze across the plain. Yangtze's arm hung heavy on my shoulder as we walked sadly together.

Suddenly I realized we were in a vast, empty grave in the spirit world. The surrounding hills were freshly dug grave mounds. The abandoned huts scattered on the plain belonged to the buried dead. And the red light above shone down from the dusty human world where the living still struggled fearfully to survive. I woke in terror in the dark. And I knew which way I would go.

We said good-bye in the Garden of Spherical Brightness. There were no parting words—only a tacit understanding too delicate, too painful, to speak. On Beijing's edge, the Qing-dynasty Garden of Spherical Brightness was once a World Wonder, a vast garden-city unrivaled on the earth, whose central jewel had been a palace filled with ancient treasures.

In 1900, the Eight-Power Allied Forces—British, French, Russian, American, German, Italian, Australian, and Japanese—invaded China to help our dowager empress, threatened by a popular uprising, the Boxer Rebellion. To keep her rule she allied with these invaders against her own people. After crushing the peasant rebels, the foreign armies pillaged Beijing and ransacked the Forbidden City, killing, raping, and maiming thousands of Chinese citizens.

Then they stormed the Garden of Spherical Brightness and looted the palace and hundreds of surrounding buildings, and the dowager empress fled. They razed and burned the great palace and its vast garden-city to the ground. For two weeks, the soldiers guarded the fires, day and night, making sure they were not put out.

Eighty-four years passed. The Garden of Spherical Brightness lay, a ruin of rubble and char, strewn across a vast, skeletal plain. Stark white marble pillars and archways rose like tombstones from the scarred earth to lean in the silence. The people were barred from this garden when it was paradise. Now a realm of desolation, its gate was open to us, and we came to mourn our loss.

"Nothing left," Yangtze murmured. "Nothing."

We followed an ancient road lined with maple and poplar trees, through fields of rubble and grass, turnips and cabbage, past a methane-generating pond and farmers digging lotus roots from water-filled paddies. Ramshackle peasant huts crept into the garden. Chickens pecked the dirt and barefoot children herded goats through the fields. A young girl and her mama gathered firewood together. Ahead lay a field dotted with rough-hewn peasant tombstones. The wild road led to a graveyard.

Yangtze and I walked under the archway of trees. Red, golden, purple, and silver autumn leaves descended like spirits. We walked in silence to the end of the road, Yangtze's arm over my shoulders. We stood for a long time, holding each other. A bell rang in the wind. We had reached the end of his poem.

> *Go on, my little girl,*
> *at the end of the good-bye road.*
> *If fate dooms our meeting to a moment,*
> *let us hold each other tightly,*
> *and wordlessly separate,*
> *though it may be our last farewell.*

Let go of the hand once held,
at the end of the good-bye road,
on the day we must say farewell.
For my shoulders are no longer young.
And my heart cannot bear too much joy.
Go on, my little girl!
Before the sun sheds his last ray
and the dusk wanders by.

Preparation

My family's campaign to get my passport passed its third year. All Ba's clever scenarios had failed to outwit the Security Bureau. And we had found no inside connections. As a last desperate strategy, though I couldn't show the financial support required to get a student visa, I sent my school records to an American college and applied for admission. I was accepted. The school sent me the admission forms. When I took them to the Security Bureau, they simply gave me a passport. Half the battle was won. But how would I trick the American Embassy into giving me a visa?

Then my aunt found a rich American friend who kindly sent me the necessary financial-support document. On my second trip to the American Embassy, my destiny was irrevocably decided. I put my priceless American visa in my coat pocket and rode my bike down the broad avenues under a pale, gray sky. A chill wind whipped through the winter streets. My three-and-a-half-year ordeal was over. I was leaving China.

Now that I was leaving, Ba and Mama decided to put me through a practical life training to learn the skills I would need to survive in

America. For weeks I spent many hours a day with them. Mama reviewed with me much she had taught me over the years: how to converse and behave politely, knit a sweater, cook a seven-course meal, make wontons, eggrolls, and dumplings.

But I felt her emotionally distancing herself, hoping to lessen the pain of the day I would leave her. Mama and I had grown bound together. Now I felt a sad dilemma. To leave would require a tearing apart, a separation, like a new, painful birth. But only by leaving could I create a new future for her in America.

I mostly came under the supervision and teaching of Master Ba. It was a Learn From Ba Campaign, a Ba crash course, Everything 101. He showed me how to operate a movie projector, to repair shoes, to clean a toilet, and to sweep and mop the kitchen in under a minute . . .

"You must be quick and efficient! Every second counts!"

How to bargain, keep an expense account, balance a bank book . . .

"You must be sharp with your money. Break every penny in half and spend it twice!"

To scale a fish, kill and clean a chicken . . .

"We must get rid of your bourgeois delicacy," Ba said. "No one is going to clean your chickens for you in America."

To repair a radio, a clock, a watch . . .

"Here's the screwdriver, now suck this uni-lense in your eye. No, not the left eye! The right eye! Be intuitive!"

To glue broken things back together flawlessly. To make mulch and grow vegetables.

"Use everything as fertilizer," Ba said.

I recalled the time he brought home a dead cat he had found in the street and buried it near the root of our grapevine. I hadn't eaten our grapes for a year after that.

Ba even explained the cycles of various crops, proper planting and harvest seasons for each, when to rotate crops to replenish the soil, and how much to charge per jin after harvest. He explained how to paint a house and build a fence. And he demonstrated how to use a file, hammer, saw, drill, pincer, pick, spade, sickle, mend a flat bike tire, rewire a broken switch, develop film, replace a window, a screen, a door.

Was I going to land in San Francisco with Ba's toolbox?

"Never count on anyone else for a single thing," Ba said. "Be prepared to build your own mountain and grow your own forest!"

And he meant it. It was a whirlwind course. Ba tested me at every step. In the end he decided I was hopeless. Who could meet Ba's expectations? But at least he and Mama could now send me off feeling they'd done everything they could.

"We forgot something," Ba said one morning. He stood before the mirror performing his daily ritual of one hundred face-slaps and tugs on his thick black hair. "Hair, you must learn to cut hair. This is the best business, an iron ricebowl. Hair is always growing somewhere. The whole world never goes bald at once. Someone always needs a haircut. Come to my studio starting tomorrow. My makeup lady can teach you the tricks."

So I went to learn haircutting tricks from Ba's makeup artist. She worked with me for a week. Then I practiced on old wigs. Ba came in randomly to offer his own theories, criticisms, and advice. Finally he declared me ready. And in an unexpected act of courage and trust, he volunteered to be my first customer. I was nervous. I knew how highly Ba valued his long, thick, hundred-tugged glossy hair, carefully cut in a cool, cavalier artist style. I tried a woman's chic doll style first, barely trimming and shaping Ba's wavy locks.

"Not smooth enough," Ba criticized.

Next I tried a man's style called the Watermelon Cap, shorter, with matching fringe all around, as if I had placed a watermelon cap on his head and cut around the rim.

"Good enough for a farmer," Ba said, looking in the mirror, "but I wouldn't pay for it. Even it out."

I would be leaving soon. I thought about Mama left behind to suffer Ba's indifference. And I grew mad at his hair. On this last trim I stood between Ba and the mirror and intentionally cut one side much shorter. He became disturbed when he saw what I had done.

"Hey, barber! It's shorter on one side! You've got to fix this. You can't have unsatisfied customers. In America the customer is God!"

Ba preached more wisdom about America while I blocked his view and fixed his hair again, cutting the other side even shorter.

"Are you blind?" Ba was really agitated when he saw himself in the mirror. "If you can't make both sides the same, what kind of brain do you have? Do it right! This is your last chance. And don't block the mirror!"

Ba didn't trust me at all now. He watched me like a prison guard. His eyes never left my scissors as I trimmed the sides perfectly even, much shorter than he liked. But he couldn't see in the back, where I snuck in a wide bald patch. I had invented a new hairstyle, the Dog-Chewed Watermelon Cap. When I nervously held the mirror behind him and he saw the patch, he was furious.

"You rabbit whelp! What did you do?"

"It was an accident," I told him.

He called the makeup lady in a panic. She turned pale when she saw what I'd done, fearing the blame for my mistake. Ba intimidated her for several minutes, as if he could frighten her into salvaging his ruined hair. Finally she choked out the obvious truth.

"It's too late," she said. "You have to shave it all off."

Ba smoldered in his chair at this news, glaring at me in the mirror, his arms folded under the sheet. He suspected.

"Take the clippers and finish it," he finally ordered.

I quickly went to work, like a smooth professional. Ba sulked as his defeated hair fell, lock by lock. My clippers hummed along as I shaved his head skillfully like a happy little barber. I felt only a small twinge of guilt. When I finished, his hair was even all over. Ba was completely bald. The makeup lady timidly approached, clutching his cap, and handed it to him. He put it on before we left the room so his coworkers couldn't see. He didn't say a word all the way home.

"I look like a criminal!" Ba told Mama, showing her what I had done, regarding me with an injured look.

Mama criticized me for being so disrespectful. Ba sulked in the house for two days, refusing to go to work, grumbling about his lost hair. He even wore his cap in the house. I began feeling guilty for betraying his trust and hurting his feelings. These last busy weeks of my Learn From Ba Campaign were the most quality time I had ever spent with him. In spite of all my resentments, I had started liking him a little. Ba had a sense of humor and a natural, proletarian charm. And he was trying to help me. I would never have gotten my passport without him. I felt lousy the day he gathered his strength, put his cap on, and went to his studio to lose face in front of all his comrades. To my surprise he came home that night beaming, his head uncovered, his cap gone.

"You won't believe it," he told Mama as he came in. "People— everybody—*loved* my new hairstyle. Ya!" He rubbed his black-splintered scalp excitedly, making sandpaper noises. "They said this is the Japanese movie star Takakura Ken's new 'tough guy' look from his latest movie, *Capture.* I'm leading the vanguard of a new fashion wave!" he bragged. "My director wants to get the same haircut! He says America's leading actor, Yul Bu Nar, has a shaved hairstyle too. And he's the American sex symbol." Ba rubbed his head again, unable to keep his hands off it in his enthusiasm. "It's very masculine! Not like our skinny, domestic actors in women's makeup, with their long greasy hair. They're like the offspring of eunuchs and Beijing Opera concubines! Gross!"

Ba beamed ecstatically. "Kitten, what a barber you are!" he praised me. "Such skill! You'll always have a rice bowl in America! Who wants to go see *Capture* with me tonight?"

Of course, we all went. We walked together to the movies for the first time since I was five years old, a family at last. Everyone wore wool scarves and caps against the cold. But not Ba. He stood out from the swarming crowds by the unashamed nakedness of his head. Brighter than a lightbulb, he carried it proudly through Beijing's winter streets like an emperor's crown.

Flight

I've told none of my friends I'm going to America. Is it guilt? Am I a traitor going to wag my tail for the capitalists? A coward fleeing the fire for the safe side of the river? I fear envy and criticism. Yet who would not grasp the opportunities I gain by leaving? I'll vanish overnight and leave no shadow; fly like a butterfly over a fence top and disappear into fields beyond. My secret flight will be known only when I am gone.

Days after returning from the American Embassy with my visa, a middle-aged stranger comes to our door, skinny, slightly stooped, with a smiling, simpleton's face. His blue proletarian uniform is buttoned all the way to his throat. Mama's eyebrows rise in a show of delighted surprise.

"Ah! Comrade Wu!" she says. "So good to see you! Come in!"

I hear the Beijing Opera opening rattle, gong, and drum. A curtain rises. Mama's painted mask is transparent to me. She is not surprised, nor is this man her friend. His wide smile and tiny frame make him appear harmless. But she is nervous. I've seen too many of his kind of "pure proletarian comrade."

"Greetings, Comrade Lin!" he says. "Happy New Year's! Here, I brought a little guest."

He hands her a small frozen chicken in a plastic bag. Mama accepts it gracefully. New Year's, 1985, was weeks ago.

"Jaia, this is Comrade Wu," she says.

"Call me Uncle." Comrade Wu smiles and shakes my hand, looking into my face. His small eyes are intrusive and somehow impersonal.

"Jaia, go make us some tea." Mama says, and hands me the chicken.

As I prepare tea in the kitchen, she and Uncle Wu sit at the dining table exchanging polite remarks.

"Where is the tea, Jaia?" Mama calls in an awkward silence.

I bring in the tray, pour three cups of tea, and sit down beside Mama. The air is tense. Uncle Wu forces a smile and decides to keep his hands in his lap. Mama smiles too. They both look at me. Then Uncle Wu breaks the silence.

"So, I hear you are going to study in America, Jaia."

"Uncle Wu knows much about America," Mama says. "He's been there and is an expert on the education of young people. If you have any questions to ask, here is your chance."

"I would be glad to answer your questions," affirms Uncle Wu.

Suddenly I realize why Mama is so nervous. Skinny Uncle Wu is "KGB," from the Ministry of Public Security. Mama should have told me he was coming. We could have prepared. I must be careful what I say, how I behave. I see Uncle Wu considers me a naive young girl. Now a look of harmless simplicity becomes my own convenient mask.

"Mmm . . . I'm not sure." I look puzzled.

"Aren't you afraid of going to America?" Uncle Wu asks.

"Should I be, Uncle Wu?" I ask nervously.

"Yes!" He's suddenly serious, full of grave concern. "You're going into the jaws of capitalism. You'll need all your wits. Do you know what will happen in America?"

"What?"

"The Americans hate communism. You are a Youth League member. They'll hate you, but they'll pretend to be your friends to tempt you with their sugar-coated bullets and weaken your vigilance. They'll try to brainwash you and use you as a weapon against our Party." Uncle Wu's manner softens. "You're a good, patriotic girl, Jaia. You must sharpen your revolutionary will! If you ever meet or hear of anyone betraying our beloved Party in America, you must report it! Do you want to serve your country?"

"Yes, Uncle Wu!"

He hands me a printed card from his jacket bearing the name Mr. Li and a San Francisco address and phone number.

"If you want to report anything, or need any help, call my good friend Uncle Li and mention my name. He'll be happy to help you."

So, I'm to be a little spy for the Party in America.

"I'll certainly call him if I have any problems, Uncle Wu."

Relieved by my performance, Mama smiles as if grateful for Uncle Wu's help. No doubt he believes he's guiding me down the best path for myself and my country. But to me he's a puppet, parroting Party words like so many of Mao's good followers grown old.

Good and loyal comrades can be most dangerous, betraying with the best intentions. How many lives were ruined by such friends and even loved ones who believed they were helping? The lessons of my life taught me to walk this tightrope. My mask is flawless. My balance perfect. The art of survival is in my blood.

"I hope our chat has been helpful." Uncle Wu grins politely.

"Oh, it has been, Uncle Wu!" I assure him. "Thank you!"

"Study hard, Jaia. Your motherland looks forward to your return. When you come back, you'll certainly be valued accordingly and contribute to our modernization."

After he leaves, Mama uncomfortably avoids my sardonic gaze. Through the whole meeting, I've been afraid for her, spoken every word for her protection. Now I feel sad.

"Supervisor Lai's KGB cousin?" I joke to relieve the tension.

Mama gives an apologetic smile.

"How could I tell them no?" she says.

She goes to the table and begins clearing away the teacups.

Chang An Avenue's streetlights flicker on in the twilight of a fading winter. And I leave Beijing, crossing borders of winter and spring, day and night, old and new, standing on a crowded bus with an aching heart. Packed in the aisle like pressed ducks, we squirm and struggle, clutching baskets, babies, and bags. Familiar odors of sweat, diapers, cigarette smoke, and machine oil fill the dusty air.

"Hey, watch it!" a man yells at someone. "You stomped my foot!"

"Who are you, Comrade Delicate?" the someone shouts back. "Deng Xiaoping's son?"

"Fuck your mother!" yells the first man.

Other people start cursing, too. And someone else yells at someone else to step outside and settle something in the street. Our buses boil like tea kettles.

I arrive at the crowded station. Ba and Big Honesty are waiting beside my train. They rode their bikes to meet me. Mama is in Canton, leading a tour for a French Writers' Delegation. I'll meet her there in two days, then cross into Hong Kong and fly to San Francisco.

"Write often, Jaia," Big Honesty says.

"I will."

"Enjoy your trip," Ba says.

He looks away as our eyes meet. I search his familiar face for signs of my unknown future. Ba always said I was more his daughter than Mama's. I wonder what parts of him will be my bittersweet inheritance? His invincible warrior's strength? His demon shadow? He has fishtail wrinkles at the corners of his eyes. But he looks twenty years younger than his age. He could be the elder brother of Big Honesty, who looks older than thirty-two.

"Seventeen years ago Ba saw me off to the countryside from this same platform," Big Honesty says. "You were only four. Now we are sending you to America. How lucky you are."

He watches me, silent. Behind his quietness I feel his fear for his little sister's unpredictable future. And his sadness at our parting. But he hides these feelings he cannot express. I will miss him.

"Everyone envys you," Ba finally says. "Even me."

We glance at each other again, our eyes afraid to meet. He and Big Honesty help me load my luggage on the train and I take a seat. Then they stand on the platform beside my open window.

"The train leaves in two minutes!" a woman's voice screeches over the loudspeaker. "All passengers please board immediately!"

Ba blinks, suddenly looks around, and pushes out through the crowd. He elbows his way into a pile of customers hovering around a vendor's cart.

"I wish I could go with you, Little Jaia," Big Honesty says softly. "Take care of yourself."

Now Ba comes squeezing out of the vendor's cart area, pushing toward us. High above his head, protected from the crowd, he holds a stick of red sugar-frosted plums. The train whistles and shudders as he reaches my window. "This is for you, Kitten," he says. He gives me the sugar plums with a hopeful, guilty smile. I take them now, as I took his sweets through the window of my kindergarten bus so many years ago.

He doesn't know how else to say what he cannot say.

"Thank you, Ba."

With a lurch and a sigh, the train rolls forward, slowly picking up speed. We wave hurriedly. I watch Ba and Big Honesty float away, till they are only a blur on a crowded platform.

The train ride from Beijing to Canton takes two nights and a day. Most people still wear proletarian uniforms. They sit at the tables gossiping, smoking, playing checkers, and cards. Dusk fades to darkness. And the barren fields outside Beijing, scarred and furrowed from last autumn's harvest, stretch to the stars.

The Yellow River shimmers in the morning sun across miles of flatlands. This river is our source, our chosen symbol, the water of our birth. Our first tribe sprang from the Yellow River as the first Egyptians sprang from the Nile. Our first emperor, Yellow Emperor Huang Di, came out of this Yellow Tribe. We say we are all children of the Yellow Emperor, our original ancestor, and of the Yellow River. Her waters fed us like mother's milk.

She has flowed like time itself through our five millennia, witnessing plague, drought, flood, famine, and numberless corpses littering her shores; tides of blood in the slaughter of unarmed peasants by their landlords, warlords, and the emperor's own armies; the endless cycle of wars, catastrophes, revolutions, and the rise and fall of dynasties.

She has watched over the sandbag children who today, as five thousand years ago, spend their early life bound in bags of yellow sand. Unable to move, they stare, eventually silent, into the fields where their parents labor. The peasants say this teaches obedience. But we have learned too well this double-edged virtue, pivotal root of our culture, bowing and scraping through fifty centuries to this era of unparalleled madness; worshiping our Sons of Heaven, surrendering body and soul, building exalted monuments to their glory on a mountain of human corpses. Our lives are only dust motes in the winds of imperial history.

But our numberless, obedient deaths never touched our emperors' hearts. Our last breaths cooled their faces like summer breezes. Our tears watered their gardens. Our lifeblood colored the crimson jewels adorning their crowns. And our veins and arteries became the intricate threads embroidering their Dragon Gowns. Even now we live in bondage to this ancient wheel of suffering. Our past is a ransacked illusion. Our future is blind. Our history echoes with the howl of chaos. And the Yellow River flows on.

Countless are the villages she floods and destroys and the lives she plucks and consumes. She gives and nurtures, takes back and devours. We are careless with her and she turns on us, our vengeful mother, with nature's exacting fury. Deceptive and dangerously unpredictable, she is like the masses themselves—seemingly docile and dependable, yet given to periodic, stunning eruptions of terrible violence. Both hold tremendous power in store and must never be taken for granted.

On the second afternoon the barren fields become vast, green rice paddies. The sky is dark with clouds. Yet the moist tropical air is full of the sweet feeling of spring. Half a day's journey from Canton, we cross another river, the mighty Yangtze. I look down on this powerful giant, boiling with raindrops and her own churning force. Twenty-three years ago, Chairman Mao plunged our nation into chaos from this river, swimming for an hour with the current like a river god while tens of thousands crowded the banks and millions listened to radio news of it with awe. When he passed by, people crowded so thickly into the water to be with him that many drowned.

A real god should have walked across the river, or swum against the current and turned the tide. But a man or woman who gathers enough power by genius, intrigue, or even simple inheritance may presume and claim godhood, as many have.

Across the Yangtze River lies the city of Wuchang in Hubei Province. Hubei, where I lived three years to be near Mama, has become more cultivated in the thirteen years that have passed. But these bright yellow fields of boi choi appear the same. We stop half an hour in Wuchang to add water and coal. I walk along the platform and buy the salty tofu jelly Mama used to buy me on her bimonthly visit to my kindergarten from her camp. It tastes satisfying and mysterious, like a memory itself.

The train sails through broad, half-cultivated fields snaked with muddy peasant roads, past a thousand lakes covered with pink and white lotus flowers. Melon-size blossoms crown swan-neck stems high above floating jade umbrella leaves. As a child I was drawn to these miraculous, flower-jeweled lakes and fed by their beauty. I scavenged in the lotus hearts for sweet seeds, as large water buffaloes sat half submerged like coarse Buddhas, serenely munching the green leaves.

Beautiful images are engraved in my memory from my childhood exile in paradise: flower-petal lakes and lotus seeds, smiling farmers in peaceful rice paddies, wild frogs and crickets singing under a river of stars, and the bright yellow Hubei sun burning fields where Mama labored for five years, turning her skin into lined parchment.

The next morning Mama meets me at the Canton train station. She's staying in the White Swan, China's first five-star hotel, built with Hong Kong money five years after Chairman Mao's death. It is twenty stories tall. Its guests are mostly foreigners, Party officials, and a few diplomats like Mama.

Mama shows her pass to the door guard and we step inside onto a thick burgundy carpet, to the music of splashing water and singing birds. Behind a long marble counter, a dozen lovely uniformed receptionists smile and move about with the grace of dancers.

The center of the grand lobby is an indoor garden. A huge rock hill covered with green moss, lush ferns, and exotic orchids rises twenty stories to a glass skylight. A waterfall cascades down from this summit, splashing into an emerald lake surrounded by tall palm trees. We stroll across an arched wooden bridge overlooking the water. Huge, golden, gargoyle-faced fish swim leisurely about. The Pearl River meets the ocean at the back of the lobby, where the tide rolls in to lap at the bottom of a tremendous wall of glass.

In the lobby rest room, a Cantonese woman in a hotel uniform stands by the sink. She watches me go into the stall. I'm almost afraid to come out, thinking she must be hotel police. When I do, a well-dressed European tourist is washing her hands at the sink. The Cantonese woman approaches her. Lowering her eyes, forcing a smile, she offers a paper towel.

Curious, I watch in the mirror, washing my hands. The foreigner reaches into her elegant purse. Coins jingle. The Cantonese woman receives them with a bow. This is her job. Now she approaches me with her paper towels. But I have no money.

"Oh, no! No need!" I say awkwardly, and hurry out of the bathroom, my hands wet and dripping.

On our way to Mama's room, two plainclothes security agents follow us into the elevator. We get off at her floor and they trail us down the hall to her door.

"Excuse me, Miss," one of them addresses Mama. "May we see your papers?"

They enter our room and politely ask who we are and why we are staying in this hotel. A Chinese in a hotel is suspicious. And a young Chinese girl in a hotel is very suspicious. Perhaps I'm a prostitute hunting foreigners, or a cheap girl fishing for a ticket out of China. After studying our papers, they are satisfied.

"We must do this for security reasons," one explains. "Many girls come here to do dirty tradings with these foreigners."

The next day we are followed, stopped, and questioned again by two different security teams with walkie-talkies—once after an innocent cup of coffee with several writers from Mama's French delegation tour.

On the afternoon of my departure, Mama and I wander through

Canton's crowded streets before going to the train station. Canton, on the Hong Kong border, is China's most Westernized city. Capitalism's influence is strong here. Giant billboards on every corner, once covered with Chairman Mao's pictures and slogans, now bear strange new propagandas: glamorous advertising posters with larger-than-life pictures of Yamaha motorcycles and Sony refrigerators; handsome men and beautiful women smoking Western cigarettes and drinking Coca-Cola.

Big-character posters still cover the walls, overpasses, and electrical poles, but these are not the hand-brushed political posters I saw throughout my childhood. These are slick, mimeographed sheets proclaiming, "Cures baldness! Hair grows back again!"; "Home-grown mink! Cheap like dirt!"; "Emperor's Secret Remedy banishes impotence! Kills hemorrhoids too!"; and "Confidential, no-pain abortion."

Cantonese Southerners have a distinctive look—short, compact, and tan, with broad foreheads and deep-set eyes. The men are more flashy and aggressive, the women more graceful and angry, than we Beijing Northerners. Yet we share a common mask and watch our world through eyes that have bartered hope for survival. And from every passing window my own mask stares back indifferently at the stranger I've become.

Crowds of purchasing clerks and greasy-haired salesman from all over China and Hong Kong look for deals at the Canton Trading Center. Tourists sit along the flowered terrace and surrounding sidewalks, eating self-prepared steam bread and boiled eggs and drinking tea from thermal bottles and jam jars. The streets are littered with newspapers, fruit peels, soda cans, and food and cigarette wrappers. And the fragrance of sweet tea roses and winter lilies in the sidewalk planters faintly permeates the afternoon pall of factory fumes and car exhaust.

Japanese cars and motorcycles are everywhere; they've occupied our cities again with their Suzukis, Hondas, and Yamahas. Fancy new hotels and skyscrapers spring up to dominate the skyline. The pace here is faster. People seem to be hurrying somewhere, chasing taxis, clutching briefcases and handbags, rushing in all directions wearing fashionable dresses, business suits, and ties.

I move among the flooding masses, my heart a knot on a rope. Mama and I navigate perilous torrents on the pedestrian-filled sidewalks, across streets swollen with cars and the endless bicycle river. Drivers honk and swerve, tires squealing, shouting war cries into the battle zone.

"Fuck your mother!"

"Fuck your grandmother!"

"Fuck your ancestors!"

A traffic cop stands on a platform island, dazed by the raging flood. Like a farmer trapped on his roof watching a monsoon river rise, or a toy soldier posted on a battlefield, he is the helpless witness of an ancient chaos whose only law is fate.

Who could rule this tumultuous mass with its terrifying primeval power? The emperor sails on us in his Dragon Boat, a mad captain on a doomed ship, believing he rules the sea. He arises haunted from our formless depths to dance in mortal terror on the ripples of our dreaming. The he dissolves back into our churning vastness. We are a millennial sea engulfing the earth and all the cataclysms of history. We rise and fall forever, born blinking and curious on the earth, to stumble blindly through an endless, mad, enchanted dream.

Though horror and chaos surround us, we are suffused in radiance and our nature is sweet. Though darkness covers our world and blinds our vision, we float in a cocoon of infinite life. If only we could see—how we would love our vibrant motherland and the people of the earth, swarming with joy on this unbelievable, mysterious globe, shining across history like numberless stars in the womb of space, breathing and pulsing in the vast flowing rhythm of life. We are painted dancers on a whirling lantern, lit from within, casting shadows on the earth. We are children of the primordeal mystery. We are the seed and the light in the hollow of the seed, burning till the resurrection, imperishable and fated for freedom.

In the dark, numinous, timeless nights we lie in multiple-generation rooms, in apartments, houses, and socialism yards, in thatched-roof huts and mud-brick shanties; a planet of sleeping souls dreaming a fated myth, an unalterable destiny . . . our Long March across history together toward a Great Liberation.

Mama and I stand at the customs gate on Luo Hu Bridge. Last night after I went to bed, she shut herself in the bathroom till I fell asleep. This morning her eyes were red from crying. Now we smile to hide our sadness from each other. I want to hug her, but I'm afraid I will start to cry and lose the strength to go. Mama taught me never to cry.

The customs officer rudely searches my luggage. I refold and repack everything. I wear the gold bracelet and necklace Mama gave me to sell in America for my college tuition. They are listed on my declaration sheet. The officer glares at me.

"You can only take one piece of gold out of the country!" he says accusingly, as if I'm a traitor taking China's treasure to the foreign devils in the West. "You must leave one piece here!"

No room for debate. I remove the bracelet and hand it to Mama.

"You'd better go." Her voice quavers. "You'll miss the train."

"Take care of your health, Mama," I tell her.

"Study hard. And don't starve yourself," she says.

This is as close to "I love you" as we can come. I start across the bridge with a rushing in my ears, my stomach churning, hot tears filling my eyes. I pass the last five-starred red flag in the middle of the bridge under the setting sun. A cool breeze blows, moist with the smell of rain clouds above and the Luo Hu River beneath my feet. I wave at Mama one last time.

On the train across the aisle, a mother sleeps, her infant suck-

ling her exposed, sacklike breast. Across the table the father sits quietly, eating a bowl of instant noodles with a pair of chopsticks. The
baby looks at me—so serious, pure, and solemn—from out of the
vast depths of an ancient well of being. Her eyes shine in the dim,
smoky train like beacons through a distant gate I left behind, long
ago. She blinks and looks out into the dusk flooding over the blurry
mountains and misty plains. A narrow shaft of sun slants through
the clouds, a dazzling ray of fiery light. And I feel closer to myself
than I've ever been.

For the first time, my life belongs to me, and the future is mine
to make. A battle lies ahead where I will find my heart. Let the storm
winds come from twelve directions. I will stand in the center and
not be touched.

Epilogue

Before leaving China, I dreamed I saw Chairman Mao in a denim apron, selling bonbons near Zhong Nan Hai Compound as Red Flag limousines zipped past. No one noticed him but me.

"You'd better eat less candy," he told me gently. "It's bad for your teeth."

I bought a bonbon from him. He rubbed his nose, searching for change in his apron pocket with a quivering hand. I felt very sad. I told him he could come home and live with me. I would take care of him for the rest of his life. He would never have to sell candy again. He was very touched.

"Only you understand me," he said.

I woke up and realized, in some strange way, I still loved Chairman Mao. Even today, we Chinese regard him with a paradoxical mixture of love, hate, cynicism, and awe. We have yet to recover our faith, shattered by the events of the Cultural Revolution. But life goes on.

Mama has retired in Beijing. She and Ba still live in our old apartment.

Jaia at age nine.

Ba, now a successful businessman, has recently converted to Buddhism. He and I have made peace.

Big Honesty also lives and works in Beijing. He is still loyal by nature to the Party, which has betrayed all his hopes. He is an isolated point of integrity in this corrupt, crumbling system that he feels is the only alternative to chaos. He and his wife have a teenage daughter.

Uncle Sea was finally allowed to join the Party in 1980, four years after his release from his labor camp. He is retired now, and no longer plays the violin.

Little Curly Hair, now married, lives and works in Beijing.

Round Round married a wealthy businessman. I haven't seen her in years. I don't know what happened to her father, Captain Chen.

Auntie Willow is retired. She and her husband live in their old apartment in Three Li Village.

Bing Mei came to America as a student before I did, and also stayed. I've heard she works in a law office. I don't know if she plays the piano anymore.

Wang Ma, my old nanny, married the widower for whom she once worked as a housekeeper.

Grandma Yang and Grandpa Li, long retired, still live in their old apartment in the Ministry of Culture backyard.

Little Plum has finally returned from her reform camp. She lives somewhere in Beijing. On my last two trips to China I tried to find her. Her socialism yard has been torn down and a skyscraper now stands in its place.

My school friends are all married, have children, and work in dead-end government jobs. Like most Chinese, they are trying to become entrepreneurs. All are deeply saddened by their lives under the Party, and were horrified by the Tiananmen Square Massacre, in which they lost several college friends.

Yangtze is now a businessman in Shanghai.

Uncle Tao still lives in his Jasmine Alley home. His loyalty to the Party is stronger than ever. He insists the Tiananmen Square Massacre never happened, but was made up by Western television to humiliate China before the world.

In 1988, I married a "foreign devil" from the West, a blue-eyed, furry monkey named Doug. Together, we wrote this book.

In 1989, the spirit of the Chinese people was resurrected during the Tiananmen Square Rebellion. Thousands of students fasted, demanding freedom, justice, an end to Party corruption. Millions of ordinary citizens flooded into the streets, risking their lives to defend them against armed soldiers. A hero, Wang Wei Lin, stood in front of a tank. The Chinese people stood up again, for one another, our country, our freedom. This spirit has kept us alive for five thousand years. It still lives in China today, in the soul of its people, like a lotus seed buried in the frozen earth, waiting for spring.